The River Amazon from Its Sources to the Sea

Paul Fountain

BIBLIOBAZAAR

Photo Underwood & Underwood

EL MISTA FROM AREQUIPA

THE RIVER AMAZON

FROM ITS SOURCES TO THE SEA

BY

PAUL FOUNTAIN

AUTHOR OF "THE GREAT FORESTS AND DESERTS OF NORTH AMERICA"; "THE GREAT FORESTS AND MOUNTAINS OF SOUTH AMERICA," ETC. ETC.

NEW YORK
DODD, MEAD & COMPANY
1914

PREFACE

IT is several years since my last book appeared. I thought that one was to be *my last;* but (and let the evolutionists note this) if there is not a survival of the *fittest,* there is of the *toughest.* So here I am again.

Twice have I promised that if my poor efforts were *generously* supported the public should have another taste of my quality. *Now* I promise them that if they *do not* support this renewed attempt, they shall have another sample. Perhaps this *threat* will improve my luck.

The first two chapters are the real preface to this work; so I have but little more to say here.

The book covers the same ground as my former work on South America, but the material is nearly entirely new: for I by no means exhausted my notes in "The Great Forests and Mountains of South America." Where I have been compelled to tread in the old footsteps I have done so with the permission of my first publishers, Messrs. Longman, which was most kindly and graciously granted. I do not think, however, that the reader need fear a monotonous repetition of old incidents. The great bulk of the material used is quite fresh; and the book is put together on new lines. There is less of the personal, and more of the descriptive, in the present work: as for the rest, each reader must judge for himself.

I am greatly indebted to Captain Whiffen for kindly allowing me to reproduce his map of the district, which contains the very latest information obtainable.

CONTENTS

LIST OF ILLUSTRATIONS

THE RIVER AMAZON

FROM ITS SOURCES TO THE SEA

CHAPTER I

THE DISCOVERY AND NAMING OF THE AMAZON

GOLD! The lust for this metal was the force that led to the discovery and colonization of South America. Gold: it was sought by the Spaniards and Portuguese everywhere in Central and South America, from the north of California to the shores of Magellan's Strait—sought in fierce excitement as often as in dogged perseverance—sought, but too frequently, in a fury of blood. The very Andes, at frequent intervals, are honeycombed with ancient mine shafts and burrows, made by monomaniacs in search of the precious metals and precious stones, for the possession of which they sacrificed souls and bodies, and slew multitudes of the harmless people of the lands they invaded.

It was the longing for gold that led to the discovery of the mighty Amazon, by far the largest river in the world.

Nearly four hundred years ago (precisely, in 1540) a

band of Spaniards stood and listened to the wondrous stories of gold and silver, of spices and other precious things, told by Indians who well knew how acceptable such tales were to the tingling ears of their greedy auditors.

The spot where these stories were told was near Quito, then the capital of a native kingdom bearing the same name; and the eager listeners were Pizarro and his band of adventurers. The alluring accounts seem to have referred to the country in the valleys between Cotopaxi and Antisana, where several considerable tributaries of the Amazon take their rise.

Pizarro detached a party under the command of his brother Gonzalez to seek for the treasure. These men seem to have passed the base of Cotopaxi, and embarked, in boats or canoes, on a river which could hardly have been other than the Napo. They were not accompanied by a guide; or, at any rate, by an efficient one; and do not seem to have stayed to examine the eastern slope of the Andes: hence they probably missed the object of their search. For it is known to the writer that there are evident traces of gold and diamonds in this region; as well as of less sought after, but really more profitable, minerals. It is strange: but to this day the treasures referred to have remained undiscovered—at least I believe so.

Gonzalez Pizarro and his companions reached the huge forest which still covers the centre of South America; and must have penetrated it to a considerable distance. It was then, as now, scantily peopled by naked savages: and what big game there is must be diligently sought for: consequently the adventurers, who looked more for wealth than food, soon began to be short of stores. Then there arose a subaltern officer, one Francisco Orellana, and offered to push on alone in search of supplies. This offer was accepted by Gonzalez; and Orellana, in one boat, and with but few companions, dropped down the Napo to the point where it joins the great river. He made no attempt to return to his commander. Why is matter for conjecture, and conjecture only. His real reason is not known, and never can be. Probably he realized that he had made a great and wonderful discovery, and ambition induced him to take a desperate risk rather than be robbed of the honour of this discovery, as he undoubtedly would have been had he carried the news back to his self-seeking chief—the grasping Pizarro.

From actual experience I can state that no man could enter the Amazon from the Napo and fail to perceive that he was floating on as mighty a stream as any on earth. Orellana must have known that he was a vast distance from the Atlantic—must have seen at a glance that the wonderful river he had discovered was rushing with calm, but tremendous force, straight for that ocean: and, like hundreds of Spaniards of his day, he resolved, on the moment, with indomitable energy and bravery to take all risks, and push on until he had completed his discovery: and so he became, not only the discoverer of the greatest of rivers, but also the first European to cross the vast American continent.

Of his adventures on this perilous journey we have no complete account. How he lived, fared, escaped dangers, and finally reached the huge mouth of the great river, is told to us in few words, and many of these, disfigured with the superstitions of the age, are not very reliable: but he did perform the wonderful voyage; of that fact there is no doubt whatever. More than 2000 miles of the Amazon's course he traversed; and was deservedly honoured and rewarded for the remarkable feat.

From time to time he encountered the native Indians who dwell on the shores of the great stream. Whether it is true that he met with amazons—female warriors—is very doubtful—it is so contrary to the habits, laws, usages and *prejudices* of these savages, that we are justified in thinking he must have been mistaken: but we may believe that he honestly thought he encountered some such viragoes; and of his right to confer their name (or any other) on his great discovery there can be no question. He called it the Rio del Amazones; this, therefore, is its proper name. But jealousy, or love of interference, has given it several others, of which that which is most defensible is "Orellana," the name of the great man who first saw, and navigated, its majestic waters. It is also called the Marañon, and the Solimoes. The last name is but seldom used, and only locally. "Orellana" has, also, almost completely dropped out of use. There is some excuse for these divergences of name in the tremendous area covered by the river and its tributaries, which drain nearly half the South American continent. The source of the Amazon is as far from its mouth as the Thames is from the Black Sea! It may well, therefore, bear several names in different regions, especially as it is joined by nine or ten tributaries, each one of which is, in itself, a river of vast dimensions, exceeding the Rhine in both length and drainage area: and three or four of them rival the Nile in size, and more than double it in volume of water. Indeed the Amazon is not only itself a huge stream, it is really the parent of the most extensive river system in the world. After much careful thought and calculation I have concluded that the streams connected with the Amazon which exceed a brook in size must have a total length of at least 100,000 miles. The brooks and runnels larger than those a man could leap across are countless: they may safely be put at tens of thousands. For the valleys of the Amazon, and its affluents, are the best watered on earth.

In many books, and on many maps, the name is spelled "Amazon": but Orellana called it the River of the Amazons. It cannot be proper, therefore, to use the singular number; though the English, and modern, form of spelling may be permissible, and is that which is followed throughout this book. The Portuguese form of the word is "Amazonas."

It may be well to remark at this point that in many instances there is much confusion in Spanish-American names owing to the circumstance that many mountains, rivers and cities have three, four, and sometimes more, different appellatives. This confusion arises partly from the frequent revolutions in South America. Don Pedro, being in the ascendant, must remove all names, and all things, which remind him too vividly of his predecessor, Don Thomaso; or, worshipping a particular set of tutelary saints, must honour these holy spirits by bestowing their names on the most prominent objects in the revolutionized district. Hence the Mary of to-day frequently becomes the Martha of to-morrow; but the old name, having become fixed in the memories of the majority of the inhabitants, is parted with reluctantly and slowly.

CHAPTER II

THE SOURCES OF THE AMAZON

AS is often the case in a great river, there is some divergence of opinion concerning the true source of the Amazon, some geographers favouring the Ucayali, others insisting that Lake Lauricocha is the parent water of the principal stream. The chief point in favour of the Ucayali is its superior length, which adds about 480 miles to the course of the Amazon: but most authorities take Lake Lauricocha for the head waters of the great river: and I think they are right.

The lake, which is small, scarcely more than a tarn, situated in an elevated valley of the Knot of Pasco, is fed by streams issuing from the mountains which form the Knot. These springs owe their origin to the snows which settle on the elevated ranges of Pasco, but melt almost as soon as they fall, the mountains being well within the tropics. The streams are consequently intermittent; but the lake is deep, and never sinks to a low level. The river which issues from it, and forms the beginning of Amazon, is called the Tunguragua, by the people of the district, and, more generally, the Upper Marañon by geographers. But to thoroughly understand the sources of the Amazon some knowledge of the Andes is necessary.

These vast mountains form a range which really

runs the whole length of America: for, notwithstanding what Dr. Bell says in his work "New Tracts in North America" (1869), I am convinced that the Andes of the South, the high lands of Central America, the Sierra Madre of Mexico, and the Rockies of the North continent, were originally one continuous range. They are hardly separated now. But here I have to deal with the Andes of the South continent only.

Broadly the Andes form two parallel ranges, with a much elevated valley between them. At a few points they diverge from this general arrangement. The Knot of Pasco is one of these divergent points; and is formed by the junction of subsidiary ranges, forming a cluster of peaks of great height. Perpetual snow does not remain on them: for they are only ten degrees south of the Equator; but there can be no doubt that several of them verge on the line of perpetual snow. As a fact, snow often lies on them for weeks at a time; and when it melts forms torrents of great volume and depth, which deeply plough the mountain sides.

At this point the Andes run north, slightly west, and the Upper Marañon follows their trend for about 400 English miles before breaking through the rocky barrier on the right and dashing with tremendous impetuosity into the forest-clad plains which form the basin of the Amazon.

But though the Upper Marañon is the beginning of the Amazon, it is by no means its only *head-water*. These number at least a hundred large streams, extending, on the line of the Andes, from Caylloma on the south, where the Ucayali (here called the Apurimac) takes its rise, to the Granadian wilderness on the north, where the Ucayali rushes from the Andes to form, seven hundred miles lower down, and, after bearing half a dozen different names, the Rio Negro (Black River), one of the largest tributaries of the main stream.

A remarkable feature of these hundred streams, more or less in number, every one of which is a river of dignity, and not a few streams of majesty, is that they all have their sources within a space of four degrees of longitude, though they spread across twenty degrees of latitude. Rivulets and brooks are not considered in this estimate. These are so numerous that the best maps in existence do not show a tenth of them. I can go much farther than this, and assert that even in this day of restless search for new lands, and new methods of obtaining wealth, there are thousands of square miles on the eastern slopes of the Andes, and in the forests which cover, like a thick cloud, the valleys of the Amazon, which have never yet been pressed by the foot of a white man. Nay, there are districts of no mean extent which have not even felt the stealthy tread of the prowling Indian. These tracts were more numerous, and more extensive, in the days when I wandered in these regions, and explored many of them. What I saw, what I found, what I heard, have to some extent already been given to the world in my book on South America. But in that book much was necessarily passed over, much abbreviated. In the present volume I stop to give details. It is all a personal narrative; not of one journey, but of several, made at different times, and under diverse conditions, the chief object being, not to give a series of adventures and experiences, but to describe a very remarkable river as it appeared to the eyes of one who endeavoured to make himself a close observer and careful narrator of what was seen and heard: for these huge waters and forests have sounds as well as sights and silences.

These two preliminary chapters contain a necessary series of explanations, without which something must have been felt wanting by the reader. It is unnecessary to say that I have not visited *all* the head-waters of the Amazon. No one unaided man could do that; but I may, without boast, say that I have seen as much of this mighty river as any one unaided, and unrecognized, man could see.

It is not my intention to give a continuous narrative of my experiences; but rather a connected description of the river, based on these experiences. It could not well be otherwise; for if I attempted to describe my journeys when, how and as they took place, this would become a book of travels rather than a monograph of the Amazon. What I have said in these two chapters might have been embodied in a preface; but the pith of a preface is its brevity. Moreover, this introduction is a necessary part of the book. Without more words, therefore, I plunge at once into a description of the river as it is known to me, beginning, as is proper, with its acknowledged source, the Upper Marañon.

CHAPTER III

THE UPPER MARAÑON

BOILING, roaring, rushing, the Marañon cuts its way through rocky beds from the very moment it leaves Lake Lauricocha. The lake itself, surrounded by stupendous rocks and mountains, receives, and discharges, larger bodies of water than would be imagined considering its small size. It is a picturesque sheet of water, as all mountain lakes are; but no time was given me to explore it, as I was compelled to go on with a band of *contrabandista* with whom I had crossed the Andes by a little-known pass from Pasco.

Pasco deserves a word or two. It is the most elevated city in America—the Spaniards say in the world, and they are probably right, as it is situated nearly 14,000 feet above sea-level; and some of the mines and houses are placed much higher than this, one silver mine near the top of the mountain on which Pasco is situated being said to be 16,000 English feet above the sea. I doubt, however, if any of the mountains of the Pasco Knot exceed 16,000 or 17,000 feet in height, and the city is not on the highest in the district.

The city is, however, a wonderful place, and probably unique in its circumstances and environments. The openings to the shafts of nearly all the mines are situated in the middle of the public thoroughfares; and in some instances the miners have to step only two or three yards from the entrance to the mines to the shops which supply their needs, or trap them of their hard-earned money for things which they *do not* need: for the beneficent Jew and the widcawake Yankee are here; and the Spanish equivalent for "Dey ish most peautiful articles, my tear; and varanted to lasht for ever"; or "I guess they lick all creation slick, and no mistake about it," may be heard in most quarters of the city.

Many of the shafts are abandoned; and the visitor must look after his neck vigilantly; for the authorities take little, if any, precaution to prevent accidents at these disused shafts, many of which have become full of drainage water. The ascent and descent of the mines which are worked are by means of ladders. At any rate this was the case when I visited Pasco some thirty years ago. There was no winding gear of any kind; and the smelting work was performed in a very primitive and wasteful way, the fuel used being mostly timber, brought up from the forests miles below at great trouble, and camels' (*guanacos'*) dung; yet there is plenty of coal in the mountains close to Pasco.

The climate at Pasco is intensely cold all the year round; there being but little variation in the temperature; but the heat of the sun at midday is strong enough to melt the snow, which seldom lies long on the ground. The vegetation is ultra-alpine, and the animal life exceedingly scant in species at this great height, although

Photo Underwood & Underwood

A STREET IN PASCO: THE HIGHEST INHABITED SPOT IN AMERICA

rats and mice abound in the mines and private houses. These little animals, some of which (e.g. the brown rat) are of European species, have been brought here in barrels and boxes of imported goods; and apparently they have found a suitable habitat in which they are flourishing exceedingly. Neither these nor the *guanacos* find any difficulty of respiration, although human new-comers pant for breath. The miners do not suffer in this respect very much, although they complain of loss of strength owing to the extremely rarefied state of the atmosphere.

These men live an exceedingly arduous life, and thousands of them break down, and die a premature death. The ladders by means of which they reach the bottoms of the shafts, are placed perpendicularly; sometimes joined together, one beneath another, by bands, sometimes leading to a series of platforms. I descended one which contained 648 steps; and, although I carried no burden, I was very tired when I returned to the top. But the labourers carry up loads of ore which weigh 200 English pounds. It takes them half an hour to reach the top, and they carry up twelve loads per man every day. This is the regulation amount of work, and no man is required to do more, I was assured by an overseer. I should think not! it is work for an elephant. All the labourers are Indians or half-breeds; and all classes of men here, labourers, miners and officials, are polite, kind-hearted, and very hospitable.

There are very few women in the city, these being mostly the wives and daughters of the tradesmen. The population is largely what is termed floating, and seldom exceeds a total of 10,000. Sometimes it sinks as low as 2000. Tradesmen grow rich very rapidly. Few of the miners remain longer than two or three years; many are unable to endure the rigid climate, and leave within a few months, or even weeks, of their arrival. I have heard that criminals are compelled to work in the mines of Pasco. I do not think this statement is correct. I saw nothing of any prisoners there; but I believe that some of the Indian labourers are indentured, or bound, in some way, for a number of years. They are all very respectable, obliging fellows, with nothing of the criminal type about them; but there is a number of loose characters lurking about the city; as there is in all the mining centres of America in both divisions of the continent. These live by preying on the honest workers, cheating them at play, and hocussing them in various other ways; yet those mortal quarrels which are so frequent in Spanish-American towns, are not common here; and a police officer told me that years often passed unsullied by the committal of a murder in Pasco.

The silver in the mines is found in conjunction with iron, and there are traces of copper and other metals. The silver is smelted on the spot, but very badly. Since my visit I have heard that English and Scotch mining-engineers are now engaged in the conduct of the mines; and many improvements have been made.

Lakes are not numerous in any part of South America, except saline pools on the Pampas; but there are several in the Knot of Pasco which resemble Lake

Lauricocha in character, though most of them are tarns of only a few hundred acres in extent; and some not a hundred yards across, yet they are very deep, and never dry up or diminish in area.

I examined one, situated about twenty miles from Lauricocha, which evidently occupied the crater of an extinct volcano. The banks shelved down so steeply that it was dangerous to descend to the water, which was, in places, nearly 800 feet deep close to the shores. Thousands of ducks and other water-fowl frequented its surface, which was less than half a mile across; and shoals of tiny fish were seen swimming slowly in the water. If there were larger ones they kept well out from the shore, and persistently refused to take the cunningly baited hooks with which we tried its depths.

Other lakes in the district were found to contain trout-like fish ranging in weight from a few ounces to a dozen pounds. There were also caught fish resembling the white-fish of the northern lakes, and a kind of bream of small size.

All extinct craters, and deep depressions amongst the mountains, contained water, which must have collected from the melting snow. Only Lakes Lauricocha and Chinchaicocha, and one or two more, have visible outlets. Chinchaicocha is the largest lake in this region, having an extent of surface at least four times as great as that of Lauricocha. It appears to be about a dozen miles long, and three or four broad: but I am calculating by appearance to the eye, as I had no opportunities of taking measurements; though the lake is only a short distance from Pasco, and a few thousand feet below it. it is not in any way connected with the source of the Amazon.

After leaving Lake Lauricocha the Upper Marañon rushes turbulently through a rocky country for a distance of between twenty and thirty miles. This part of its course is, by barometric measurement, about 10,000 feet above sea-level. There are no actual falls, but several cascades; and the bed of the river is full of huge rocks and boulders of all sizes. The depth does not seem to be great at any part of this upper course; but the force of the current is undoubtedly great, and no boat could live on the stream for one moment. A little lower down a few quiet pools alternate with the wild torrent; and there are spots where the river is fordable. Care is required in passing it: for there are often deep holes in these pools which are only two or three yards in diameter, and though the water is absolutely clear, one does not see them until about to step into them. They are of the nature of "pot holes"; being very symmetrical in form, and occasionally a dozen feet deep.

At this point the scenery surrounding the river is very sublime, though of the wildest character conceivable. Huge ranges of mountains tower above it 6000 or 7000 feet, and enclose it on all sides. These summits are snow-clad after every storm-burst, but the snow does not lie long except there is a continuance of bad weather. The mountains verge on the line of perpetual snow, but do not, like Chimborazo, Cotopaxi, and some other mighty summits to the northward, actually enter it. Only occasionally does the snow lie for weeks together

Photo Underwood & Underwood

on the extreme summits of these enclosing mountains, which form a wall on each side of the valley through which the river tumbles and rolls rather than runs.

The rocks, both in the valley and in the bed of the river, are often covered with lichens and mosses; but vegetation of higher classes is scarce; and the tall mountain ranges and peaks are completely bare of it, and have a hard and austere appearance.

The condor, the typical bird of the Andes, may be seen any day soaring in the sky until it is a mere speck. It would be more correct to write condors: for it is a rare thing to see a solitary bird of this species, or even a pair of them alone. It is a sociable bird, and flies in flocks usually numbering about forty individuals, and sometimes twice that number. It depends on the amount of persecution it has undergone. In very lonely places, far from the habitation of cruel man, I have seen as many as 800 together; a fine sight as they sail majestically round, and in and out amongst themselves; sometimes descending to within a few hundred yards of the spectator, and again ascending until out of sight, and only betraying their presence by an occasional hoarse cry. At what height they cease to be visible to the human eye I do not know; but I have watched them disappear when I was standing on heights so great that I had to struggle for every breath I inhaled. They certainly ascend at least six miles above sea-level, and suffer no inconvenience or loss of physical power. But it should be mentioned that there are two species of these birds; and the smaller one does not fly nearly so high as the larger.

Guanacos run wild on this part of the Andes range; but they are so much harassed by the hunters and others who visit these elevated regions in pursuit of various callings, that they are seldom seen. They must feed largely, if not entirely, on moss and the few dwarfed cacti found on the lower ranges: though there are spots where these cacti are abundant and flourishing at much greater heights than 10,000 feet. The cactus is a plant of the desert and the desolate mountain range.

A dipper, or water-ouzel, also haunts the tumultuous Upper Marañon. It is a bright little bird, with a brilliant chestnut breast, and amused me much with lively habits, and daring ventures, as it flew, as it seemed, right into frothing torrents which one would think must sweep it under and away.

No doubt flies were the objects of its pursuit; and insect life is abundant enough in this bleak valley. Besides gnats, or mosquitoes (always, and everywhere, in America counted amongst my chief tormentors), there were clouds of a very minute grey fly, a mere speck of a thing, but which caused me much suffering, to the great amusement of my friends the bandits; for I was the only man of the party whom they attacked. They bit me cruelly at the back of the neck on those bosses which, I believe, the phrenologists declare denote philoprogenitiveness in the individual, until these "bumps" were swollen to a very conspicuous size.

"Why should they sting me, but none of you?" I enquired, pathetically.

"Beef!" was the cool reply of the chief of the party; an evident reference to the size of my person, and the fleshiness thereof; which, I must admit, were in strong contrast to the leanness and small figures of my companions.

I have described these men as *contrabandista*, the Spanish word for smugglers, which is really what they were. I do not think they were worse; but they were armed to the teeth as the saying is; and I have no doubt of what would have happened if they had come in contact with the customs officers or soldiers. We did, indeed, receive information at a lonely hut, tenanted by a goatherd, that an armed force was on the look-out for us; and the information caused us to hurry through a great part of the valley. Having a lively remembrance of what happened to me when I fell into the hands of some customs officials in Mexico on a previous occasion, I was by no means happy for a day or two until the danger blew over.

Why was I found in the company of such characters? Travelling alone, or at most with one or two attendants, and with very inadequate means, I often found it both convenient and safe to join myself to very shady characters. Such men, having an intimate knowledge of the remote parts of their country, could guide and assist me to reach places I should have been unable to visit alone. With but a scant knowledge of the Spanish language, and not too well acquainted with the laws and customs of the land, I should often have been stopped and turned back if I had not, as it were, squeezed through in a crowd of determined characters who were sure to make their way by "force or cunning," and often with a considerable show of "funning," which I was not adverse to witnessing. I was there in search of wild scenery and wild adventures, and not at all disposed to be too particular in the choice of my associates. Besides, while in their company I was immune from that fleecing process they were disposed to inflict on " stray birds," to use their own phrase, and I was often passed on from band to band. How did I become acquainted with these men and secure their confidence and friendship? I do not feel called on to reveal this: sufficient to say I never partook of any action which I deemed unjust, or even dishonourable, or in any way countenanced unrighteousness.

The first falls on the Marañon are of the nature of cascades, or rapids, rushing down sharp slopes, generally for short distances, but in some places for the length of a mile or more. There are spots where the valley narrows to a mere gorge; and here the river flows through cañons which, though not comparable to those of the Colorado, are grand and impressive beyond the power of pen to describe.

The river, in these cañons, glides with a silent force which is misleading to the eye. Possibly a boat could live on it, and pass through in safety; but though I have had a great experience in dangerous river navigation in all parts of America, I should not care to risk running through any of the Marañon cañons. I noticed that the force of the current had cut away the base of the rocks and undermined them; in some places causing heavy falls which had partly blocked the channel. The debris, and smaller fragments, had been swept away; but many huge blocks remained firm in the stream, causing the water to hiss, boil and dash into spray, in a way that inspired one with deep awe to witness.

The circumstances of my journey in this region precluded exact measurements, as I have already hinted; but guessing, without exaggeration, I should state the longest cañon to be about twelve English miles; and the greatest height of the environing rocks 400 feet. On an average they are 200 feet above the surface of the water, which they often overhang. Nowhere is there a beach, or sloping bank, like that found at the bottom of the Colorado cañons: but every feature here is on a much smaller scale than in that marvellous district, and the general features different. For instance, the rocks forming the actual sides of the cañon are placed much closer together proportionally than they are in the Colorado river: although the vast height of these last named have a far more imposing effect.

In the Marañon cañons the rocks are often not 200 feet apart, giving a very gloomy effect to the chasm between, in spite of the brilliant skies and bright light above: but something must often be allowed for the shadow of the enclosing mountains of the outer ranges, which, in two or three places, approach to within 600 or 700 yards of the river, towering over it at least 5000 feet, and perhaps 1000 or 2000 feet more. In one place, mountains 8000 feet high approach to within much less than a quarter of a mile of the top of the cañon, which is here more than 800 feet deep.

Through such regions as those the Marañon dashes and rolls for an extent of country which is said to be 150 leagues in length, or more than 400 English miles. Judging from the time it took me to traverse it, and the known distances between many places on the course, I should believe that the upper reaches of the stream extend fully this distance.

The gorge where it leaves the Andes and drops to the low lands of Brazil is one of the wildest I have seen in any of my wanderings in the two vast continents of America; and this is making a very strong assertion indeed.

CHAPTER IV

THE DOWNWARD RUSH TO THE GREAT FOREST

A REMARKABLE feature of the Andes Range is that, running due north and south, or, at least, practically so, the eastward face or slope is far more steep, or abrupt, than the western. Why it is so I do not know: but it is a fact that it is so: not here and there, but throughout its entire length in South America.

A result of this peculiar feature is that these rivers, like the Marañon, taking their rise in the elevated valley before mentioned, and flowing eastward, reach the central plains of the continent in a series of cascades and falls, many of which are of superb grandeur. There are not, within my knowledge (and it is very extensive) any such large and heavy falls as are found in the Yosemite Valley, and Yellowstone Park, of the North continent; but many of the falls of the rivers which form the head waters of the Amazon are incomparable for depth, and for picturesque beauty and wonderfulness.

The west wall of the Andes, in the valley of the Upper Marañon, is the highest; and many rivulets and brooks flow from it to the Marañon. Some of them have their origin in springs in the rocks; and others are formed by the overflow of small lakes, or ponds; but I think I may safely say that all these springs and ponds are collections of snow-water. Not all of them are permanent; but many are. In every case the current is very rapid; and falls and cascades are numerous. In the wider parts of the valley some small rivers have a course of fifty or sixty miles before joining the Marañon; and on one I saw a fall of at least 200 feet in an unbroken stream, though the quantity of the descending water was not great. In many places the cascades meet projecting rocks, or ledges, and are dashed into clouds of spray. There are also dry watercourses, which are probably torrents after heavy snows and rains: for tropical showers of great violence are frequent: and I thought the heavier falls always took the form of rain, and the lighter that of snow. Something, of course, depends on height; but heavy rains were experienced at greater altitudes than 12,000 feet. Only one or two brooks join the Marañon on the east side, before it bursts away from the Andes.

There are a number of isolated huts and houses, and a few small hamlets and towns, in the valley, of which the chief are Llata, Huari, Caxamarquilla and Jaen. Most of these places are engaged in the mining industry; but there is no made road between them: indeed the country is so high, so rough and broken, and so little used, that this circumstance is not surprising.

The sea is not more than 100 miles, in a direct line, from the centre of this valley; in some places it is not seventy miles; and it is visible from some of the higher peaks of the western wall. Such passes as there are hardly deserve the name of "secondary." Only fatalists, and persons with no particular respect for the safety of

Photo Underwood & Underw

RAILWAY TO MINES NEAR THE SOURCE OF THE AMAZON

their necks, would be likely to attempt them. The first regular pass is that running from Truxillo, through Caxamarca to Moyobamba. It crosses both walls of the Andes at a great elevation; and passes over the Marañon by means of a terribly rickety bridge, which is never repaired until an accident calls the attention of the Peruvian authorities to its dilapidated state. This bridge is near the little town of Ulco, where my smuggling companions left me. Thirty miles farther on the river reaches the forest ground by a series of leaps and cascades of great beauty and grandeur, though only a few of them make sheer drops of any great height. The fall of Virmapantando is a series of three great cascades of about 100, 50 and 60 feet respectively, with some intervening torrents; the whole occurring within about a mile and a half. A dozen miles lower down there is another cataract of about thirty feet; and then a series of rapids which carry us almost to the junction of the Chito river, which runs through Ecuadorian territory.

Long before we reach this point boats can be used on the Marañon; but frequent portages are necessary. I have shot some of the rapids in a canoe; but the practice is dangerous here on account of the great number of submerged rocks; and several treacherous whirlpools, the cause of which is very obscure; but I suspected that some of them were formed by the escape of water through underground channels. After a very narrow escape of drowning I abandoned the intention of descending the river by boat; and, in fact, my knowledge of the lower Amazon was acquired in an ascent of the river from its mouth, in the years 1884–85.

In this region there are two distinct species of condors, one being much smaller than the other, and of lighter plumage, there being little or no black colour about it. It resembles the Californian condor; and farther north is the only kind met with.

The condor is a bird which ought to be well known by this time; but the actual experiences I have gained of it are greatly at variance from what I find written by professional naturalists. I shall not start an argument; nor shall I directly contradict any man: but it must be noted that the information I give here, and elsewhere, in this book is all gained at first hand. It will be found, however, to differ much from many almost universally received opinions. I am sorry it is so: but it is obvious that only two courses are open to me. I must either state facts as they appeared to me or fall into line with the herd of professed naturalists, and repeat the fine old fictions, which have been repeated fifty times in the hundred, or two hundred, years which have elapsed since the first observer made his erroneous observations, or was misled by the statements of Indians who did not fully understand the questions put to them. Perfectly honest and truthful men make mistakes, and grave ones. A great many of the remarks of Darwin on South American natural history are not worth the paper on which they are written; yet nobody would think of accusing that great man of intentionally misleading the public. The simple fact is that he was not in the country long enough, and had not a sufficient general knowledge of it, to make exhaustive observations.

However, I shall say no more concerning the mistakes

and errors of others. I simply give my experiences; and add, as an explanation, that if they differ, or seem to differ, from those who may be worthy of as much, or more, credence than I am, it is an unfortunate circumstance. But I certainly do differ from many credited authorities: and, as a case in point, about the condor amongst other things.

It may be gross nonsense to describe the bird as wheeling round Chimborazo—I believe it is: but it ascends, in its flight, to a much greater height than that mountain, as I have already described. Why it does so is one of those problems of nature that no man can solve. So far as I could perceive the chief object seemed to be to enjoy life, and the wonderful power of wing with which these magnificent birds are endowed by the Almighty. It was certainly not to search, or watch, for prey. Of that there can be no doubt whatever.

Condors are gregarious, as previously stated; and they usually breed in one another's neighbourhood, but not in association. Near the spot where the Marañon passes through the mountain barrier there is a rugged knot known as "Condor Rocks," where these birds rear their young in great numbers. They also nest in the rocky highlands, which abut on the Amazon near the mouth of the Chito river, and south of it. In their breeding habits all the species, or varieties, resemble eagles; and lay the same number of eggs, viz. two or three. It has been asserted that the Californian condor lays only one. I have repeatedly taken two from the same nest. Condors sometimes make a nest, and sometimes do not. The Andes condor, which we may call the common species, since it has the greatest range, and is the most numerous, usually lays its eggs on a mossy crag, or ledge of rock where there is a growth of herbage; and always seeks the shelter of an overhanging rock, tree or protective object of some kind. Sometimes they occupy a crevice; or hole, which has been scooped out by some other animal. The eggs are usually described as white: they are not pure white; but a kind of pale grey, and dirty in appearance. Those of the Californian condor are a pale dove-grey.

Two errors concerning the condor are persistently repeated, by modern writers. The first is that condors attack men, and other animals. I am sure they never do anything of the kind. Of course they may destroy newly born animals if they get the chance to do so, and they may commence operations on moribund creatures that are too far gone to offer resistance: but this is the full extent of their depredations. Carrion is their natural food; and they seek nothing else. The ignorant herdsmen, and other people of classes who are in the habit of placing their beliefs and suppositions in the place of actual knowledge, may assert the contrary to this; but they are no more to be relied on than the people of Lancashire who believe in witches; or the peasants of Devonshire who consult a "wise woman" instead of a doctor.

The second mistake, a piece of guesswork, based on a peculiar formation of the larynx, is that the condor has no voice. It rarely makes any sound except when on the wing; then it utters a peculiar hoarse cry, which is indescribable, as it is quite unlike that of any other bird I am acquainted with. It seems to consist of a single note—a prolonged guttural sound, which can be distinctly heard when the bird is at a very great height in the air.

Before reaching the forest region the traveller from the Andes towards the Amazon must pass through some curious zones of vegetation. The region of lichens extends nearly to the summits of the mountains that form the Knot of Pasco, which may be put at 16,000 or 17,000 feet. Elsewhere they are found on all parts of the rocks. Mosses abound up to about 10,000 feet; and, in places, much higher; and are often conspicuous owing to their profusion, remarkable forms and brilliant colour. Favoured by the protection of these cryptogamic growths several pretty wild flowers are found at unusually great heights for such plants; amongst them several kinds of calceolaria; and almost the first woody-stemmed growth that is met with is a crimson-flowered azalea. The majority of plants and flowers, however, were quite unknown to me; many of them being now seen for the first time.

It was very curious to suddenly drop from a region of flowering shrubs and aromatic plants, to an intermediate zone of cacti of gigantic size, reminding me of the "Staked Plains" of Texas. The candelabra cacti were here of great size, denoting a barren soil, or, perhaps, the presence of alkalies in the detritus of these mountains: for in the western states of the North I invariably found such deposits in the soil where cacti flourished most. "A little learning is a dangerous thing," sang the poet Pope. Men have perished of thirst amongst groves of cacti plants. Had they possessed "a little learning," one slash of a knife on the nearest trunk would have furnished them with several quarts of excellent fluid, and saved their lives.

How the cactus attracts and collects moisture from the deadly aridness of the most desolate deserts, I know not; but I have found the taproot of a candelabrum cactus descend thirty feet into the ground, and then have not discovered the end of it. I do not know that "root" is a proper term for the curious prolongation of the trunk which is capable of penetrating ground which seems hard as rock to the footsteps of man. Why does Nature protect this natural reservoir with thorns long and strong, which wound cruelly if they are not approached carefully? The wild horses of the plains, and other animals, guided by instinct, or reason, know the value of the cacti; and feed eagerly on the moist substance of these plants; but the only way in which they can get at it is to kick it to pieces with their hoofs. In doing this they often badly lame themselves.

There are several other kinds of cacti on the mountain sides; all growing above the belt of forest; but lower than the lichens and mosses. The presence of cacti on the ground seems to be fatal to the existence of the cryptogamia, yet the two classes of plants appear to be closely allied. I think it would be out of place to point out here the numerous similarities between the two genera; but some of the cacti have the creeping habits which so greatly distinguish the cryptogamia; and which so often make them appear like a disease of the earth's surface, insomuch that "lichen" has been adopted by the medical profession as the descriptive word of a large class of skin diseases.

Not that all lichens and cacti have a repulsive appearance: but a forest of the candelabra cacti has a curious, and artificial, look to the eye. This is not altogether displeasing; but there is a kind of low-growing cactus which resembles a scab; and which creeps and creeps until it has covered large tracts of country in an irregular, patchy way; and which is not only an unsightly thing; but is, also, a source of much trouble to the traveller; as it bristles with large thorns strong enough to cripple a horse.

There are but few evils unfurnished with a "compensation balance"; and this creeping cactus bears a very delicious and refreshing fruit. The fruits of all cacti appear as warts, or excrescences, on the trunks of the plants. Some of them are well known as the "prickly pears" of the shops; and not infrequently are exposed in the markets of all European and American countries. The flavours vary much. Most of them are sub-acid, like those of the currant and gooseberry; but in the New Mexico and Arizona district there is a variety which tastes much like a strawberry. Both the sap, which is very abundant, and the fruits of these plants, have a remarkable strengthening effect on the human system; and I am surprised that this fact has not been more noticed than it seems to have been. Perhaps this neglect of a useful remedy is owing to the fact that cacti grow only in very desolate and unattractive regions. I think invalids suffering from consumption, and other debilitating complaints, would benefit greatly from a prolonged stay in a cacti forest.

Not only are the curative properties of cacti ignored or unknown; but their common uses are neglected in an amazing way. I have passed through districts in the

"Wild West" of the United States, which could not have been traversed by a party unprovided with a water-cart, were it not for the abundance of these curious plants.

I have also found, and assisted in the tracking, of men who have perished of thirst surrounded by an abundant growth of cacti. On one occasion I was present at the burying of four men who had died raving mad as a result of drinking the water of the "soda ponds" in an insane effort to relieve their sufferings. They all lay under huge cactus plants; and one of my party, cutting off a limb of one of these plants, and suspending a bucket under it, obtained two gallons of cool and refreshing fluid in less than half an hour. So do men often perish with salvation within reach of their hands.

The huge forest which occupies the centre of the South American continent; and which, in spite of much wanton destruction on its outskirts, still occupies at least a million square miles of surface; and, allowing for some breaks, and its extensions into Venezuela and Guiana in the north, and Bolivia in the south, may stretch to nearly double that area, climbs some 6000 or 7000 feet up the slope of the Peruvian Andes. The height varies in different districts, for no perceptible reason. In the highlands, which extend into the interior about 800 miles, along the whole length of Peru, and where the rivers have a strong current, vast quantities of timber have been felled, and sent floating down-stream to such places as Santiago and San Ignacio, on the Upper Amazon, where it is collected into rafts, and taken down to Wanta to be shipped. But the heart of the forest (and a vast heart it is) is impenetrable to the lumber-man, and will probably long remain so. Much of it is swamp—the most extensive swamp in the world: and where it is cut by large rivers, these mostly have currents so slow, and are so choked in places by the trees, which crowd into them, and environ them so closely, that no breeze strong enough to fill a sail ever ruffles their surface. Consequently timber cannot be rafted and towed down to the ports on the main river.

Years ago the Brazilian Government placed a torpedo gunboat on the Amazon; and a sort of police-boat specially constructed to steam up the many great tributaries of the great river, and explore them. But even these failed to effect many discoveries, or gather materials for maps. The difficulties are great in the navigation of rivers with all sorts of hidden dangers uncleared from their channels: and commanders of torpedo craft are not exactly the kind of gentlemen to explore such regions as Matto Grosso. The Brazilian sailor has yet to learn the meaning of such nautical phrases as "Show a leg and save the tide"; and to do a thing in "a brace of shakes" is quite beyond his capacity, even with a smart sergeant of marines and a rattan cane behind his back: and I have seen sailors of the Brazilian navy caned in a way which one might have thought would make even a tortoise lively. The first explorers of the Matto Grosso must be men who, like myself (let the boast be forgiven), can bump an old tub over a mud flat without spilling the stores, and live on dried monkeys' tails for a year at a stretch. Something of this sort has been my experience on many a weary journey in South America, and I have been without bread for so long a period as almost to forget the taste of it. Bread, I should mention, was not used by the Brazilians of the back-lands; pulse and rice taking its place; and many families living entirely on flesh, with small quantities of fruits and vegetables.

I do not intend to dwell on the natural history of the Andes; but I wish to make a few general remarks about some of the birds and mammals which are found at a great height in the range. A vast mountain range may be a barrier to the migration of many species of creatures; but it is not so to the extent that "systematic naturalists" represent. There are animals on the Andes to the height of 12,000 or 14,000 feet that one would not expect to find there considering the barrenness of the ground and the severity of the climate. The humming-bird, for instance, seems to be out of its element in such a region, where flowers are few, and the cold bitter, yet several species haunt the rocks of Peru to a height of 12,000 feet at least. I am not sure that they do not even cross the ridge to the plains of the seaboard. At any rate, the same species are found on both sides of the Andes: it cannot, therefore, have formed a barrier to them.

Mice, too, are abundant throughout the range, from Patagonia to Ecuador, and this in places where I could find no food to support their numbers! They, and the humming-birds, probably feed largely on insects, which are numerous amongst the moss, and lurking in the cracks and fissures of the rocks, consisting mostly of moths and minute beetles. The lichens maintain a considerable insect colony of their own, mostly of very small creatures, which harmonize so well with their surroundings that they easily escape a careless human eye. Do they escape the mice and the humming-birds? I think not. These little creatures know where to find their prey; and they find it in spite of protective colouring. They would soon cease to exist if they did not: and amongst the lower creatures existence is not so great a struggle as we are taught by scientists, who must find something new to talk about, if they wish to keep their names before the public. Left to herself, Nature keeps an exact balance.

There is a fox, or wild dog, of small size, in the higher Andes; and this handsome little creature, I know, feeds chiefly, perhaps entirely, on the rats and mice. These rodents are of American species. There appear to be no fewer than six kinds of mice inhabiting the higher Andes of Eastern Peru. They are all short-tailed, "white-footed" mice; and one species, approximating the European brown rat in size, is probably confined to this region, as I have not seen it in any other part of America, or in any museum.

There are two kinds of rats, both long-tailed: one, weighing about a pound, is scarce (or perhaps nocturnal in its habits), and dwells on the ground occupied by the cacti groves. I did not often see it; but trapped three or four specimens. The common rat of the Andes is a water-rat which is found in all parts of those streams which contain fish. It also preys on other aquatic animals and insects; and makes a very beautiful and symmetrical nest amongst the small reeds (a kind of stiff grass) which grow in the shallow water of many of the mountain streams. The entrance to the nest is in the side; it is made of fine grass, interwoven with moss, and sometimes entirely of moss; and lined with fur which is evidently torn from the breast of the little animal.

The structure is so little like that of other rats or mice that I mistook it for a bird's nest until I found four young rats in one of them.

These are in addition to the European rats and mice which are found in many of the towns amongst the Andes, from Pasco downwards, until they may be said to swarm in the cities, and even the villages, of the coast-line and interior.

Probably no animal has fixed habits which it never varies. I have noticed that many creatures easily adapt themselves to new conditions of life. Thus many observers have fallen into great errors through supposing because they have never seen a particular kind of bird fly higher than a hundred yards that it never ascends so high as a mile; because it has only been noticed at the margins of pools, that it never swims to the centres of large lakes.

Large flocks of birds were seen flying from the interior of the country across the Andes. To do this they must have passed at an altitude of at least three miles. Amongst them were dense flocks of ducks, geese, and gulls; all probably bound to the sea coast. Gulls, or tern, breed in immense numbers in the marshes and swamps eastward of the Peruvian Andes, in the neighbourhood of the Ucayali, fully 800 miles inland from the sea! Thirty years is a long time in this modern progressive era; but about thirty years ago the birds had been so little disturbed in the valley of the Upper Amazon, that at the proper season (when the breeding was over) ducks and gulls might be seen passing the Andes in flocks numbering hundreds of thousands. I have seen them flying all day in batches of ten to twenty thousand; and at night have calculated that at least 2,000,000 birds have passed over my head, so high up that they appeared as mere specks though I was standing on a peak 16,000 feet (*three miles*) above sea-level!

Small birds passed in smaller, yet very large, flocks; and multitudes of others, the species of which could not be told by their manner of flight.

CHAPTER V

THE UCAYALI

THE Ucayali must be described in considerable detail. It is not merely one of the chief head-waters of the Amazon: it is, in the opinion of many persons, the actual source of the main river.

Like the Marañon, the Ucayali is essentially a mountain stream in its upper courses; and like the real source of the Amazon it flows through inexpressibly grand and wild scenery. There is more variety in the country through which it flows than is the case in the Marañon; and it is a much longer river than its rival for chief honours.

But those persons who think the Ucayali is the source of the Amazon are invariably, I believe, those who have not visited the two streams. It is true that many Peruvians claim the Ucayali as the parent of the Amazon; but their opinions are of little worth, as they are those of ignorant men who are guided by prejudice, national pride, and any reason except hard fact.

As is the case of the Marañon, the name of Ucayali applies to a portion of the stream only—the lower reaches in this instance: and it is doubtful which of two great branches is the source of the Ucayali. These two branches run parallel for a long distance, divided by a lofty range which forms the western wall of the eastern range of the Andes: for here the mountains divide into two huge branches, running, like the rivers, parallel to each other. There are, besides, subsidiary or outlying masses; and the scenery is of such a varied and remarkable character that one hardly knows where to begin a description of it.

The left branch of the river, the one I believe to be its source, rises in a vast bend, or bay, of the Andes a few miles above the town of Cayllama, through which it runs. It bursts forth from the mountain-side; but would probably be dry a great part of the year, were it not fed by the melting snow from the tremendous rocks which surround it, from which a great number of babbling brooks and graceful cascades are constantly running.

The people of Cayllama believe they are situated at a fabulous height above the coast towns: by barometric measurement (the only kind it was in my power to make) I made the place about 9000 feet above the sea. The country in the neighbourhood is a plateau enclosed by mountains; and there is some cultivation of the ground, which, however, is miserably poor, and unproductive of the most necessary things for man's existence. Terrific sand-storms occur, as they do in all parts of the elevated valleys of Peru; and whirlwinds are one of the commonest sights on this plateau. I have seen them apparently from 100 to 150 feet high; and so dense that I have deemed it necessary to gallop away from them. The speed at which they travel seems to be from six or seven to about twenty miles an hour; and they are often very destructive. Men and animals lose their lives by being overtaken and buried to a great depth. When they break, a huge cloud of fine dust rises in the air, and can be seen a vast distance away. It sometimes floats hundreds of miles, especially if a strong wind continues to blow for a considerable time.

The river skirts this plateau, running at the base of a rocky wall as far as the little town of Parura, about twenty miles from Cuzco, which is known to be nearly 12,000 feet above the sea. It here takes a turn to the north, the course at first being nearly due east, and becomes known as the Apurimac. Lower down it is the Tambo; and it is not until its junction with the Urubamba (just as often called the Vilcanota) that it is called the Ucayali, a name which it bears to its junction with the Amazon.

The distance to the meeting of the Apurimac with the Urubamba is about 800 miles from Cayllama. Beyond this point the Ucayali is a mighty river with a total course of about 1000 miles; but its stream is very tortuous and it has never been accurately measured.

Its upper reaches flow, or rather rush, through a country studded with snow-capped peaks; and as the line of perpetual snow under the Equator is 16,000 feet, these vast mountains cannot be much under this height. Some of them undoubtedly exceed it.

It is right that I should state here that I am not acquainted with every part of the Ucayali's course. I simply claim to know enough of the river to give a general description of it; and a particular account of certain parts of it.

The whole region abounds in remarkable features. The country lying between the Urubamba and the Apurimac is entirely occupied by the remarkable ridge before mentioned, which does not vary much in height, and towers 6000 or 7000 feet above the valley below it: that is fully 14,000 feet above the sea. There are but very few known passes over it; and here and there it rises like a wall above either river, with an awe-inspiring abruptness.

This range takes its rise much farther south, in Bolivia on the eastern shores of Lake Titicaca, the largest lake in South America. The cluster of peaks in this district is the most tremendous in the whole system of the Andes, several of them much exceeding 20,000 feet in height: as Serata, Ancolum, Illimani, and others; and the whole region is volcanic; ancient, slumbering and active.

This part of the country is, however, outside the scope of the present work; and I must confine myself to the Apurimac range, often called the Nevada Cuzco, and bearing half a dozen purely local names. Only a few tiny cascades fall from it into either of the rivers which closely embrace its base, like huge ditches; but at a spot on the Urubamba, a few miles above the embouchure of the Paucartambo, there is an unbroken cascade from the rocks which appears to drop at least 1000 feet, yet the volume of water is so small that when the wind blows with force it sweeps it aside like a ribbon.

The distance across the ridge from river to river is from twelve to thirty miles, above Cuzco: and I tried to cross it at seven or eight spots before I succeeded in doing so. It is a stiff piece of climbing, and dangerous. Often we had to swarm up the faces of cliffs which were as perpendicular as a wall; and for more than half the distance up a slip of the foot would have meant certain death. The descent on the other side was even worse. It was nearly all rope work; and we had often to lower one another 100 and 150 feet; and several good ropes were lost, as it was found to be impossible to disengage them after the last man had descended, though one of the guides had an ingenious device for effecting this work.

The Apurimac before effecting its juncture with the Urubamba becomes the Tambo; and this portion of it wends its way through defiles as gloomy as those of the Colorado, though not so high and impressive. At one place the cañon was so narrow that I could throw a pebble from one side to the other; and the cliffs above, 800 or 400 feet high, hung over so much as to almost shut out the view of the sky, and exclude the daylight. Some of the masses above seemed to be loose; and as there was plenty of evidence of heavy and frequent falls of rock, I was quite relieved when we had passed through this terrible passage.

On the whole the plateau and valleys of this district seemed to be more fertile than those farther north; but possibly the difference of season must be allowed for. Many of the plants and flowers seen here may not have been in leaf and bloom at the time I visited the northern provinces. At any rate, there were scores more of flowers here than I saw in the country adjoining the banks of the Marañon. Amongst those well known in Europe, and which I suppose have been acclimatized in the last-named country, were beds of heliotrope, giving forth a delightfully sweet scent as we tramped through them. Acres of the hill-sides were covered with red and yellow calceolarias and verbenas; besides hundreds of beautiful blooms, the names of which I knew not. Fuchsias here form shrubs, or bushes, fourteen feet high, and bushy in proportion, the blooms being so thick as to quite eclipse the leaves, and almost hide them. One splendid flower appears to be a dahlia; and what I think is singular, and almost unique amongst wild flowers, there are four distinct colours in its blooms—yellow, white, a beautifully rich crimson, and scarlet.

The cultivated plants are such as one usually associates with a tropical climate, though the degree of cold is sharp, not only on the mountains, but also in the sheltered valleys; yet the coffee and tobacco which are raised are both of very fine quality; and while grain (except rice) will often not ripen or prosper, the climate being either too hot or too cold, the sugar-cane, and cotton shrub, both flourish on the mountain-sides; and the coca (not *cocoa*) plant comes to perfection. It is one of the most extraordinary vegetable products in nature; and why it is not better known and more used in other parts of the world is very puzzling. Probably the accounts of it seem too marvellous to be true; and are regarded as "travellers' tales." It is a species of tea which has the power to arrest the waste of the human system to so wonderful an extent that a person using it can sustain severe labour without other food for several days. Muleteers, and other persons travelling in the Peruvian Andes, always carry it with them; as it is a stimulant of far more use than spirits; and some of the poorer wayfarers perform journeys of several hundred miles with scarcely any other refreshment. The statement seems an exaggeration; but it is not. Bread is not used in Peru; and the poor traveller starts on his journey with no other provision than a little tobacco, and the never-forgotten coca leaves—the part of the plant in general use, though it flowers and fructifies five or six times a year. It is used all over Brazil, and in most other parts of South America; but chiefly in the Andes.

It is very singular to pass from a highly cultivated mountain-side, or coffee patch in a valley; and after an hour or two's travel to find oneself in a horrible desert of sand, without even a blade of grass visible; but it is a frequent experience in the southern and north-eastern districts of the Peruvian Andes. That part of the elevated valley which lies to the eastward of the rivers Paucartambo, Urubamba, and Ucayali; and also the Pampa del Sacramento, westward of the upper reaches of the last-named river, contain deserts of a very pronounced type. Some of them are knee-deep in sand; and several are declared to be impassable. Men have made the attempt and never reappeared, and would-be rescuers who have followed them have also disappeared. I have myself penetrated them so far as to see that the continually moving clouds of fine sand must be a very real danger to man and horse; and I crossed one of them with some persons who did not fully realize the risk we were taking. Until this time I had not believed there were such utterly desolate spots, even in Sahara, and the central steppes of Asia. Nothing of life is found in them—no bird of the air ever crosses them. There are spots where, though they are as dry as the dust of Sodom, the sand is so loose that if a man inadvertently steps into them he will sink and disappear as readily as in a quick-sand. Blade of grass! The very lichens refuse to show themselves on the rocks, which, here and there, crop up from the sand, like breakers in a sea. An absolutely worthless tract of country; one of Nature's dust-heaps—an elevated Atacama, without the one feature which makes that Chilean wilderness passable —fixity of soil. A railway can be thrown across the desert of Atacama; the sands of the desert of Sacramento would swallow up railroad, and railroad workers, and its sand-laden winds howl for more!

Few men of the country are mad enough to attempt the passage of these sand deserts: the people think it is a sign of insanity to propose to do so. Personally my whole series of adventures in South America were the outcome of an overwhelming sorrow which made me, not altogether reckless, but desperate, and careless of consequences. So I was led to undertake, and do, many things that seemed rash; but which have, at any rate, made me acquainted with some little-known, and unfrequented, by-paths of the world.

It is strange that these sand tracts should exist surrounded by a country that is probably the best-watered region in the world. No other division of the earth can show a land teeming with rivers so large, and so numerous, as those which form the system of the mighty Amazon: and it is probably only water that is wanted to turn these barrens of dead sand into gardens of Eden. If one or two of the rivers of the elevated valley were turned into them what might not the result be! Or the waste might gradually be won by planting poplars and North American pines on the outskirts of them. The poplar has been introduced into many parts of the Andes, and flourishes apace; but the pines are strangely neglected.

After the junction of the Urubamba and Tambo, the river (now the Ucayali) runs for a long way through a wide valley which is, as I have just described, bordered on both sides by some of the worst deserts of South America. There is vegetation on the banks of the Ucayali; but no tributaries join it from either side for a distance of more than 200 miles—a very remarkable circumstance. One river only, the Pachutea, runs into it on the left bank. Any other brook, or runnel (nothing larger can possibly reach it), that perchance reaches its channel is certainly dry during three-fourths of the year. I did find a few dry beds of streams; but these could only have been torrents for a few hours, or days at most, immediately after those terrific rain-storms which are common at the season we may term "the fall" in this region.

The course of the Ucayali is, in its upper reaches, through rocky channels, which are only occasionally deep enough to be described as cañons. The stream is rapid with shoots and cascades at frequent intervals; but as far as I know the river at this point, there are no falls of magnitude. The last 200 miles of its course before joining the Amazon are navigable for vessels larger than boats; and there is much cultivated land in this region, with several towns and villages on its banks. The last hundred miles, at least, down to the main river, are through a dense primeval forest. Large quantities of the timber have been felled; but at the time of my visit these inroads had not made any very perceptible diminution of the forest near the river. The "backwoods" were still impenetrable to any ordinary traveller; a tract of swamp so closely overgrown with huge trees, and closely knitted vines, that, as was proved by an experiment in my presence, an experienced axe-man, after eight hours of incessant hacking, had not advanced twelve yards from the spot where he commenced operations!

CHAPTER VI

THE SEARCH FOR THE HEAD-WATERS OF THE PURUS

ACCORDING to the best maps I could procure, the head-waters of the Purus, another great tributary of the Amazon, are not more than thirty miles from the junction of the Tambo with the Urubamba. At this time I had been up the Amazon as high as the first cataract (from the mouth of the river), and had also explored a considerable portion of the Purus; and I would have gone a much greater distance than thirty miles to see the source of this interesting river. So I struck inland accompanied only by a personal servant, a Venezuelan sailor named George Maccara, two Peruvian Spaniards and two Indians to serve as carriers.

At this time I was not in a good state of health. The change of diet forced upon me had unpleasant results. I suffered greatly from the lack of bread. After a time the eating of much fruit and vegetables became impossible, and I lived almost entirely on flesh; but the meat of all kinds in this part of South America is almost devoid of fat; and the craving for fat took the form of a disease with me: so much so that when I obtained some olive oil I used to drink large quantities of it daily. This condition lasted until I returned to the coast towns and obtained the food of civilization. It is only at hotels, however, that bread is to be obtained, and that only at hotels frequented by United States tourists and Europeans. It is always in the form of French rolls—a yard long. These remarks apply also to Brazil. The people of the land eat no bread, except a few of the rich, who have acquired the taste for it in North America or during their travels in Europe.

The elevated valley of Peru stretches farther towards the interior than is shown on maps. Thirty years ago there were no accurate maps of the country to be obtained in Peru. Those published in the United States, and in England were better; but even these were of very little use to a traveller. They were on much too small a scale; and were only approximately correct—often not even that. Places were marked upon them which did not exist, and many that did exist were completely ignored, or overlooked.

Let it be clearly understood that throughout nearly the whole extent of Peru there is a double set of elevated valleys; and a dual set of enclosing walls also. The valley to the eastward has the character of an enclosed plateau; and the two sets of ranges are, also, divided by a valley which is several thousand feet above the level of the sea. As a rule, these two ranges run parallel to each other; but there are many breaks; and some conglomerations of peaks; the Knot of Pasco, for instance. In a general sense—a very general sense—the whole country is eminently a mountainous one—even more so than Switzerland: but it must not be supposed that I am making a comparison between the two countries. No two mountain regions could be more dissimilar. Glaciers abound in Switzerland; but this formation is almost unknown in Peru; owing, no doubt, to the American country being situated entirely within the tropics. Pine forests, larches and firs are the characteristic forests of Switzerland: these trees are unknown in Peru, the pines of the Andes being very different in appearance from those of Europe and North America. Neither are they a prominent feature of the landscape, as they are in other countries.

The slope of the first, or western, range of the Peruvian Andes is more abrupt than that of the eastern; but both are far more steep than is usual in other countries. To the east, I found it difficult to find a pass through which I could descend to the forest-covered plain below. This part of the country is not occupied permanently, except by Indians and a few isolated planters: and these were singularly ignorant of the valley country to the eastward of their homes.

The Indians of this region are not so intelligent as the red men of the North; and not so adventurous. They may be of the same race; but their habits and proclivities are very different; and their mental development much inferior to that of the northern tribes. They do not wander so much; and I found both Indians and Spaniards who had never descended to the forests which lie at the base of their tremendous mountains. Why? After some time I met a Peruvian who could give a reason. "I went once," he said: "but it took me two days to reach the plains. I went after gold. An Indian of the forest had come up to us to buy knives, and brought a little dust of the precious metal to pay for them. He explained where he found it: so praying to our Lady of Good Intent, I went in search of more. Our Lady must have been angry with me: for I found no gold; but instead was nearly killed by a jaguar; and I trod upon a big snake which bit me, and made me very bad. I sought for gold five or six months, and did not see a trace of it; and then it took me five days to climb back home. As there is nothing to be found I never went again."

This is just it. "There is nothing to be found"; and so the people, Indians included, do not take the trouble to go up and down the difficult mountain-sides. There may be more to be gained by a little enterprise than these supine people suppose; as will be noticed presently.

The gentleman whose words I have quoted showed me the skin of the jaguar which had attacked him. It was that of a very fine animal; but it had been killed without trouble; and the injuries my friend had sustained, as evidenced by the claw-marks about his body, did not appear to have been very severe. I have seen men who had been mauled to a much greater extent.

I induced this gentleman to go with me about twenty miles, to show me the pass by which he had descended to the plains. We had first a stiff climb of about 4000 feet up the barrier range; which was covered here with beautiful flowers, shrubs, bushes and small trees, amongst which the lauchamar was noticed. The Indians, and lower-class Peruvians make clothes of the bark of this tree; which is first soaked in water, then well beaten with mallets; and thus becomes nearly as soft and elastic as woollen cloth.

The scenery viewed from the top of this ridge was superb. It was clearly seen that we were on the last eastward barrier of the Andes: for below the forest stretched away to an enormous distance, on ground that, from our eminence looked quite flat. No hills, undulations, or other inequalities, could be perceived; and only the larger rivers gleamed in the light of the sun.

The colour of the landscape was sombre, with no appearance of green anywhere. Greys of various shades, with blue in the middle distance, and a pinkish haze on the horizon, were the prevalent hues. Here and there were long strips of blackish shade, and others of brown: in fact, the whole land was quite different in appearance from what one might reasonably expect it to be; and had we not known the character of the country, nobody could have guessed that it was a dense forest. There were no details, and no individual trees distinguishable; and the grandeur of the scene consisted entirely in its immensity. Broadly it was similar to what I afterwards witnessed 500 miles farther north in Ecuador; where, however, the colouring was very different; which is singular, as the character of the forest is the same throughout its whole extent. Indeed it is remarkable that the general appearance of both mountains and forests changes but little throughout the central parts of South America.

Viewed from the spot where we were now standing, many clouds were seen floating thousands of feet below us, and obscuring portions of the distant landscape. Above the sky was perfectly clear; and bright to the verge of dazzling brilliance; yet the air was shrewd and biting, as it is in England on a frosty December morning.

Some wild guanacos were seen, but escaped before we could get within shooting distance of them. I discovered the tracks of a puma, too; almost the first I had seen since I had been in these mountains. For all the wild animals are much persecuted; and guanacos and pumas nearly exterminated. The pumas are so scarce that I never actually saw one in the highlands of Peru, but these animals, and jaguars, I found to be exceedingly abundant in the forests of the plain, where no hunters come to destroy them. At the present time we could not follow the puma the footmarks of which were seen on account of the inaccessibility of the ground.

The descent to the plains was down a gully with walls so close together that often I could touch both at the same time by stretching out my arms. I passed through a fissure in Ecuador of a very similar kind, but far more gloomy and difficult of passage than this one, the walls of which were seldom more than forty or fifty to a hundred feet high. The most difficult part was a cliff-like drop of twenty feet, down which we clambered by means of a roughly made grass-rope ladder; which was left in position to assist us to mount when we returned.

When we came to the side of the mountain our real difficulties commenced; for it was covered with loose stones, which gave way beneath our weight, and dangerous rolls and falls were frequent, the stones flying down with us, and sometimes inflicting nasty cuts and knocks. Slipping, sliding, falling, we did not reach firm ground until sunset. The forest was then still several thousand feet beneath us, but we could distinguish the trees quite easily, and smell the peculiar aromatic odour which arises from some of them.

The moon was about a quarter old, and gave sufficient light to reveal the landscape dimly to a great distance, and I remained awake the greater part of the night viewing the wonderful scene, the like of which few men have the privilege of seeing even once in the course of their lives. It would be futile to attempt to judge the distance over which the eye could range. In a former work, writing of the Ecuador Andes, I have put it at hundreds of miles. This may be an exaggeration, and probably is so; but the range of eye over a flat country, from a height of 10,000 to 16,000 feet, is enormous, and quite possibly does not fall short of 100 miles. There are no points, or natural objects, which serve to fix the distances viewed—all is one apparently flat expanse of the densest forest on the earth's surface.

Humming-birds abound to the very summit of this outer ridge. Five species were noted, the largest not bigger than a wren. Parrots and macaws keep to the lower forests, where they are abundant. Large condors were almost continually hovering about us at a great height. These birds seldom approach very close to men; but they do sometimes come within gunshot. I have killed a few from curiosity and desire to examine them; but I soon gave up shooting them, as their destruction is going on too fast. Prejudice and obstinacy say they are mischievous birds: I know differently; and the time will come when the people of South America will regret the extermination of these handsome and elegant birds. A mountainous and rocky country is essential to their existence; and although they visit the plains, they do not dwell in any part of the level country.

Small birds were seen on the mountain-side, but no large ones besides the condors; and no mammals except mice and chinchillas, which are marvellously abundant. They live in colonies; and the faces of the cliffs are so honeycombed with their holes that they look like the homes of multitudes of sand-martins. These little animals have the power of running up a perpendicular surface, like a mouse; and their holes are self-burrowed and of great depth, and communicate one with another —to a considerable extent, at any rate. There are several kinds of chinchillas; but in this district those which I saw were the Peruvian short-tailed species. They are of a very light slate colour with black mottlings, and are as active as squirrels. During my night watch hundreds of them approached our camp, apparently attracted by the light of the fire; but on the slightest movement, or noise, from me, they bolted in a body, reappearing in half an hour. When any sound came up from the forest below, they sat up and evidently listened with some anxiety, turning their heads from side to side, probably on the watch for enemies.

Though the forest was fully a mile beneath us, many sounds emanated from it during the night. The howling monkeys were busy, and kept up a dismal succession of horribly mournful sounds—like those of a person suffering unutterable torment. Several birds, also, disturbed the serenity of the night, amongst which the most active was probably a species of night-jar; or it might have been an owl. Other noises I could not allot to any particular creature, never having heard them before.

It is singular that there is always a great deal of noise in the Brazilian forest until long after midnight; but during the day the silence of death reigns in all parts of it. The monkeys are responsible, mostly, for these night noises. The howlers mourn, and groan, and yell in a very human-like tone of voice; but every now and then a sharp scream of mingled pain and horror announces that the jaguar has pounced upon an unfortunate simian; or that it has become the victim of a lurking boa-constrictor. The jaguar makes short work of its prey: but the horrid, creeping serpent, never active but during the momentary dart on its victim, is as cruel as a cat with a mouse; and the screams of a monkey, as it is slowly crushed to death, are dreadful to listen to.

Continuing our journey down the mountain-side we came to an extensive cane-brake, which was so thick that we had frequently to cut our way through it. This was easily done, and did not delay us much; but it was afternoon before we reached the lower slopes of the mountain. There are no foot-hills, but the actual base slopes down gradually to the lower ground; and cannot be described as steep for the last 2000 feet. The forest belt here ascends from 4000 to 5000 feet. It would undoubtedly grow much higher up; but above 5000 feet the cliff-like face is too perpendicular to afford the trees a root-hold. A few odd ones, and some clumps, may be seen here and there, where the winds or the birds have carried up the seeds to ledges and crevices; but these find so little soil for their support, that they are always small, and of puny development.

The forest proper is simply magnificent, and differs from all other arboreal tracts on earth. As is well known, in all countries, North American, Asiatic and European, one species of tree supplants another; and thus we get forests of one particular kind, to the exclusion of all others. But in this vast tract—Matto Grosso—The Great Forest—there is nothing of this kind; but the variety of trees is endless, all growing together in mag-

Photo Underwood & Underwood

A "BELL-LLAMA" LEADING A HERD THROUGH THE INDIAN STREET OF PASCO

nificent confusion: and nowhere, so far as I have seen, does one species predominate over more than a few acres; and even such instances as this are of rare occurrence.

To name the trees which compose this wonderful forest, even those of the commonest kinds, is a task of which I am incapable. Many of them are quite "unknown to science"; hundreds are well known to botanists, and have been described by more competent hands than mine. Some of the more curious will be described from time to time in this book, as circumstances bring them into prominent notice. Here I can only record that some of the largest I met with in Matto Grosso were found at the foot of the Peruvian Eastern Andes. It is not for height, so much as for extent, for bushiness, that they are noticeable, though many are giants. Trees of 200 feet in height are numerous; and this is a very considerable size: as trees exceeding 100 feet are very rare in most wooded countries.

Branches and boughs of these trees often exceed 100 feet in length and are eight feet in diameter, the parent trunk being sometimes as much as twenty in diameter. Probably the weight of the whole tree would be several hundred tons. Many of them are miniature forests in themselves, supporting large trunks of other species as parasites, the whole bound together by creeping plants of huge growth, the bines of which exceed a foot in diameter. These tremendous vines are the boa-constrictor of the vegetable world. It may take years, perhaps ages, but in due course they crush to death the mighty trunks they embrace. One reads about the immense creeping and climbing plants of the African forests, and sees pictures of them; but they do not seem to attain so vast a size as those of Brazil. To measure them, except the girth of the stem, is impossible; but as they turn and twist in convolutions that must do much more than double the length; and as they climb to the tops of the tallest trees, a fine specimen is probably at least 600 feet long. These huge vines ramify, and throw off hundreds of shoots and bines; so they are plants remarkable for size in themselves. Some of them bear splendid blossoms, as the trumpet-flower, which is so large that the Indian children and women wear them on their heads like helmets. The naturalist Bates was, I believe, the first to notice this fact. Trumpet-flower is not, however, a good name for these flowers: for there are at least half a dozen kinds of them, borne on plants which differ very widely in their characters

CHAPTER VII

THE HEAD-WATERS OF THE PURUS

THE first night we passed in this region we camped close to the base of the mountains; and in the morning at daybreak one of the Indians called my attention to a herd of guanacos up among the rocks at a height of fully 1000 feet (about 850 yards) above our heads. I shot at them five times before I struck one. The sound of a rifle must have been new to these animals: for at the first shot they only remained still with their heads stretched up to listen. At the next discharge some of them moved a little; but others resumed their munching at the dry herbage on the rocks.

The one that was struck tumbled off the ledge where it was standing, and slipped and rolled almost down to our feet. It frequently caught against projecting crags; but none of these were large enough to prevent its descent; and the carcass was a good deal cut and rent by the sharp points and stones; but it afforded us an abundant supply of excellent meat.

Guanacos, vicuñas, alpacas and llamas are all closely allied to one another, being simply varieties of the same species. Llamas are domesticated guanacos; and there are many breeds of them, just as there are of horses and sheep; and the alpaca is one of these breeds. There is no more difference between alpacas and llamas and guanacos than there is between south downs and merinos. The vicuña, or vicugna, is a local variety of the guanaco. It was probably a mountain guanaco, the last-named species taking to the mountains at a much later period than the former. The larger guanaco is found wild in the pampas, or plains, which the vicuña never is. Vicuña is the Spanish form of spelling of the name—I do not know on what authority modern writers have changed it to vicugna.

The guanaco, and all its varieties, are certainly camels; and have all the habits, as well as the nasty temper, of these "ships of the desert." All describers of the animal notice its revolting trick of "spitting" at persons who approach it or stand near to watch it. The "spitting" is really a blowing out of the mucus of the nose; and why there should be any fastidiousness in plainly saying so I cannot conceive. They have another nasty habit of emitting the urine at one, in a straight stream like the fluid of a skunk: they also pair in quite a different way from that of other animals. All of them, domestic and wild, are surly and spiteful, and bite and kick without any provocation; and they are incessantly quarrelling amongst themselves, and fight as viciously as dogs. But the flesh of all is excellent food—the best meat of any animals in South America. In the elevated valleys of the Central Andes, including the whole of Peru and Ecuador, and a great part of Chile, there are numerous herds of llamas and alpacas—the largest I have seen contained about 7000 animals. The wild guanacos and vicuñas number about ten to twenty per herd, except in the uninhabited

Photo Uuderwood & Uuderwood

A HERD OF PACK-LLAMAS AND INDIAN ATTENDANT

wildernesses, where they congregate in much greater numbers.

To number and describe all the animals and plants of the luxuriant district which gives birth to the head-waters of the Purus, would be to write a natural history. It may be noticed, however, that owing to the forest being on much drier ground than that it occupies farther northward and eastward, there is some modification of both flora and fauna. Monkeys and sloths are more abundant, and serpents less numerous; and caimans, or alligators, altogether absent: but these reptiles may have been estivating, or enjoying their summer sleep, at the time of my visit.

Though serpents are not numerous here, I saw several of large size. One monstrous-looking creature was dragging itself from tree to tree a hundred feet overhead, and as it stretched its repulsive body almost in a straight line, I thought it appeared to be quite sixteen feet long.

I nearly walked over another as it lay semi-dormant in the herbage at the foot of some trees. To avoid accidents I destroyed this creature, and it proved to be nearly thirteen feet long. A bullet through the head was not sufficient to quiet it; and it was finally killed by cutting through its spine with an axe. Both these snakes were boas.

The tender spot in a serpent is the tail. If it is cut through in this quarter it is rendered quite incapable of rising to attack, or of writhing away; and will not long survive.

The ground immediately eastward of the Peruvian Andes has a gentle, and almost imperceptible, slope to the north-east, and the country is full of brooks and rivulets with beds of mingled pebbles and sand. The grass on the banks is green, and the ground meadow-like; but generally the water-courses run through a thick canopy of foliage, many of the trees being heavily laden with fruits and flowers. Very few of the streams in this neighbourhood are too deep to be fordable; but some of them have deep holes in their beds; and most of them pretty rapids and cascades of no great size. The babbling of brooks is incessant; and the songs of birds greet the ear in the early morning and late at night. For several species of the birds of the district have charming songs; and a kind of bell-bird is very frequently to be heard tolling. Tolling is a good word to express the sound this most extraordinary creature makes: for the notes are not produced in very quick succession—at any rate by this species, which is about the size of a blackbird and of a mottled brown colour.

It differs much from those I have seen in eastern Brazil, which are mostly white-plumaged. The species which I am now describing is furnished with a long, horn-shaped appendage at the base of the upper beak, which is not, so far as I could perceive, erectile; and has nothing to do with the remarkable sounds the bird produces, which are very similar to those of a musically toned bell, of considerable size.

I am afraid no words of mine can describe these sounds, and the extraordinary effect they have on the human ear when heard in the solitudes of a vast forest, so far removed from human habitations that one easily feels as lonely as a modern Adam. No person hearing the notes for the first time, and unacquainted with their origin, could possibly guess that they proceeded from the throat of a tiny songster. "Tong! tong! tong!" then a pause. "Tong! tong! tong!" followed by a dozen more notes, none of them uttered in quick succession; but with an interval, like the notes of a slowly rung bell.

The bird seems to be strictly arboreal, as I have never seen it on the ground. It keeps at a good height, up amongst the densely growing leaves; which makes it difficult to see; but I have, on several occasions, witnessed it in the act of tolling. The head is thrown back, the body stretched upward and the beak opened widely, while the sound is emitted.

The bell-birds are decidedly shy little creatures; and are always difficult to discover, even though the plumage of some of them is pure white; a circumstance that shows that Nature is under no necessity to clothe an animal in "protective" garb to render it safe from the attacks of its enemies: for no hues could be less likely to secure an animal's immunity to danger, than the pure white of some of the bell-birds, the scarlet of the macaws, and the black of the toucans.

The fact is that in one set of circumstances, and under a peculiar class of conditions, not only are the fur, feather and scales of any and every living creature imitative of its surroundings; but there is no object, animate or inanimate, that does not, also, in a particular set of circumstances, and under peculiar circumstances, closely resemble some other object. The very clouds are often mistaken for mountains; and "Sheep's Tor" means that the Devonshire rustic found some difficulty in distinguishing his flock from the boulders of his native downs.

Difficulties, and lack of means, prevented me from

penetrating farther into the interior of the forest than about fifty English miles. To do this I followed the courses of the streams, usually walking in a foot or two of water. For though the forest is not so dense as it is towards the heart of Matto Grosso, and for hundreds of miles inland from the banks of the great rivers, it is thick enough to prevent the free progress of men.

In some of the " leafy tunnels " passed through, and in which we walked distances of twenty miles, or more, without seeing the clouds, the gloom was so great that all objects appeared only as shadows. To prevent accidents we advanced in file, roped together, like mountaineers; so if the leading man stepped into a hole, a mischance that often occurred, the others were warned, and pulled him on to his feet again. The rearmost of the party carried the arms, ammunition and other articles that a wetting would spoil; and the vicinity of dangerous animals was announced by the barking of three or four dogs which we had with us; one of which fell a victim to a puma or a jaguar, we could not tell which in the prevalent dimness.

Both pumas and jaguars were unpleasantly numerous. We could hear them crying and screaming at night; and they often came so close to our camp that we could hear them purring; for all three sounds are uttered by both jaguars and pumas. The screaming sound, much like that of the domestic cat when it is quarrelling with others, indicated that these larger animals were also settling their disputes with tooth and claw.

According to the book-naturalist the puma is not a dangerous animal; but I am afraid he has never met it in the wilds: at any rate all writers are pretty well agreed that the jaguar is a creature not to be played with. It has the very dangerous habit of lying stretched on the limb of some great tree, where it is impossible to distinguish it; not so much because its "protective colouring harmonizes with the rough bark and mosses of the trunk" as because it takes care to keep the body of the bough between itself and the passing victims for which it is watching. It is not at all particular what this victim is. It usually has to put up with some forlorn spider-monkey, or howler; and perhaps with a dry old sloth; or still drier ant-eater; but it is partial to domestic animals of all kinds; especially dogs and men: and though it is true that carnivorous animals are slow to attack men as a rule, unless they are provoked, the jaguar is one of the exceptions that prove the rule: and if a plump specimen of the family Primates, genus *homo*, happens to pass under its favourite lurking tree, it drops silently, and swift as a lightning stroke, on the back and shoulders of that unfortunate lord of creation; and then there is a tragedy in which the best man is the victim, thus proving that the victory is not always to the strong; though, in this case, the race is certainly to the swift.

For, I have actually seen a jaguar pounce on its prey; and the swiftness and suddenness with which it descends are certainly amazing. The animal resembles a flash of light, rather than a springing body; and the death of the victim is assured; for the position of the jaguar on its back, renders resistance impossible. The assailant is a brutal enemy, too. It is never in a hurry to put its prey out of its misery; but likes to suck the blood from the living animal. I once sawa living monkey in the clutches of a jaguar. I was not aware of the near neighbourhood of the beast of prey until the screams of the monkey called my attention to them both as they struggled in a tree seventy feet above my head. The jaguar was holding the victim down with one paw, and growling over it; while I was nearly helpless, as I was shooting birds and had only a fowling-piece and a revolver with me. However, I fired both barrels into the brute's flanks; and was drawing the revolver with the intention of giving it a further peppering; but it did not wait. Giving me a startled look, it bolted higher up the tree where I could not see it. The monkey fell to the ground, and was quite dead when I picked it up; but the poor little animal's cries rang in my ears for days afterwards.

Pumas are not so dangerous as jaguars; but the gentlemen who write of them as gentle and harmless beasts, etc., have evidently never seen them, except in cages. Both animals will fight desperately if wounded and unable to escape; and the jaguar is ever ready to pounce on man if it can take him unawares: indeed there are reliable accounts of its having boldly faced men and destroyed them in broad daylight.

Which of the streams that rise in the lower mountain slopes of this region is actually the Purus I am unable to say: nor is it likely that it could be ascertained without following it down to some known point; but of the twenty, or more, that I examined, it is probable that all find their way into the main stream as tributaries. They are all remarkably similar in character and dimension—all equally beautiful to the eye: and this district is one of the most delightful and Eden-like of any I saw in South America. The trees were often masses of bloom, white or crimson; and the ground studded with flowers of a hundred kinds, and a hundred tints, wherever they could find light and air enough to exist. But in the thick forest creeping plants usurp what little space is left by the close-growing trees. These also bear curious and splendidly coloured blossoms; and there are a multitude of orchids, mostly white or light purple in hue.

Here I saw the cannon-ball tree, a kind of calabash, I think. Its huge round fruit is hollow, and bursts with a loud noise, like an explosion, when it drops to the ground. Fern trees and palms were exceedingly abundant in places; though these seemed to be choked out of existence in the dense forest.

There are three kinds of spider-monkeys inhabiting the woods, one of which, remarkable for its length and extreme slenderness of limb, was quite new to me: and I never saw it in any other part of the continent. The howler was a large animal, and powerful of lungs; and seemed to be very plentiful, judging from the noises they made every evening and far into the night: but no matter how numerous monkeys may be in the forests, it is difficult to see many of them. They are cautious in showing themselves too freely; and usually remain all day in the tops of the tallest trees, where the leaves completely enshroud them. No doubt this is their safest place; as snakes cannot ascend to the extreme tops of the trees without being seen; and the branches are too slender to support the weight of their arch-enemy the jaguar. The safety of the sloths also is assured by their habit of keeping to slender branches; though they do sometimes get surprised by their wily enemies. Of sloths there are many in the Peruvian forests. I often saw them clinging to the boughs. They always hang back downwards: and are never seen in any other position, except when climbing upwards, or shuffling along the ground. But their visits to the earth are very few and far between. In the trees they can be so active as to show that the word "sloth" applied to them is a gross misnomer: on the ground they are so helpless, that I am not sure the tortoise could not outrace them. They are most harmless and helpless creatures; and if captured make no attempt to defend themselves. It is a fact that they weep piteously, and make a moaning noise, when they find themselves in the hands of that universal destroyer of all things, living or otherwise—man: and I should think they are the most tenacious of life of all mammals. The Indians are often very cruel to them; and when one was brained and cut open, I noticed that its heart and lungs were still working. If they are shot as they hang to the branches they are seldom or never killed: if they die afterwards, the carcass remains clinging to the bough. It may fall, many hours afterwards, when the muscles relax; but this is exceptional; and the Indians of Guiana, and North Brazil, who shoot them with poisoned arrows, always climb the trees after them. The wourali poison is as fatal to sloths as it is to all other animals. Bates' assertion that he has seen a sloth swim 500 yards across a river, I do not believe. He must have been mistaken; and the beautiful fiction that all animals, except man, swim naturally, should be classed with those funny illusions, the barnacle goose and the Scythian lamb.

The sloth has a great dislike to water, or even dampness; and is found only in the drier parts of the forest;

and if surprised in an isolated tree, and driven to the extremity of a branch, it will suffer itself to be captured rather than drop into a river, or pool: and that this reluctance to drop is not the result of fear of the consequences of a fall is shown from the fact that rather than be at the trouble of descending a large trunk where its hold is never very firm, it will precipitate itself from a considerable height. I have known one drop forty feet to hard ground to avoid capture, and sustain no injury whatever.

It is not correct that the sloth completely strips a tree of leaves before proceeding to another, nor does it live entirely on leafage; but fruits enter into its diet. They eat the young leaves and buds; and must be destructive to trees. They also consume an apple-like fruit of a rank acrid taste; and the berries and gourds of several vines, and other wild fruits of the forest, all of which are known to me only by their Indian, or local Spanish, names; and none of which are in much repute among the people of the country. The sloth seems to delight in strong acrid flavours. Observing that it is very frequently found in a particular tree, I tasted the leaves of it, and found them quite biting to the tongue, with a strong acid flavour. It is much the same with the berries and fruits they esteem: they are all harsh, rough, or biting to the human palate; and I never saw them eat sweet fruits of any kind.

The sloth, when reposing quietly in a tree, might easily be mistaken for a large bird's nest, or a growth of dry moss or lichen. The same remark applies to several other animals in these forests: the great ant-eater, for instance: and the circumstance, at first sight, seems to be a strong point in favour of the "protective colouring" and "mimicry" theory of the naturalist. Unfortunately for the speculative tenets of these gentlemen, I have placed it beyond doubt that colour and mimicry do not protect an animal from its natural enemies; though it is possible that these attributes serve to guard it to some extent from wanton destruction. That there is no such thing as wanton destruction in nature is another error of those exponents of wild life who have not acquired their knowledge at the fountain-head. Monkeys catch hundreds of birds, and destroy hundreds of nests containing young, for no purpose whatever but the love of mischief: the otter of this region (a huge creature three times the size of the European species) destroys ten times more fish than it can eat: the jaguarondi, and a species of wild cat in this region, destroy any small animal they meet, whether they are hungry or not, and often leave it on the spot where it is killed: there is a species of large wasp, or hornet, here, which has the same habit as the common wasp, of shearing off the legs and wings of captured flies, and then dropping the writhing carcass: and it is almost a proverb that a well-fed Tom Mouser is the best catcher of rats and mice, destroying them "in sport." Nor does this end the list. I could enumerate hundreds of wild creatures which kill in wantonness.

Now for a few final words on "protection" and "mimicry." The first time I saw a tree porcupine I mistook it for a bird's nest: and on another occasion I thought a great ant-eater, with its tail over its back, was a tuft of dried grass; but having discovered my mistakes I *never afterwards was deceived.* Nor is the

Indian enemy of these two animals ever misled in the least degree. When his stomach cries cupboard, he goes straight to their haunts, sees them in one moment and bags them in another. It is the same with the cunning puma and sly jaguar. These gentlemen of "the wild" know all about protection and mimicry. The jaguar looks up into a tree and perceives the sleeping sloth. "Bird's nest, or tuft of brown moss!" Far more likely he muses thus: "Not exactly what I want. Not much juice in this old stager; but pot-luck is better than an empty stomach: so here goes!"

Silently as the Shadow of Death the spotted villain glides up the tree; and the first intimation the poor sleeping leaf-eater has of danger is a terrific blow on the side. It does not kill him: for he is tougher than leather. But he is cuffed—clawed up into convenient position for the murderer to finish his work. In vain the wretched victim sighs and weeps (as do all his kind when in tribulation). He is in the paws of one of the most merciless of all cats; and his sufferings are not so very much prolonged—if the jaguar is keen set. "Not so bad, after all," exclaims the rascal (in the cat language, of course) as he drops a few fragments of his victim's hairy hide, and licks clean his blood-wetted whiskers. "'Protection' and 'Mimicry'! Oh! ah! my bright amber coat with velvet spots is quite invisible amongst the dark leaves; or looks like an old lady's shoulder-shawl against the black trunk! Just so. I'll try that dodge again some day."

A "stick insect" and a "leaf butterfly" are freaks of Nature like a "mandrake carrot," and the "Death's-head turnip," and the "ghosts, nun's-veils, weeping ladies and old man's heads," which are so numerous in the caves and mountains of North America; and so exactly like the objects after which they are named as to arouse the wonder of all who see them.

Although not strictly a part of the declared object of this work, I should like to say a few more words about the cats of this region; and it will not be altogether out of place, since they abound greatly on the banks of the Amazon and all its tributaries, great and small.

The word "jaguar" is pronounced "ya'wah," which is the Indian name of the creature, just as puma ("poo'mah") is that of its cousin, or brother: for there is not a halfpenny worth of difference between them, except outwardly, in colour. The jaguar is simply a leopard. I very much doubt if a "trained," or "professional," naturalist could pick out with certainty the American animals from a mixed band of jaguars and African leopards—in fact, I am sure he could not. There is said to be a characteristic "boss" on the skull of the jaguar. Of that I know nothing and care less. I believe that a "separate genus was established" for the tinamou (South American partridge) because a "bump" was discovered on its skull, which no ordinary eye could perceive without the aid of a magnifying glass! Such finical nonsense may amuse the book-naturalist: it cannot carry much weight with those who are acquainted with something more than the skin and bones of an animal.

I have never seen a Senegal maneless lion; but judging from pictures of the animal there is absolutely no difference between it and a puma. A gentleman from the shires went up to London to hear Mr. Joseph Chamberlain speak. "I were towld," said he, "that I should know Joe by the orchard [orchid] in his button-hole; and blow me 'twer'n't nothin' but a tater blossom!"

This gentleman, I am sure, would be unable to distinguish the differences between a jaguar and a leopard; and a puma and a maneless lion.

The most remarkable circumstance, or characteristic, of the two largest American cats is the curious variation in size of fully grown animals of both species. If large pumas were found in the north and small in the south the divergence in size would not be so surprising; but the pumas, and also the jaguars, of a given district may vary in size so much as fifty per cent, or even more.

A full-grown animal, indeed, an old one, as evidenced by the condition of its teeth, shot by me in Arizona, was only thirty-four inches in length from the nose to the root of the tail; while another killed in South Nevada was six feet two and a half inches from snout to tail. It is the custom to include the tail in the total length of a beast of prey. This should never be done, as the tail varies in length more than the animal; and a very small specimen may have a very long tail; and vice versa.

Six feet, within an inch or two, is the maximum length for both jaguars and pumas; but the puma is, on the whole, and in the generality of specimens, much the smaller animal. Otherwise the two animals differ in habits, and mode of life, in only a few particulars; though a number of misstatements and errors have, not crept, but been boldly thrust into natural histories by book-makers; and these mendacities have been repeated and copied by credulous, and ignorant, though possibly honest, naturalists to a lamentable extent; insomuch that one feels he can trust no modern work on the subject.

The chief differences between these two felines are that the jaguar is more restricted in its habitat, by fully one half, than the puma; and is a forest-haunting animal. It appears in the open country, and in cultivated districts; but only in very limited numbers. The puma, on the other hand, frequents pampas, the deserts of the north, and bleak and bare mountain-sides; as well as dense forests. It has been disputed that the puma does frequent forests to any great extent. Against these disputatious statements there are the assertions of this book: that is all I have to say on the matter.

Another statement of mine, appearing in a former work, provoked a gentleman of some position in the naturalist world to write and ask, with evident scepticism in his tone, if I had not made a mistake. This was the account I gave of seeing a jaguarondi kill a great ant-eater by breaking its neck. There is no mistake whatever in the statement. The jaguarondi is a large and powerful cat, nearly, and, perhaps, sometimes quite, three feet in length *not* including the tail; and I should be very loth to approach one which was not completely disabled. The muscular strength of all the cats is enormous, compared with that of herbivorous animals; and both jaguars and pumas are capable of pulling down the largest animals in America. It is only their cowardice that prevents them from openly attacking the horned cattle at the haciendas and ranchos. Horns are nasty things to be progged with, and a bull with its "dander up," as my American friends would say, is a "lively cuss;

and well able to write his ten commandments on any cat's hide."

The courage of jaguars, pumas, jaguarondis, all the smaller wild cats, and lynxcs, is that of the domestic tabby. Hurt or frightened, and driven into a corner, they will show the *fury of fear:* they have no real courage. The jaguar is more sly and cunning than the puma, but in no degree bolder: the jaguar habitually resorts to trees; the puma only occasionally does so; and most frequently to avoid pursuers.

The jaguarondi also climbs trees; and is more strictly a forest animal than either of its larger congeners. It runs the lynx a close race for third place amongst the American cats; and is certainly the third largest in South America. I have not seen a great deal of it, and all I can state about it is embodied in my "Great Mountains and Forests of South America."

The small wild cats of the Amazonian forests are very shy little animals; and it is difficult to learn much of their habits. The moment that they observe a person watching them, they disappear; and as they are not only lynx-eyed, but gifted, also, with acute powers of scent, it is not much use concealing oneself near their haunts. What they cannot see, they sniff; and guess the rest, I think. All I can say with certainty is that they prey chiefly on birds, catching some in the trees, and some pretty large ones on the ground. One that I shot weighed less than four pounds; but it had a rail which weighed two in its jaws at the time, and was running pretty quickly. It was much the same colour as a domestic tabby cat; but was profusely spotted with black.

All the wild cats of the Amazonian region which I saw were spotted, though the ground colour varied much, some species being bluish or slaty, one dark grey, another sandy or fox-coloured, and a fourth nearly white, with dark brown spots. It is a little strange, I think, but I never saw a South American cat with a striped skin.

Jaguars and pumas, if taken when young, are easily tamed; and become much attached to their masters. I never heard of their becoming treacherous; as tame lions and tigers are said to sometimes be.

CHAPTER VIII

MORE ABOUT THE HEAD-WATERS OF THE PURUS

A LIVELY gentleman whom I once knew, describing the passengers on board a South American steamer, said that amongst them were twelve Spanish soldiers, very small of person, very fierce of countenance, returning from a revolution, or going somewhere to make one—he was not very clear which. Nobody can be very clear about South American revolutions; and this must be my excuse for ignorance of circumstances in the political history of the countries I am now concerned with.

Studying my old maps, and more modern ones recently procured, I perceive that some South American editions of Prince von Bismarck have been at work, making annexations, and rectifying frontiers with a liberal hand. Places which, in my time, were in Ecuador, are now in Peru; and others which were claimed by the land of Pizarro, are now included in Brazilian territory; but in one thing I must disagree with the latest maps. Even admitting the modern frontier, the head-waters of the Purus are within Peruvian limits. Of that fact I am well assured: but the maps place them within Brazil; and instead of showing more than twenty streams, indicate only a dozen or so. This seems strange, because I know the Peruvian Government has sent several expeditions to explore the country I am now describing; and many European travellers must have visited it since I was there twenty-seven or twenty-eight years ago.

I have said that all these streams have similar characteristics; and that none of them take their origin in lakes or pools. Some rise from springs welling from the earth; and some gush from fissures in the rocks. One or two run from marshes in the low ground: none seem to rise at a greater height above sea-level than 1800 or 1400 feet. Snow-water must occasionally augment the volume of these streams: for most of them are near the mountain ridge; but I do not think there are any glaciers in this part of the Andes. The only ones I saw in any part of Peru, were very small, and situated in the highest parts of the range: in fact, I suspected that none of them were permanent, but subject to disappearance in exceptional seasons. However this may be there is no permanent stream flowing eastward from the higher range; and the few cascades that descend from a greater height than 1400 feet, run, or fall, only in the rainy season.

Having proceeded as far into the heart of the country as I felt to be safe with my slender provisions, I halted for a time at the village of a band of Indians, who received us with great hospitality and kindness, as these people usually do in districts where they are well treated. At this time, at any rate, the Indians were not much interfered with eastward of the Andes; and the Peruvians, I believe, have always in modern times treated them well. The people of this country act up to their profession of republicans; and all persons, except those who may justly be classed and treated as vagabonds, are granted the rights of citizenship without reference to breed or creed: and, in a word, Peru is undoubtedly one of the most honest and high-principled countries of South America.

The Indians of the village here mentioned number about fifty, viz. sixteen men, twenty women, and thirteen children under the apparent age of fourteen years. Children are never numerous amongst the Indians; and I fear that many babies are destroyed. Parents, too, are not so prolific as those in civilized countries. Few of the Indian women have more than four or five children before they cease bearing; and many of them only two or three.

In the towns, and settled portions of the country, a certain amount of respect for decency is enforced; but in the wilds and woods the Indians are a law unto themselves and do pretty much as they like, or as their pee-ai-men enjoin. They go about unclothed, and perform their superstitious rites in pools of blood. For instance, an abominable doctrine, preached from one side of the country to the other, is that if a woman has twin children she must have committed adultery with the devil, who is the father of one of them. As the pee-ai-man cannot tell which is the black soul, both must be burnt; and the woman, likewise, as a punishment for her supposed sin. It is rare for Indian women, in either the north or the south, to bear twins, but a few painful instances have come under my notice.

About two years ago I saw a paragraph in a newspaper to the effect that a pee-ai-man named "George" had been sent down to Georgetown, British Guiana, to be tried for murder—I presume some such case as that I have mentioned.

Many years ago I offered to blow the brains out of this scoundrel, for the benefit of his tribesmen; and to save the lives of a poor woman and her newly born babes; but the people were horrified and begged me not to do so, as George's spirit would haunt them, and they would have to slay me to appease it. So, as there were no police within call, or Europeans to help me stop the horrid act, I took my gun and went off into the woods that I might not hear the cries of the doomed. When I came back I found the red-eyed husband glaring at a heap of ashes and a few white bones, all that remained of his home and family.

No untoward incident marked my stay at the Peruvian Indian village. Indian encampments never have a name: the Peruvians refer to them by the name of the chief, or pee-ai-man. In this case (not an infrequent one) the pee-ai-man was the chief, and he rejoiced in a cognomen which ran to fifteen words, and eighty-three letters as I spelled it, the meaning of which was that he was father of all the snowy hills of the west. He was otherwise a much-married man; as he had four wives but only two children. I called him "Snow Hill," as I found my tongue unequal to the task of drawling out his patronymic: and as he, on his part, was ignorant of the irreverent brevity of the sobriquet, he took it as a great compliment, which perhaps it was, viewed in the light of the customs and prejudices of these people. For it is considered an insult to ask an Indian, of any rank, his name; and to confer a fresh one on him is equivalent to acknowledging that his actual name is too exalted to be lightly mentioned. In his turn he conferred on me the title of "Big Mountain"—whether in reference to my physical or moral attributes he left me to surmise.

Indian villages are not usually permanent: it depends on the abundance of food in the districts where they are situated; and sometimes on the interference of the lords of the sail—the so-called white men. The wigwam is a form of dwelling unknown among the South American Indians. Their huts are never tent-shaped; but usually square or oblong, with roofs which are as often flat, or nearly so, as sloping. In a warm country, with rain as the only vicissitude of climate to guard against, light materials suffice for the erection of the huts; and the frameworks are made of boughs of trees, and the walls and roofs are packed with grass, reeds or large palm leaves, and similar materials. The size depends on the taste and industry of the occupier and his family. The women, and larger children, do a great part of the building; and often the whole of it: for the head of the family is a gentleman who has a great disinclination to over-exertion; and thinks, if he provides game for food, he has well performed his share of the duty of life.

The food of these children of the forest consists of such fruit as they find growing in the woods, wild rice, and several nutritious piths of the tapioca kind, roots and game. This last, consisting of any bird or beast of the forest the hunter is fortunate enough to capture, is obtained in various ways—by shooting with bows and arrows, by trapping, and by spearing when driven within a narrow enclosure.

The bow and arrows do not seem to have been a

favourite weapon with the South American Indians: at any rate none of them I have met with ever showed much skill in its use. I have not been able to find much evidence of the degree of perfection to which our ancestors brought the art of archery; but according to a book published by the Messrs. Longman "twelve score," i.e. of yards, was considered a long shot in the days when bows were used in the British army. The statement seems to me extraordinary, because I have actually seen an arrow sent double that distance by a North American Indian. If the statements in the "Badminton" book on archery are reliable, then the American red men must have been the strongest and most skilful bowmen that ever existed. But would an arrow sent with a force that would carry it only "twelve score," or 240 yards, be able to penetrate iron armour? And does "twelve score" (an expression confined to Shakespeare, I believe) mean twelve score yards? The arrow of an Indian would not penetrate sheet-iron the eighth of an inch thick. I have had the experiment tried many times by the most powerful bowmen I could find. At long ranges the arrow was always stopped or turned: at short distances it was crumpled up like a piece of straw: yet we find it repeated hundreds of times that the arrows of the British bowmen easily pierced the armour of the Middle Ages.

As to distances, 300 to 350 English yards was a fair shot for a Red warrior; exceptionally strong and skilful shots have sent it about 500 yards in my presence. Shooting with the bow was very uncertain at distances exceeding 100 yards; and none of the yarns of splitting sticks, hitting dollar pieces, and "barking" squirrels at the tops of tall trees, have any truth in them. They cannot be true, since the red men always approached as close as possible to an object before shooting at it; and though they could send an arrow completely through the fore-quarters of a bison, a feat I have known a rifle-ball fail to do, they could not be sure of hitting the animal at all at a greater distance than from eighty to a hundred yards.

Here, in eastern Peru, the savages could not approach to such strength and skill as those I have described as distinguishing their northern brethren. Few of them could send an arrow more than 120 yards; and the best man amongst them sent one only 155 yards, after a dozen tries. They could not hit an object the size of a man at eighty yards, except by what was evidently mere chance: and shots were so feebly delivered that none of the hunters relied upon them to stop animals exceeding a monkey in size. They attempt to poison their arrows, but not with wourali poison; which is unknown among them, even by repute.

The favourite way of taking large animals, such as the small deer of the region, capivaras and pacas, is to surround them with a large party of men and boys, and gradually close in on them. They are speared as they attempt to escape from the circle. The inhabitants of several villages usually join in forming the ring; and a hunt seldom fails in producing a plentiful supply of game.

How the Peruvian gentleman referred to in a previous page failed to find traces of gold in this country I cannot imagine. He must have gone in the wrong direction. For I found dust in nearly all the streams; and indications of there being extensive, if not plentiful, quantities of it. I mean that in this region there is gold scattered over a wide area. I discovered several large quartz reefs; but could not, of course, say how rich in metal they were: probably not more than six or eight ounces to the ton; but this is a good paying quantity.

Where there is reef mining, there is also placer mining, especially where the streams show good signs of the precious metal; but though I searched long and diligently, I found nothing to reward my labour. Placers are always miner's luck. That is, one man may find half a dozen of them, and clear several thousand pounds; and a score of his mates search the land for months, and not obtain a piece as big as a pea!

Finding it impossible to do more in this region I returned to the highlands by the same route I had come hither. I thought, at one time, that I would risk everything, and, making a canoe, drop down the stream to the Amazon. But consideration convinced me that the scheme was too desperate to be put into execution. The current is sluggish, and progress could not be great: and the country through which the river passes was, I knew, inundated for a great distance on both sides, therefore, game difficult to be procured, and I could not collect more than a week's provisions for two men—myself and servant: for I could not take either Peruvians or Indians so far from their homes. And, above all, I had not fifty charges of ammunition left. So back to Peru's elevated valleys I went.

CHAPTER IX

SOME OTHER HEAD-WATERS OF THE AMAZON

TO avoid monotony I must group together a number of interesting descriptions of streams which form the sources of a great number of the north-western tributaries of the Amazon. These all rise on the eastern slopes of the Andes in Ecuador and Colombia, there generally spoken of as the Granadian Confederation, and extend over *nearly nine degrees* of latitude in the very centre of the tropics—from 5° S. to 4° N.

No map in existence indicates a tithe of the streams which rush south, and south-eastward, to swell the mighty current of the Amazon. Without including the courses which cannot claim to be more than brooks, they number hundreds of them. The great rivers, with courses of at least 400 to 1500 miles, are the Rio Negro, with a dozen different names; the Caqueta, the Ica and the Napo. Other rivers of this system, all of which exceed the Thames in length and size, are the Guaviare, Ipaminare, Gujazu, Aguarico, Curaray, Tigre, Chambira and Morona.

The beginnings of all these rivers are in turmoil and rushing torrents. Some of the finest and most picturesque falls in the world are found in their upper courses; but they are at present little known, or known not at all. These falls are remarkable for their height, or the depth they descend; which is not strange when we consider that Ecuador contains a huge knot of the loftiest summits in the Andes, as Chimborazo, 21,424 feet; Gayamba, 19,586; Antisana, 19,187; and Cotopaxi, 18,877.

There are others verging on these heights; and the eastern wall of the Andes, here even steeper, and more rugged and abrupt than in Peru, must often be nearly 14,000 to 16,000 feet in height; and is full of the most dizzy and appalling passes, cañons, and valleys of any I have ever seen, Colorado itself scarcely excepted.

I have already mentioned that the Napo rises on the very slope of Cotopaxi, the snow-water of which drains into it on the north-eastern side, a circumstance of much danger to the inhabitants of the river valley: for when by accident the snow of Cotopaxi's cone suddenly melts, the river rises with overwhelming rapidity. That heat should penetrate the vast mass, in its lower section at least three or four miles thick, and melt the snows and glaciers of generations in a few hours, shows clearly the frightful intensity of Cotopaxi's heat.

Some of the huge crevasses which seam the mountain's side are occupied by glaciers of immense thickness, the whole cone being enveloped in snow from twenty to sixty feet deep, and running 6000 feet down the slope. In the year 1808 all this melted in one night; and the Napo became a raging torrent. Whole villages were swept away, and hundreds of people were drowned, or dashed to death, in a moment.

The effects of Cotopaxi's eruptions are always awful beyond compare with those of other volcanoes. Its explosions have been distinctly heard at places 500

Photo Underwood & Underwood

A GLACIER IN THE ANDES NEAR OROZA

miles distant; and its flames have been seen to shoot up to a height much exceeding half a mile. The floods brought about by the sudden thawing of its snows have caused destruction of life and property at towns and villages 800 miles distant; and the ashes have travelled as far.

Snow, and especially glaciers, are, however, not common in these mountains, even on the high peaks. Being situated under the Equator, or within a degree or two of it, the line of perpetual snow is very high; and rather variable, I may add. Of course, there is always snow on the summits of those gigantic peaks which rear their crests 20,000 feet; but the amount certainly varies: and taking Chimborazo as an instance, I do not think there is a glacier on it that descends 2000 feet from the summit. There is snow lower down; sometimes as low as about 10,000 feet; but it only remains a few hours. It falls at night; by midday on the following morning it is nearly all gone!

It is probably these sudden thaws which seam the mountain-sides so deeply with ravines, and cover them with loose stones; one of the great difficulties the mountaineers have to contend with in the peaks of the Andes. The rainfall in these regions is often very erratic. There are spots in the elevated valley where it never rains. These are dreadful sand deserts, where death lurks slyly for the unwary traveller, sometimes slaying him with fiery thirst, at other times choking him with almost impalpable dust. It is surprising that we hear so little of these deadly deserts; but I suspect that few adventurers visit them, or stay long enough to learn their real character.

As a set-off to these remarkable instances of dryness, I may mention that there are other spots in these valleys where rain at the rate of an inch an hour is not uncommon; and I have known thirty inches fall in a day and a night. The result is torrents of tremendous size and power, which sweep everything before them, and leave great rocks in their channels which are sometimes hundreds of tons in weight.

For the beds of most of the larger torrents are dry three parts of the year—that is in the absence of the wet season, which is often erratic in its appearance, coming as much as two months behind the usual time.

Some of these mountain streams empty themselves into the head-water streams, which thus vary their actual sources: others dry up entirely; and have water in them only two or three months in a year—in the winter season of these regions.

It is possible to look down from the Ecuador Andes and see a dozen of these head-waters from one spot; and trace their courses for an immense distance. Clouds may be cumulative a mile beneath you, but you see over them; and the atmosphere is so bright and clear that there seems to be hardly space between you and objects known to be fifty miles distant. Fifty miles is certainly a comparatively short distance to view over from a "coign of vantage." Probably one can see at least double that distance; but the landscape fades to dull streaks of neutral tints, blue-greys, purple-greys, light browns, tawny hues, and an endless number of tones. Here and there one of the larger rivers reveals a gleaming reach; and one can realize what a splendid view of lakes it would be a privilege to view from such an alti-

Photo Underwood & Underwood

CHAUPICHACA RAILWAY AND BRIDGE; 9,472 FEET, PROBABLY THE HIGHEST IN THE WORLD

tude; but lakes of any size do not exist here; and no large sheet of water is visible. Cities, towns and villages, too far off to be seen in detail, are revealed by the clouds of haze (dust and smoke, I suppose) which float over them. On one occasion a balloon was seen, rising from some fête in an interior town. It seemed to be miles below us, and never rose to anything near the level of our feet, and it remained in view an hour before it dwindled to an undiscernible speck. I mention the fact; but the sight seemed to be so singularly out of place in such surroundings that it had quite a disturbing effect on my mind.

Roads there are in these mountains; but such roads! Now a mere track, with an occasional cross of small size and rough workmanship by its side, to mark the spot where a brutal murder has been committed; and with more frequent crosses, of larger size, and decorated with tawdry pictures of the Virgin, or some saint, to invite good Catholics to prayer, the road presently crosses an awful chasm, with a torrent rushing and thundering at the bottom, so far down that it is lost in the mist which lurks in the deep, narrow gorges; crossed, I say, by a narrow suspension-bridge constructed of poles, reed-matting and ropes, all apparently rotten, and with interstices between the flooring through which one catches glimpses of the terrible gulf below. The bridge sways, and its side poles shift position as one tests its stability with the foot. It is too awful; and all our little party, fearful that it will not bear the weight of a mounted man, look about for materials to mend it. These are bought from a guanaco herdsman who lives in a tiny hut a mile away; and nearly the whole day is consumed in the work. The herdsman comes to watch and grin: for the much-needed repairs will benefit him; and he is well paid into the bargain. Thus, by private enterprise, are most of the mountain bridges of this region kept from falling bodily into the gulfs they span, perhaps with a man or two on them. Such accidents do happen.

The narrow gulfs which are thus bridged seem to be cracks occasioned by volcanic commotions. When they are of great depth they are invariably traversed by a water-course with a turbulent current. Probably they were mere crevices, not a foot wide, at their beginnings and torrential rains are responsible for their more or less rapid increase. That they are all much water-worn is obvious to any eye. In some cases they are wider at the bottom than at the top, and the rocks bulge, or overhang, the water below. Sometimes they are so wide, and the sides so rugged, that it is possible to climb down the cañons: but this is always a dangerous, and generally an impossible, feat. A slip could not be recovered, and the fall would be almost sheer.

Some of these cañons form passes across the range, from side to side. In this case they are always larger, or wider; but not necessarily deeper than those I have just described. Where they form passes they, of course, run down the slopes of the mountains, and have no water in them during the greater part of the year. They are liable to be blocked by snow; or deluged by sudden rain-storms; and if a traveller is caught in one of them his fate is sealed. The snow fills the crevasse, in some places where it is narrow, to the depth of 100 feet, or even more; and the doomed man is caught like a mouse

Photo Underwood & Underwood

THE CRATER OF EL MISTA. OCCASIONALLY ACTIVE

in a trap. It is still more dangerous to be overtaken by a storm-burst, even of moderate boisterousness. The water collects so rapidly, and runs from the hills in such quantities, that the torrent is formed in a few minutes, and sweeps everything before it. Rocks above, loosened by previous tempests, or by earthquakes, fall with a crash, and are dashed into thousands of fragments; from those no larger than grains of sand, to masses weighing tons: and all are rolled and bounced along like balls, beating overtaken men and animals into a sodden pulp.

Seismic action is almost continual in all parts of the Andes, I think. It certainly is here; and I have felt as many as seven or eight shocks in one day: and heard rumblings and sharper noises, which were alarming enough at first; but, like the inhabitants of the country, I got used to them. It is not an uncommon occurrence for men, horses, and even the sure-footed mules and guanacos to stumble and fall, from the effects of shocks. If I remember right, Darwin was thrown down on one occasion: and in both Peru and Ecuador I have heard parents ask their children "What made you tumble? Did the earth roll?" Localisms often correctly describe objects and effects. "Earth roll" is the usual description of an earthquake among the people of this region; and it more correctly describes the phenomenon than "quake." The earth does seem to roll from beneath one's feet; and it is very difficult, and often quite impossible, to avoid being thrown down.

This may seem a very terrifying state of things to people living in Europe and the eastern parts of North America: but the reverse of this is the case in Peru, and other countries in the Central Andes, and the cessation of these shocks is a cause of terror: for it has been well established that before one of those awful eruptions which devastate hundreds of miles of country, and destroy thousands of persons, there is a complete cessation of all minor convulsions. This circumstance is well known to the people of the land; and those who are timid, or wise, or cautious, make preparations for the safety of themselves and their property, whenever there is a prolonged period of quiet. "I have not noticed a shock for a week: have you?" I heard one ranchero ask of another. "No," was the reply. "Ah! that is bad!" And these men were delighted when, in the middle of the night there was a series of explosions like the firing of a battery, and pots and pans were tumbled about in the hut in wild confusion. "Pedro has blown off his gas!" said one fellow to me quite cheerfully. Amongst the lower classes, and herdsmen in particular, the spirit who presides over subterranean fires is always alluded to as Pedro—why I could never learn. Perhaps a sailor of the old school could not have told who "Davy Jones" was, though of the existence of that personage (or spiritage!) he would have no doubt. Possibly, like "Chucks the marine," he is a widow's man; i.e. has only a mythical existence.

In this region vegetation, in the form of herbage and bushes, attains to a greater elevation than in other parts of the Andes; but, probably owing to the extreme steepness of the barrier range, the forest does not ascend higher than about 7000 feet. Odd trees are found up to 10,000 feet: and many which are exotic to the region have been planted in the elevated valley, and flourish

Photo Underwood & Underwood

ANOTHER VIEW OF THE CRATER OF EL MISTA: LOOKING ACROSS

well. Fuchsias, calceolarias, and flowers which I supposed to be species of dahlias, peonies, verbenas and azaleas appeared in so great profusion amongst the wild flowers that many of the rocks presented a magnificent sight.

The higher peaks, for a few thousand feet below the snow-line, were generally bare of all vegetation except mosses and lichens; but there were some exceptions. On Cotopaxi and Antisana, for instance, there is a creeping plant bearing a pretty blue flower with a white centre, found as far up the slopes of those two mountains as I could reach; and where no other plant exists higher in the botanical world than a lichen. That it should exist on Cotopaxi at all seemed to me to be a wonderful thing. Every time that King of Terrors revolts, and streams out his fiery death and destruction, all things on his sides must be burnt to cinders. The sides of this mountain are actually calcined to an immense depth if not right through to the volcanic throat: and all roots, large or small, must be completely destroyed every time an eruption takes place; though I was not impressed with the quantity of lava on Cotopaxi's sides. It appeared to me from what I saw and heard, that the principal ejecta from this remarkable volcano are ashes and stones. The water from the melted ice and snow must be boiling hot when it runs from the great crevasses that seam the mountain-sides; but owing to the extreme steepness of the cone it runs down in such heavy streams that it washes the cinders and other volcanic matter into the valleys at the base of the mount, where rich crops of various kinds are raised upon it—particularly potatoes, which, my informant declared, in this country always do well on "burnt ground of any kind."

But as several of the large tributaries of the Amazon take their rise on the bases of the great mountains of this district, it cannot be out of place to give a particular description of some of them; and this I can best do by narrating my attempts to ascend them.

Photo Underwood & Underwood

UNDER THE EQUATOR IN THE ANDES: PEAK OF PINCHINCA

CHAPTER X

ATTEMPTED ASCENTS OF MOUNTS COTOPAXI AND ANTISANA

"NOBODY ever has ascended to the crater of Cotopaxi; nobody ever will succeed in doing so," I was told. I had a good look at the mount; and was disposed to agree with this dictum: its ascent would be on all fours with an attempt to climb a huge sugar-loaf, I thought. Still, if everybody argued in this way the thing would assuredly never be done; so I determined to have a try.

I am thankful that the natural modesty which is so conspicuous in travellers and naturalists generally, and in myself in particular, except when I am "darning up" those dear old ladies the Natural Selectionists, induced me to make my preparations very quietly and secretly.

I was never very fit for the heavy work of mountain climbing, as I always suffered from a physical infirmity which hampered me heavily. But "where there is a will there is a way," is one of my favourite maxims, which I like none the less for its extreme homeliness. So I sent George, my servant, to find guides of some sort, and gain as much general information as he could.

The Spanish American is a fatalist. "Who knows! What then! How can!" are amongst the most frequent expressions heard from his lips—not as enquiries, but as lackadaisical exclamations. Could Cotopaxi be ascended ? Who knows, and who cares ! Would he make the attempt ? What for ? What good ! Well, he might like to earn a few dollars ! Oh ! to be sure : a few dollars would be welcome. What could he do for the Señor ? Show him the best side to attempt Cotopaxi ! What an idea ! But of course he *could*, and *would*, point out the most likely point to ascend the sleeping Pedro ; and straightway pockets the dollars, and leads one to a spot where nothing less nimble than a fly could find a foothold.

Having been victimized by several of these apathetic, but knowing, gentlemen, George suggested that I should leave the matter in his hands. Then he found an old shepherd who had driven a flock of merino-sheep about the Quito district for nearly forty years ; and told him if he could find an efficient guide he would be paid *by results* : the higher the guide got the greater the number of dollars that would find their way into the old boy's palm.

He accepted the bargain ; "and who so fit for the task as his grandson, Jesus !" [The names of the Lord are frequently conferred on children by Spaniards and Portuguese : and even in the Protestant countries of Europe, modified into Jesse and Christopher. The last-mentioned form is often adopted by Spaniards, though it is of Italian origin. But Christo, or Cristo, is common enough in Brazil.]

The boy on being interviewed proved to be a stripling of fifteen or sixteen years ; but bright-featured and strong. He agreed to take us as high up as he ever had been ; but said he would be afraid to go higher : and, in fact, I gave up all thoughts of reaching the crater before I started; the task was so obviously impossible. But I wished to see as much of the character and formation of the mount as was practicable; and two more peasants having volunteered to accompany us I left Quito and took up quarters at the Rancho of San Jeronymo on the road between Quito and Riobamba. The rancho is close to the base of the mountain; well up on the slope in fact; and a magnificent view of Chimborazo, and the mountains which cluster in all directions, was obtained from it.

The ranchero was made acquainted with my intention and offered to accompany me for his own pleasure. I was only too glad to have this valuable addition to my little party, especially when I learned that he had made many attempts to climb to the cone. He scouted the possibility of the attempt succeeding; but was in sympathy with my desire to get as high as possible; and was one of the very few Spaniards I met with who were lovers of Nature, and willing to put themselves to pain and trouble to witness one of her fine sights.

Acting on the advice of my host, I deferred the attempt for three days, until some heavy white clouds dispersed. These clouds completely hid the cone, but were in themselves a splendid sight at sunset and sunrise, running rapidly through a series of magnificent colour shadows—light and deep orange, and reds in the morning, crimsons, fiery copper colour and light green at night. Words cannot convey a sense of the beautiful gradations of change, and the awe of the sights which surrounded us; but to see them once is to have them printed on the brain for the remainder of life.

All I could see of Cotopaxi during these three days

was a massive grey slope running up into the clouds at an unusually steep angle, even for an Andes mountain. I was not idle; but accompanied by the boy wandered up to a considerable height; and surveyed the difficulties I intended to attack. Water-worn and rugged, the mountain-side was almost destitute of vegetation, lichens excepted. There was no moss, and the little blue flower described just now does not appear until a height of at least 8000 feet is reached. Besides jagged rocks, and deep ravines into which one could not descend without the help of companions well furnished with ropes, there were tracts covered with loose stones varying in size from that of pebbles to masses one could not lift: but the smaller stones prevailed to so great an extent that it was difficult to walk over them. They shifted position and slipped back; so that we were frequently brought down to our knees; and sometimes had worse falls. I took care, after some experience, to well pad my elbows and knees in preparation for the grand attempt, and to make an alpenstock, which I found of great use in arresting a slip.

On the eventful day we started before daybreak, the clouds having dispersed the previous evening. There was a heavy mist lying on the mountain-side; but this dispersed as the sun arose; and was followed by a clear and beautiful morning; with an atmosphere which was perfectly calm and still. The sun, about ten o'clock, had power sufficient, notwithstanding our altitude, to cause us to perspire freely; but there was no ground heat, and no smoke issuing from the numerous rents and fissures which scored the slope. Above, the crater, which we could plainly see from our position, was sending up a thin column of black smoke, as it was always doing during my stay in the neighbourhood. It ascends for an immense distance before dispersing—several miles at least: and it gives one a curious sensation to look up the dark and rugged slope, and see it surmounted by an enormous crest of black vapour. I say rugged slope: for a near sight of Cotopaxi is very different from a distant view. Seen from any point between ten and sixty or seventy miles, the cone looks dazzling white, and perfectly smooth in contour. As a matter of fact, though perfect in general outline, the sides are exceedingly rough and steep. Some of the ravines, or crevasses, run up to the actual crest of the crater; but it is not possible to ascend them: they are blocked with snow, stones and masses of rock, which it is impossible to burrow through, or climb over by any ordinary means. What the gentlemen with the aeroplanes may do we shall see some day: and if Peter Botte could be conquered there seems no reason why Cotopaxi should not be. The difficulties to be overcome, however, are enormous; and insuperable to a small party.

Had I possessed the means I should have made an attempt at the head of 150 men, with at least a score of long ladders. What appears to be the worst place might be surmounted by a ladder of ninety feet. Shorter lengths could be carried up to the spot and lashed together. Other ladders could be hauled up these, and so on; and with the aid of plenty of ropes, plenty of men, and plenty of pluck I think the summit might be attained. The greatest fear I should have would be that of dislodging huge masses of overhanging snow, which would sweep everything before them. This would be a very real danger; but it could be risked. Peril is an element of all mountain climbing, as the newspaper accounts inform us every year; and the peril here would be considerably above the average. But nobody would attempt to surmount Cotopaxi who was not prepared to put his life in his hand.

The ascent must be by one of the huge rents, or gullies, which seam the cone on all sides. The separating ridges are certainly impracticable. The snow cape which covers the cone comes down about 6000 feet; but there are small glaciers which descend lower than this and overlap the gullies, in some cases to such an extent that we could crawl nearly a hundred yards under them. Water was trickling from the one where we performed this feat; and formed a runnel which lower down dashed over the rocks in many small cascades. Occasionally the thaw is so great that it would not be possible to ascend this gully on account of the quantity and force of the water; but the dry season would certainly be chosen for an ascent by any traveller who did not intend to deliberately court disaster. Probably immediately after an eruption, as soon as the stones were cool enough, would be the best time for an ascent. There would then be no snow or ice to impede the traveller's progress.

From the rancho to the snow-line was about 6000 feet —2000 yards—not much more than a mile (in height) yet it took us all day to attain this elevation. Early in the afternoon it became evident that we could not reach the snow-limit before nightfall. My companions wished to return; but at my earnest entreaty some of them consented to go on. The boy, who was timid, and two of the peasants went back; but the proprietor of the little farm, my servant, and three other peasants who were with us persevered, though it meant spending a night in the open in the most uncomfortable circumstances that could occur in such a region. Fortunately we had all brought our thick ponchos, or cloaks, with us; and we borrowed those of the returning peasants. We were also well supplied with provisions: I had seen to that: for I am convinced that nothing will cause the failure of an expedition, great or small, sooner than the breakdown of the commissariat.

The sun was a fiery red ball in the west when we reached the snow-line; and found ourselves abruptly stopped. It is not the snow that prevents a farther ascent; but at this point the steepness and ruggedness of the cone; and also the other obstacles, greatly increase; and there is a ragged fringe of ice where the snow has melted and refrozen; and which could in no case be passed until a way had been cut through it, a task impossible to four or five men in a limited time.

So at this point we prepared to pass the night. A fire could not be made: for there is nothing here that will burn, except in the fervent heat of an eruption. We were surrounded by calcined rocks and stones; but not a scrap of dry vegetation could be seen anywhere. The little blue flowers, mentioned twice before, were scattered about, though very sparsely; and this was absolutely the only plant I could find. The lichens made the rock masses look singular, rather than gay, in red, yellow and black stains; and there was one very remarkable cryptogamous growth lining the under sides of masses of rocks and stones which had lodged together in such a way as to form grottoes. This was a sign of dampness low down, where the snow-water had percolated amongst the loose stones. The lichen appeared on the stone as a dark green slime thickly studded with minute bright blue pedicels, which turn yellow as they die off. A trifle, perhaps; but one worth notice since it was *made*, or *evolved*, by a Master Mind of some kind, and placed in a position where trifles are wonders on account of their rarity.

I know that many unsuccessful attempts have been made to reach the crater of Cotopaxi; but I have never read an account of any of them, nor heard them described; and I do not even know if any adventurer has succeeded in getting higher than the snow-line. I should think not. For I have tried the ascent on three sides, and could neither find, nor see, any pass so good as the one on the west side. Here, and here only, did I succeed in approaching the snow-level. In many minor attempts I was turned back by insurmountable obstacles when I had ascended only 1000, 2000, or, at most, 3000 feet. This, on the eastern side, where the base-ground, and consequently the starting-point, is higher, meant that I got within 2000 feet of the snow: and it should be noted that the frigid-line is 1000 feet lower in the winter (that is the wet season) than it is in the summer. It is the snow that is the chief barrier; but supposing this all cleared away, I am convinced that only a very large and well-found party would have the slightest chance of reaching the crater. Long and heavy ladders are essential; and some of these would have to be left in the positions where they were first planted: and the ground above 6000 or 7000 feet is so ticklish that only large numbers of men could handle even moderate weights without grave risk of accident. It is unnecessary, and useless, to dwell on details; but I may say that as each man ascended he would have to be guarded and guided by rope-parties on the flanks as well as above: and very elaborate precautions would have to be taken in many spots.

We passed the night huddled together amongst the stones with which we erected a low wall, as some shelter against an icy cold breeze which began to blow immediately after sunset. No man of us attempted to sleep; and we passed the time in smoking and chatting, with an occasional nip of good old rum to counteract the effects of the rasping air which seemed to freeze in our throats. I am no tippler, and no defender of the bottle: neither am I an admirer of the non-alcohol fanatic. Midnight 6000 feet below the crest of a freezing mountain is not the time to think of total abstinence—or even moderation. And it was freezing on Cotopaxi. Our breath formed little clouds, and icicles an inch long formed on our moustaches. Our respiration sounded like the wheezings of an old pump; and to draw breath at all was a painful exertion. I prayed fervently for morning; but the night seemed to be interminable. There was a young moon; but it did not give sufficient light to reveal surrounding objects: and though there are ranchos and hamlets in the valley below, not too far distant for noises to be heard half-way up Cotopaxi, not a sound reached our ears. From sunset to sunrise a dead silence prevailed. Once or twice I did hear the wind moan as it blew over the jagged rocks: but the sound was momentary, and hardly worth noticing.

Daylight came quite suddenly. The rising of the sun

was a grand sight; but I have seen it under more magnificent conditions elsewhere—in the Colorado valley for instance. The reflections on Chimborazo and other peaks were very fine; the snow turning a bright crimson, changing rapidly to light red, and pale pink. It is not until the sun has been up several hours that the snow appears of that dazzling whiteness which is so great a characteristic of the higher peaks of the Andes.

From our highest point we could not see the cone of Cotopaxi, owing to intervening and overhanging rocks and snow. The smoke overhanging the mountain could be seen at an immense height, appearing of a sooty brown colour. There is always more or less smoke issuing from the crater; its cessation is said to be a sure sign of an impending eruption.

The volume of smoke which rises from the crater is very great, but it disperses without clouding the atmosphere. One of the wonders of this country is the marvellously clear air. Objects are seen an immense distance, and appear comparatively close when they are a long distance off. For instance when I caught my first sight of Cotopaxi from the Napo river, and was told it was fully sixty English miles away I could not believe it. It appeared to be reachable in a few hours; but after travelling towards it two whole days, I did not seem to have made any appreciable progress in its direction! Sketches I made during the journey were practically the same so far as the mountain in the background was concerned.

With the return of day my courage increased, and I wished to try to climb a little higher; but my companions were not to be persuaded to make further

Photo Underwood & Underwood

CHIMBORAZO: ABOUT 20,500 FEET HIGH

exertions; and I could not go alone. There was an ugly-looking rock, or mass of calcined matter, half buried in snow, a hundred feet above our heads, which hung over ominously. "How are you going to get over that?" enquired the gentleman who was my host. The enquiry was a conclusive argument; and regretfully I consented to climb down, quite as ticklish a business as ascending, though performed more quickly. By midday we had reached the rancho; and were very glad of a refreshing cup of hot coffee; the berries which were used having been grown on the slope of the mountains to westward, not a dozen miles from the spot where we enjoyed their stimulating fragrance.

Animal life is not absent from the sides of Cotopaxi, if it is not abundant. Formerly guanacos roamed round its base; but these had been exterminated at the time of my visit. The last puma was seen here as late as 1860, I was told by my old friend the shepherd; but it is many years since the Quito valley was a happy hunting-ground for these animals. At present there is a species of American mouse, and a kind of marmot (not the common prairie dog) on the lower slopes, ascending 2000 or 3000 feet. These are the only mammals which came under my observation.

There are several small birds found to a considerable height; but the only one I need notice here is a humming-bird, which I saw quite up to the snow-level, though what attracted it to that inhospitable height I do not know and cannot conjecture. I asked my companions if they knew. They shrugged their shoulders; and looked their contempt of the question. "Who knows!" Who indeed!

It is a pretty little bird, green in colour with a blue throat and a white breast. I shot one or two for the purpose of ascertaining what food they were seeking on the mountain, and so proved that their diet was insectivorous; and seemed to consist entirely of minute flies, which are abundant enough on all parts of the mountain where there is vegetation. The opinion that humming-birds and flowers are inseparable is an erroneous one. Many of the humming-birds inhabit desolate regions, and live on small flies and beetles; nevertheless there are plenty of flowers about the base of Cotopaxi, and in the adjoining valley.

Condors sail round the volcano, and perhaps over it; but they are not numerous. The herdsmen are greatly prejudiced against them; and destroy them whenever they get a chance to do so. The lad who acted as one of our guides had made himself acquainted with the mountain during his search for these birds, which breed on it. He obtained a reward for every egg and young bird he brought down. At what height they breed on Cotopaxi I did not ascertain; but my young friend admitted that many of the eyries were situated far out of his reach. I saw condors in pairs, perched on crags which looked like breeding-places, just under the snow-line; but as these birds seldom make a nest, and choose positions under rocks and beetling cliffs, it is difficult to discover their breeding-sites from below.

It is true that condors often dispense with a nest; but they sometimes construct a platform of dry herbage, and cover it with fragments of skin, feathers, etc., from the creatures whose carcasses they prey on. When there

Photo Underwood & Underwood

COUNTRY NEAR COTOPAXI: VOLCANO HIDDEN BEHIND CLOUDS

is a nest, therefore, the stench arising from it is unendurable to human nostrils.

Failing to scale Cotopaxi, I next assailed Antisana; but though I passed two days and nights on the east side of this mountain, I failed to reach the top by several thousand feet. The difficulties are similar to those on Cotopaxi; and although there is no steep cone to surmount, deep ravines, jagged rocks, and overhanging cliffs render it impossible for an ordinary individual, unprovided with a proper outfit, and without a sufficient number of assistants, to climb these stupendous peaks. The areas of loose stones are greater on Antisana than on Cotopaxi; and there is a far greater amount of vegetation on the lower slopes of the first-named mountain, including bushes, shrubs and a few trees. Large tracts of the sides are gorgeous with wild flowers of beautiful tints; and amongst the shrubs are a few fuchsias covered so thickly with small red blooms that no leaves appear.

Several runnels trickle down the mountain-sides, with deep channels, proclaiming that they are rushing torrents in the rainy season; and there are rents in the sides through which smoke or steam slowly rises more or less frequently, showing that Antisana is only dozing, and may awake with a bellow any day.

There is, also, the same kind of humming-bird on this mountain as that which haunts the slopes of Cotopaxi; as well as two other species, which are common in the valley. It is asserted that all the great peaks here, Pinchincha, Gayamba, Antisana, Cotopaxi and Chimborazo, have their own species of humming-birds. I saw no evidence of this; but there are certainly several species confined to the mountains which are not found in the valleys below, nor in any other district, so far as I know. Many of the humming-birds, of which there are about 900 species, are local; but it is not likely that they are so very local as to be confined to one mountain. One remarkable feature in these beautiful little birds I noticed, and that is that the mountain species have shorter and straighter beaks than those inhabiting the plains of Brazil. The reason seems to be obvious. The flowers in the mountains are smaller and less deep than those of the lowlands; and the beaks of the humming-birds are used to probe the bells of flowers—not in search of nectar as the popular idea imagines, but to capture the insects which lurk deep down in the tubular blossoms.

I ought, perhaps, to be careful, in writing of the localization of humming-birds, as it seems pretty certain that many of the valleys in the Andes have species peculiar to them. They were not very abundant anywhere; and this is clearly due to the numbers which have been trapped and killed to make decorations for ladies' hats and bonnets. Round some of the better-peopled countries of the Peruvian and Ecuadorian Andes they had been nearly exterminated at the time of my visit. I am afraid I destroyed my quota: for I was anxious to make a collection of as many species as possible. Ultimately I got together 157 species, besides about forty which I classed as varieties. My whole collection of American birds, insects, etc. etc., was afterwards purchased by the Emperor of Brazil for his private museum. I was sorry to part with them; but the Fates were against me; and I often had enough to do to convey myself from place to place without being encumbered with many possessions. At one time I hoped to obtain sufficient means from the sales of specimens to enable me to work on a larger and more important scale; but I soon awoke from that dream. Specimen-hunting as a business means rags and poverty. I was once recommended to a "merchant" who it was thought would buy my specimens. He looked at them with contempt in his eye. "These are no use to me. I don't want twos and threes. Catch 'em wholesale 'fines, middles, coarse.' Here's a list of the kinds and colours I want. See? Heads, legs, wings and tails. Do what you like with the bodies. Eat 'em if they are big enough."

The man was a purveyor for French milliners. Green is the prevailing colour in the plumage of humming-birds; but they are found of nearly all hues, brown, black, blue, and, in one instance at least, scarlet, or bright crimson. White, yellow and reds generally are subsidiary colours, appearing in small markings, etc.

In size, also, humming-birds vary greatly. Some are so large, and have so few distinctive characteristics, that I should not have been able to say with certainty that they were humming-birds had it not been for their peculiar flight. The flight of *all* humming-birds, without a known exception, is quite different from that of other birds; but is exactly like that of insects. It has been described so often—sometimes correctly, quite as often incorrectly—that I do not intend to say much about it here, except that, having watched it for hours and days, and under every possible circumstance, I think I may venture to state a few facts about it without hesitation or doubt. The wings vibrate so rapidly that they appear like gossamer, and it is quite impossible to distinguish their colour or markings while the bird is in flight. While the wings are in motion the bird can remain perfectly stationary in front of a flower, or any other object. It can *dart* upwards, downwards, or to either side; and also backwards as much as six or eight feet. Some naturalists have attempted to show that this last motion is impossible. It is not only possible; it is a common motion of all humming-birds. Sustained flight, like that of a rook, a pigeon, or even an undulating flight similar to that of many short-winged small birds is quite impossible with humming-birds. They *dart* from flower to flower, or from tree to tree, just like swift-flying insects. On the open pampas, or llanos, they can easily be run down, and captured with a butterfly net: for though they do not perch they make pauses between each dart, as if gathering strength for it; or hesitating which direction to take. They generally turn in a fresh direction at each successive dart. They squeak when captured, and struggle violently, and will not live in captivity. The stories of their having been fed with sugar and water, and honey, placed in paper cups, I do not believe. Honey, sap and pollen may be taken as part of the food of some humming-birds, and I believe it is so; but the whole family is insectivorous; and insects form the bulk of the food of all of them; and the entire diet of most of them. Assertions to the contrary are speculations, guesses, theories, anything but the experiences of eye-witnesses.

Humming-birds never attempt to conceal their nests: and so it happens that I have seen and examined a multitude of them. They are always placed on something pendulous, the end of a twig, or a blade of grass. It has been suggested that this position is chosen as a protection from monkeys and snakes: and I think it not unlikely that this may be so. The chief enemy of the humming-bird is the huge bird-eating spider—I was on the point of making something like a bull, and writing "bird-sucking." As a fact the spider does not actually eat the bird, but sucks every drop of blood and juice from the poor little carcass. I have seen these horrid spiders, on two occasions, crawl down towards nests, and when they could get no farther deliberately drop on to the young. I have repeatedly tried to rescue birds from these spiders, but the dreadful creatures are furnished with poison fangs. Though I have had the bird in my hand immediately after it was seized it was always in a dying state—eyes glazed and wings rigid, and the whole body apparently paralysed. I am not writing of humming-birds only, but all kinds of small birds; and on one occasion I took a bird the size of a thrush from a spider. It is generally young birds which are seized; but it depends on the species of spider. There seem to be at least three species of bird-eaters—one which is "a hunter" pure and simple; a similar species which spins a lurking-place under the limbs of decayed trees, etc., and one which spins a web for the capture of small birds and large insects. The first is the largest. It was a French lady who first drew attention to, and described, the web-spinning species—she does not seem to have seen the others. Doubt and ridicule were cast on her stories; but all travellers have to endure a certain amount of impertinence from gentlemen afflicted with the smile sardonic. This is not the place to describe these spiders, which must be referred to in the district where they are most numerous and grow to the largest size—the heart of the Brazilian forest. Incidentally, also, other humming-birds must be noticed; but here I may say that these lovely living gems, as they have justly been called, are found in all parts of South America; and, indeed, practically throughout the continent. They touch Canada in the summer season, are quite common in some of the southern states, abound in Mexico and Central America, and are found as far south as Tierra del Fuego—at least so it is said on first-class authority—although when I was there in '92 or '93 I never saw any during a daily search of the country which lasted several weeks. But probably they are migrants in so low a latitude, and may have been absent during my visit.

Where they have not been persecuted they are abundant; but in some of the long-settled portions of the country they are nearly exterminated. During the time of my travels there was no protection for birds or game of any sort in South America, and not much in the northern part of the continent. Now there are pretty (and sometimes *very*) stringent game-laws in the north; and protection for small birds and rare species: but I believe that anywhere in the southern division of the continent, an idle rascal may commit as much bird-murder as he likes, in any way he thinks proper. Cruelty to animals never shocks a Spaniard.

On the slopes of Antisana I found the green motmot; and this interesting bird is plentifully distributed throughout the eastern flanks of the Peruvian and

Ecuadorian Andes. I do not say it is not found on the western slopes also. I do not know. The bulk of the towns and cities are on the west; and I have so much of the savage about me that I do not like towns and cities—nor the false science and theories that dwell in them!

CHAPTER XI

THE PLAINS OF ECUADOR AND COLOMBIA

THE tributaries which join the Amazon from the Andes of Ecuador and Colombia (formerly Granadian Confederation) have generally a south-eastern course; and are always described as flowing through plains. The plains have, however, a very decided dip towards the main river; and it is not until the 73rd degree of longitude W. is passed that the Amazon flows through what appears to be a flat country. Of this there is more to be said hereafter. For the present I may say that there are no mountain ranges in the interior of Ecuador; and very few groups of hills of any noticeable eminence: still the country gradually and almost imperceptibly makes a very considerable dip towards the south-east, as much as 2000 to 2500 feet in a distance of 800 miles. The few hills that are met with are isolated; and never form connected ridges.

There is a parallel range of the Andes running north-eastward in Colombia, enclosing a valley of considerable width; as much as, and more than, a hundred miles in places, through which runs the Rio Magdalena, one of the very few large rivers of the earth which empty themselves into the sea in a due north direction. But this region is quite out of our scheme, and cannot be described here.

It is to be observed that all the navigable rivers of South America, the Magdalena excepted, empty themselves on the east coast of the continent; and *more than half* the entire system is connected with the Amazon: and by means of the Amazon, its tributaries, and the Orinoco, with which it is connected by the cross-cutting Rio Casiquiare, and the Rio Negro, two-thirds of the entire southern continent may be reached! It is probably the eastward flow of South American waters which tends to increase the size of the Amazon—I mean because there is no dividing ridge to divert part of the flow to other directions. A similar remark is applicable to the northern continent of America.

There is a good deal of unexplored country in the extreme east of both the republics mentioned in this chapter, though there are several towns on the Napo, and others on the Ica: but these have their trade almost entirely via the Amazon; and Peru has now possessed herself of the most important of them. The country between the Napo and the Ica; and between the Ica and the Caqueta, was almost unknown thirty years ago. A few small towns and ranchos on the larger rivers were the only inhabited spots; but a good deal of the wood had been felled in the vicinity of the streams and floated down to the Amazon to be shipped for Europe: and parties of men wandered in the forests collecting wild cinchona bark, cork and rubber, destroying the trees in so doing: for the people of these countries are usually very careless and improvident.

The rivers and streams in the east of Ecuador are very numerous, and they all drain into the Amazon; and possibly this country could be made one of the most prolific in South America; but the Andes are a barrier to its development, as they are to all the western states. The rivers on the Pacific coast are simply rivulets; and many of them are dry, or partially so, in the summer season: and there is not one that serves as a waterway into the interior of the country, or ever can do so: the tremendous range of mountains being an effectual barrier to inland water communication.

Before leaving the Andes region I would state that there are districts on the eastern slopes, where not only gold, but several kinds of precious stones, are found, if they are not abundant. I found several diamonds, but fear of provoking trouble with the local authorities prevented me from making a thorough search. I had hopes of making terms, or getting a concession; but I never saw the way clear to the fulfilment of these hopes. A person must have been in this, the most priest-ridden country in the world, to understand my position. At the time of which I am writing there was an entire absence of public morality in Ecuador. If it had been known that I was in possession of a valuable secret, I should have been required to give it up to the priestly rulers of the land. If it had been merely suspected that I knew of the existence of precious metals, and precious stones, I should have been detained in prison until I had revealed all my knowledge, and more. For the rapacious priests would never have believed that I had told them all. Everything in Ecuador was controlled by the priests; and where their interests were concerned, or where there was a chance of acquiring wealth, the liberty, property and life of an individual were accounted of no value. A solitary, unknown wanderer, without an interest, or friends, in the country; and with no certainty that I would be able to communicate with a consul in case of need, I thought it desirable that I should be extremely careful what I did or said. At any rate I determined to get out of the country before I opened negotiations with any person within its frontiers. So far nothing has come of the knowledge I acquired. Capital, and safety for that capital, are two indispensable preliminaries; and I found no American friends very anxious to risk their dollars in such a country as Ecuador. I believe some attempt to approach the Ecuadorian executive was made, but fell through because the first demand of that body was that the situation of the supposed diamond and gold mines should be revealed to them. I absolutely refused to comply with this demand until my rights were satisfactorily settled. There the matter rests.

The number of diamonds I actually found was twenty-three; and eighteen rubies. The rubies were found in the bed of a stream, the gravel of which was highly auriferous; but I failed to find any nuggets of the metal. The reef is certainly much richer than the one described as being near the head-waters of the Purus. Probably a great deal of gold-dust could be washed out of the gravel of the stream; but as I thought I was being watched, and should lose the benefits of my discovery, I did not attempt to make a present use of it. A cradle is a noisy instrument; and a man cannot even "pan out" without attracting the notice of every passer-by.

Years afterwards I offered my uncut diamonds and rubies for sale. I was assured that the diamonds were of poor quality. For the largest I obtained £8 English money. The remainder fetched very low prices; but for the rubies I obtained £85 although they were small. It is possible that the rubies of Ecuador may prove of more value than the diamond mines. Nearly thirty years have elapsed since these few stones were picked up; but I have never heard that Ecuador has yet discovered the wealth that lies at the feet of her mighty rocks; which is a strange circumstance. No doubt these precious things require looking for; but there are always indications of the presence in the rocks of gold and diamonds; and some practised eye ought to have seen these long ago.

I did not pass down the Amazon at this time; but having searched the country to the extent my time and outfit would permit, passed back into Peru; and, later still, into Bolivia. But as the drainage of Ecuador is entirely into the Amazon, and the quantity of water which is daily poured from that country into the main stream enormous, I think I am justified in devoting some space to a description of the productions of the country.

The forest is of the same general features as that of Matto Grosso; but it is not so damp: in fact there are thousands of square miles of it in which no swamp is to be found. This is a very unusual feature in Matto Grosso, where the reverse of this is the usual case; and not thousands merely, but tens of thousands of square miles are constantly underwater; and I have been puzzled to know how it is that the wet does not kill the trees. Either they are of species which thrive in moisture, or they have "evolved themselves" and "acquired aquatic habits."

I am rather afraid to write much about the trees of Ecuador, as I am no botanist: and as a naturalist, I suppose, stand to the spick-and-span professor in much the same relationship as that of "an old bodging tailor" to the "practical man." Let it not be thought that modesty, or humility, leads to this confession. Not so. I think that the old fellow who can neatly clap a patch on your what-do-you-call-'em is often of more use, and more welcome, than "Slasher, *late* with Dasher, of New Bond Street." So I will rush into a description of the trees of Ecuador, and chance whether I blunder much in my accounts of them. To avoid serious misdescriptions the best way will be to give the native names and make no attempts to classify them.

One of the finest trees in the country, and throughout Northern and Central Brazil, is the mora. It usually grows to a height of 150 feet; and fine specimens, in favourable positions, attain to 200 feet. I think I need hardly say this is a great height for a forest tree, even in the tropics, where most of the trees are large and well developed. I have rarely seen this tree without flowers: it must, therefore, be in bloom during the greater part of the year. The blossoms appear in large clusters, and are of a brilliant scarlet colour: so that the tree, from a short distance, and with the sun shining brilliantly upon it, has the appearance of a mass of glowing fire—for few of the leaves can be seen, so thickly does it bloom. The mora is not only a tall tree; it is, also, very bushy; the distance through from outer branch to outer branch being sometimes as much as fifty yards—this is, of course, where the tree has room to spread. In close forests, it still seems able to elbow more room for itself than most trees; and even miles deep in the heart of the forest it is one of the largest, as well as the tallest, of trees.

Monkeys are fond of harbouring in the mora; but sloths eschew it, I cannot tell, or guess, for what reason: but I have noticed the fact that two species of mammals, or birds, never occupy the same tree; and quite often a particular kind of tree is entirely avoided by some genus, or family, of animals. Why an inquisitive, mischievous creature, like the monkey, should avoid trees in which sloths are feeding, or sleeping, is a mystery of Nature which I cannot explain. It is even more mysterious that they seem always to know when a sloth has possession of a tree, in spite of mimicry and protective colouring; but seldom perceive the approach of their arch-enemies, the boa, anaconda and jaguar, though it cannot be pretended, with a shadow of truth, that the "colouring" or "mimicry" of any of these creatures at all approaches to that of the sloth. The fact is that it is not colour, or similarity to some other object, that enables the serpent and the huge cat to approach their victims; but silent cunning and craft. The monkey sees not, knows not, until the death-dealing paw pins him down; or the darting, fang-furnished head shoots down on him. The case is exactly on all fours with that of the prowling Zulu savages who surprised the Prince Imperial's party in South Africa. In all cases, in nature, as in war, it is the same. Cunning, or enterprise (*not necessarily* superior cunning or enterprise), wins the prize from carelessness, or forgetfulness. It is always so, according to my experiences, with creatures of prey. They surprise their victims; and if they fail to do this; if they inadvertently make the least noise, or reveal an inch of their spotted hides, off go their victims; and the would-be slayers have nothing left but to lick their chops, and sneak disappointed and supperless to their lairs.

The monkeys which favour the mora as a habitation are of the "spider" kind; but I am not able to indicate with precision which particular species. They go in troops numbering from fifty to eighty, are lively and noisy; but do not show themselves to a spectator if they can avoid doing so: in fact, I have heard them in a tree near my camp for days together without seeing one. It is only by concealing oneself and patiently watching, that a glimpse of them can be obtained. It is worth the trouble and expenditure of time, however: for they are most interesting and entertaining creatures.

American monkeys are not so mischievous and spiteful as those of Asia and Africa. I have kept them as pets; and I never knew them purloin or destroy any article; or bite any person who was not actually doing them an injury. In a wild state the mother carries her young one in her arms much like a human parent. When she jumps or runs the little creature clings to her chest, and never to the back. The leaps these spider-monkeys take are tremendous; but nearly always downwards, from a higher branch to a lower one. Of course one can only guess the distance travelled; but I am sure it often exceeds sixty feet; yet the monkey never misses its hold. They also spring laterally a good distance; I should think fully twelve feet; but I have never seen one leap upwards to a higher bough, more than six or seven feet. They never drop, not even to avoid an enemy;

but always leap: and they always go to slender branches where their heavier pursuers cannot follow them: and as soon as they are in safety scold him with noisy energy. They are all noisy; but the monkeys known as howlers make a monstrous hubbub, apparently without any cause whatever. Their cries at night are often unendurable; and I have sometimes got up and shot into the air to frighten them away—not always with success.

I have not been able to confirm the assertion, made by some writers, that howler-monkeys are natural ventriloquists; but I think that it is very likely that they are: and it is just as likely that one howler is answered by several others occupying trees at various distances. I think it was the Rev. J. Wood who first promulgated the theory that the voice of this monkey is ventriloquial. All I can say with certainty is, that when a howler commences his charming serenade, he is answered by similar melancholy sounds from the surrounding forest far and near. The noise itself is indescribable with any degree of exactitude. It usually starts with a sound that fully justifies its popular name of howler—it is a howl, rising or falling (I cannot say which) to a noise that resembles a scream. The intensity of the sound varies. Sometimes it rises to a yell that causes one's ears to quiver: then it drops to a low moan. This rises to a scream again, emanating, it seems, from a distant part of the forest; but this may be an act of ventriloquism on the part of the first howler. I can hardly think so, however, and I incline to the opinion that these monkeys answer one another from great distances—as far as they can hear, in fact.

So little is known of American monkeys generally,

and the howler tribe in particular, that modern compilers of "popular natural histories" still resort to the information given by Baron von Humboldt, which is extremely misleading. These monkeys do not hang by the tail and swing themselves until they gain sufficient momentum to catch the branches of an adjoining tree. They are strictly inhabitants of the dense forest; and leap from branch to branch like other monkeys; but they are not nearly so agile as the spider-monkeys. Neither do "a number of females follow the male in solemn procession" as asserted by the Baron. In fact we need not follow the lively German any further—his work "*Voyage aux Régions Equinoxiales du Nouveau Continent*" is very unreliable in a great many particulars; especially where he attempts to describe the habits of birds and mammals.

Howlers differ in the colour of their fur, and in very little else. The habits of them all are alike; they all inhabit dense forest, and all howl in the same intolerable way. There is a black species, and a brown, and a tawny, and one at least in which two or more shades of colour are intermingled. They are all much stouter built than the spiders; and many of them have more human-like countenances. When sitting on boughs of trees they nurse their young huddled into their bosoms; and when in motion the little ones cling round the bodies of the mothers with the chest pressed closely to theirs. Neither these, nor any other American monkeys, carry their young on their backs when running or leaping; but the little ones perch on the backs of both males and females when they are at rest in the trees, or moving slowly amongst the branches. Perhaps the males also carry them when leaping. It is very difficult to tell the sexes of monkeys when they are moving rapidly in tall trees: indeed, it is only occasionally that more than a passing glimpse of them can be obtained. I have no recollection of having seen a female with two young ones in her arms; but as they do occasionally have two, it is probable that the male carries one. As a rule, American monkeys do not have more than one or two at a birth: the majority of the species probably never have more than one, except, at any rate, very exceptionally.

Monkeys seem to agree pretty well on the whole; but squabbles and fights do occasionally occur, provoked, usually, by an attempt of a party of quite a different family to take possession of trees already occupied. Some of the animals lose their lives in these fights; for I have picked up the dead bodies from under the trees.

I think, too, that monkeys sometimes get bitten by whip snakes, and other poisonous serpents: for I have picked up their dead bodies under the trees, without finding any perceptible cause of death. On one such occasion, a young one was clinging to its mother's breasts. As I happened to be able to procure milk I succeeded in rearing the little thing; and it became very much attached to me. I brought it to England and left it with friends; but it pined when I returned to America and soon died, perhaps from improper feeding. American monkeys are not robust creatures; and I have lost several pets through the inconsiderateness of friends who gave them such unnatural food as cakes and sweets; and even meat: things which they will eat in captivity, though they would probably not look at them if met with while they were at liberty. All my pet monkeys, except some which I purchased, were reared from an early age. I never attempted to capture any; and never shot them; and I have noticed that when I have remained camped at one spot for a considerable time, the monkeys would soon get tame enough to show themselves freely, and permit me to watch them: but all the wild creatures, and especially birds, showed a similar confidence when they found they need not fear molestation. In tracts where man has seldom, or never, been, the birds were so tame that they could be knocked down with sticks; a trait of these creatures which has been remarked, very frequently, by other travellers in other parts of the world. Mammals were wilder; but even these were often unusually tame.

This is not describing the trees as I purposed doing; but I was so much interested in the creatures of the wild, that I cannot help thinking that others are pleased to learn about them; and so I am induced to gossip.

Remarkable for its blossoms, which are lily-white in hue, and as large as a half-pint cup, the shastee-pan is a large tree, though much less than the mora. The wood is soft; and I do not know that the tree is valuable for timber. I mention it because of its lovely blooms, and because it is the home of the caterpillar which produces one of the largest butterflies in America. I do not know the name of this butterfly, and I have never seen a specimen of it in a collection. It measures from four and a half to five inches in expanse of wing and is of a most beautiful ultramarine colour. It is one of the most beautiful sights of the country to see a multitude of these butterflies, recently hatched, hovering round the tree which has been the home of the first stages of their short lives. Thousands of them may be seen together. I believe this butterfly is unknown in collections; and unfortunately all mine were destroyed during my rough journeyings from place to place. Some were shaken to pieces; others perished of damp. While in South America, a mule or two had to carry all my belongings—provisions, clothing, arms and ammunition. I had so great a difficulty in carrying specimens that I was glad to get rid of them to any persons who were likely to value them. Hundreds of those I saved were purchased by private collectors: others, which I essayed to send through the post, were never heard of more; and many were stopped by the customs, who would not permit them to leave some countries, or enter others, until a really monstrous duty was paid on them. Alas! Travellers have funny experiences to narrate, as well as strange tales to tell.

There is a considerable quantity of mahogany wood in eastern Ecuador; but much of it that was accessible on the banks of the rivers has been felled. There seem to be several species of this well-known timber, one of which is so heavy that it will not float: consequently it is not cut in Ecuador, as few timber-ships come up the tributaries, and what timber was cut on them had to be floated down to the ports on the Amazon, and there shipped.

Lignum-vitæ also grows in this country; and the kind found here is so large and heavy, that if a log of it is dropped into water it sinks like a piece of iron.

These two trees, though doubtless two of the most useful in the country, did not possess the interest to me that others did which were rare and beautiful; and, at this time at least, were probably quite unknown outside the region where they grew.

I do not know that it is of much use giving the Indian, or Spanish, popular names, of the trees mentioned, as these vary in every tribe and district; but there is a tree known as the Antwa-sin-tanno; which means twisted snake tree, that is a great curiosity on account of the convolutions, not only of the trunk, but of all the branches also. It does not bear a conspicuous flower; but the small fruits which cluster on its boughs are a favourite food of both monkeys and wild men. This is the appropriate term for the Indians of the district: but I must consider these people in another place.

The "cannon-ball tree" is common; and so is the candle tree—at least, I suppose this is the tree meant by some old writers. It bears a fruit which resembles a large candle, nearly two feet long; but it is not white like wax, the hue being reddish, or brown, and it will not burn except like a stick. There is, however, a "torch tree," also bearing an elongated seed, or fruit, which burns like a pine; and is very useful for making torches. Both these trees are of comparatively small size.

CHAPTER XII

SOME NOTES ON THE NATURAL HISTORY OF THE UPPER AMAZON

I CANNOT leave the regions described in the foregoing chapters without further reference to some of the more curious creatures which inhabit them. The flora and fauna are always distinctive of a country; and without a description of them, one might as well say a river flows through a desert, and close the chapter. Unless the animals and the plants receive due attention, one description would do equally well for the Nile, the Ganges and the Amazon.

On this vast river there are animals and plants which are local, and others which are general in their distribution. Some must receive attention where they occur: it is more convenient to describe others where they are a prominent feature in the landscape.

Monkeys are often described in books as being numerous in South America. There are a greater number, both of species and individuals, on the Amazon than in any other part of the continent; but they are certainly not as numerous anywhere in America as they are described as being in Africa, India and some of the other Asiatic countries. And there are no large monkeys in America—nothing to compare with the man-like apes of Africa, and the hunaman of India, which eye-witnesses have assured me sometimes grows to such a size as to be mistaken for a man in the distance. This could never occur with any American monkey: for though two or three approach the hunaman in relative length, etc., they are, none of them, more than a third of the weight of the Indian animal. Slimness is the characteristic of the American monkey; and it does not hold a first place amongst the mammals of the continent.

But there are certain animals of which America is assuredly the head-quarters, amongst them the bats. I do not say that the Amazon is the chief haunt of these curious creatures, the only mammals possessed of true flight, but they swarm on some parts of it; and nowhere more than in those districts of Peru and Ecuador which border on the great river. The species are many; and amongst them are the vampire and the great bat. I write these words advisedly, because I believe naturalists have established a family for vampires; and recognize several, if not many, species. The one I mean here is that which has made its name notorious by its blood-sucking habits.

The great bat is the largest on the continent; but I am not sure that it is *Vampirus spectrum*. A specimen of this creature which I saw in a museum, and which I was told was an exceptionally fine one, could not have measured more than twenty-six or twenty-seven inches in expanse of wing; but I have found them on the Upper Amazon, and on some of its tributaries, about ten inches wider; and altogether bigger and finer-looking animals than this "exceptionally fine specimen." But we need not make too much of this. The finest specimens of animals do not find their way into large museums. The curators of these are usually men with a considerable amount of ledger account in their composition. Private collectors pay the best prices, and get the best specimens. I am not writing this in scorn—of the museum curators at any rate. They are appointed and paid by persons who are not always good judges of what a curator should be, and, if they are required to keep an eye on cash expenditure, nobody can blame officials for performing what they know is required of them. The point is, that private collectors like to know that they have a bigger and better specimen than a public institution; and will pay the price for it. So they get the pick of a traveller's specimens, if he thinks it worth while to put them on the market. Here is a case in point, after relating which I will not recur to the subject. It will suffice to show why I did not trouble myself to bring this or that remarkable specimen to this country. Better prices than those offered in England, or in any European country, were always to be had at the nearest American big town.

In the early 'seventies I brought to London the skin of one of the largest grizzly bears ever shot in America. I showed it to a naturalist with a view to selling it to a museum. He "hummed and ahed!" doubted if it was so extraordinarily big a specimen; did not think the museum wanted it; and finally offered me £5 for it. That sum would not have covered the expense I had incurred in bringing it to this country. So I took it to an Oxford Street furrier. This gentleman also had doubts of its value, "but would I leave it?" obviously for him to make enquiries, and try to find a customer. When I called again he placed £50 before me: which I pouched.

But if I could produce such a skin now, there are many American magnates who would readily give £600 or £700 for it; though fashions in fur rise and fall, as they do in all things.

In Ecuador, the great bat, or "great vampire," passes the day in trees. It does not cluster in such numbers as some of the so-called flying foxes; but I have counted as many as 200 in one tree; and I probably did not see them all. They keep high up amongst the branches, and are not disturbed by the report of a gun; but it is not much use shooting them in this position; as if killed they still continue to hang from the branches. They fly high at night; but every now and then one will flit within range, presenting an easy shot. The flight is like that of all bats I am acquainted with—a silent flitting, to and fro. Sometimes one will dart downwards, evidently securing an insect. I do not know if they take other food than insects. In the stomachs of several of the few I shot there was a sour-smelling mucus full of the broken remains of insects, amongst which I found wings, legs, etc., of flies, beetles and moths.

The true vampire, the little gentleman, I presume, who refused to bite Squire Waterton, is plentiful enough on the Upper Amazon; but strange to say it does not bite people very often, nor domestic animals. I have opened some of these bats, and found the peculiar modification of the intestinal canal I read of in books; but blood, never. The stomachs were full of mucus; which appeared to be digested food: but if it was blood it had undergone a great change, including loss of colour. However, that blood forms a considerable part of its food is certain; and the puncture it makes is a deep, though small, bite; not always a mere abrasion with the tongue. Altogether I have seen about a dozen cases amongst men and boys, and many more amongst cattle. I have more than once surprised the bat in the act of sucking the blood from horses and mules; but they always darted away on my approach in such a manner that it was difficult to obtain a shot at them; and I never succeeded in bringing one of these marauders down. The bite leaves a permanent, though minute, mark; and I am sure that I have frequently found this mark on the hides of wild animals, such as capivaras, agoutis and deer. But the puzzling point is the vast numbers of these bats. I have found caves full of them —clustering from the roofs in thousands; and they may be seen on some of the upper reaches of the Amazon tributaries flying at evening time in myriads. Now it does not seem possible that there are a sufficient number of wild mammals in the heart of the forests to provide all these with constant meals of blood. The forest in its innermost recesses is not a populous place. There are few mammals, which are large enough for a vampire to attack; and I could never gather evidence that they settle on small ones.

As there are few reliable accounts of the habits of the vampire, I hope I shall be excused for dwelling at some length on the subject. I believe the question has arisen, "Are there several species of blood-sucking vampires?" I know there are two, and I suspect there are more; but I have no positive proof of it. I have some notes by me which seem to refer to a third species; but they are not very clear; and I cannot distinctly remember the circumstances to which they refer. It was my misfortune often to have to jot down stray notes on any book or paper I had at hand. Consequently some got lost, and some were too scanty and hastily written to be of much use when looked up in after years. For I had no thought of writing for publication during the years of my wandering life. If this circumstance is borne in mind, it will explain many apparent discrepancies and confusing statements. It has taken me years to gather up and arrange my notes: and I find that conclusions concerning the habits of an animal arrived at in one country are, sometimes, more or less upset by observations upon it in other districts of the continent.

What I can state with absolute certainty is that there are two species that are inveterate blood-suckers, of which one is *Desmodus rufus* (recognized by comparison with museum specimens); but the other I cannot identify by reference to pictures or stuffed specimens. Apparently it is a "javelin-bat," and one of those which have not yet found their way into lists and descriptions.

With regard to the common vampire: its little stomach could not, I feel sure, contain an ounce of blood; but the sucking action seems to set up a flow of blood which it is difficult to stanch. In my "Great Mountains and Forest of South America," I have given an account of an officer who was bitten; and who mentions that the bed-clothes were saturated with blood; and he calculated his loss at fourteen ounces: and I have found horses and cattle which have been bitten with blood streaming down their flanks. It seems to be unlikely that so great a flow could be set up by a mere abrasion of the skins caused by the rough tongue of the bat. However this may be it is certain that the second species referred to bites, and that very deeply though the wound is small. This javelin-bat (if I am rightly naming it) is much bigger than the first species. The body is about the same size as that of a blackbird, and the expanse of wing fifteen inches. It flits and flies in a straight line with great rapidity; and its stomach, like that of the common vampire, is of rudimentary formation; but notwithstanding this seemingly conclusive evidence I am strongly of opinion that other food than blood must be eaten by both these bats. If it can be proved that I am wrong (and I have no positive evidence that my belief is correct), then I must fall back on the theory that the vampires attack birds as well as mammals. There are whole classes of animals which the vampires cannot attack—the monkeys and the cats for instance: and there are no wild guanacos and horses in the great Brazilian forest. Therefore if the bats do not take other food than blood, and do not attack birds, how is it that there are such enormous numbers of them in many parts of the forest?

Along the range of the Andes the vampires occupy, and breed in, caves; but in the heart of the forest, where there are no caves, they cluster together in hollow trees, where I have seen them hanging together as thickly as bees. They slumber during the day; and they are difficult to arouse, so that one may handle and capture as many as he likes. They utter a thin squeaky cry; and also a sharper, short note, of metallic tone, like that produced by twanging a piece of metal; but they make no attempt to resist capture, or resent it.

How they breed, or where they deposit their young, I could never discover; but the little bat travels much like the young monkey, clinging to the breast of its mother; only in the bat the young is carried head downwards; while the monkey bears its little one with the head upwards. I do not think they make nests; and I could not discover that they have any natural enemies. Being of nocturnal habits, they are difficult to watch, and to discover during the daytime, even in districts where they abound. I had a habit of prying into decayed trees, and holes of all kinds, in search of birds' nests, snakes, etc.; but it was only rarely that I found a colony of bats. These curious creatures are certainly all gregarious: they sleep and rest hanging by their feet very closely together; and in immense bodies. Estimates of their numbers must be guesses: for to count them is impossible. Probably I have found as many as 20,000 in one huge hollow tree. It would take a considerable quantity of blood to feed such a host! Even supposing our military friend exaggerated when he put his total loss at fourteen ounces, it is certain that the bat wastes (or causes the loss of) a great deal more than it consumes, and a fair estimate would be five ounces per meal; and if we allow a meal a day to each bat, and consider that one party of bats alone numbered 20,000 individuals, we are constrained to pause in amazement and exclaim, "It cannot be possible that they live on blood alone."

Here we have treated of the true vampires (or blood-sucking species) alone; but these do not form a hundredth part of the bat world of the Amazon. It is difficult to reveal the scenery of any country in detail so as to bring a realistic picture before the eye of a reader, especially if a preconception has been formed; but, in fact, the monkey and the sloth, the tapir and the deer, are not prominent features in the Amazonian landscape; the bat is—a very conspicuous feature indeed. Bats appear on all parts of the river and its tributaries in swarms. They flit across its enormous broads, its quiet pools, its lakes, and its rapids; and force themselves upon the notice of the traveller. On the Purus; and in Bolivia, on some of the upper reaches of the Madeira, there is a bat of enormous size, the stretch of wing considerably exceeding thirty inches; but accepting the "popular natural history" maximum of twenty-eight inches, this is an enormous creature to see flitting, twirling, turning over, and performing a dozen other tricks in the air. There may be hundreds of them together; and one's mind reverts, unbidden, to imaginations of the prehistoric ages, and the flying pterodactyls which were—I will not inflict a galvanic shock on the Natural Selectionists by saying bats, but—a bat-like race of creatures. Often, at evening time, when they appear, they are, with the exception of an occasional nocturnal bird, the only living creatures which can be seen.

The vampires (I mean the blood-suckers) never congregate on trees, though they do in the hollows of decayed ones: the other kinds do; or, perhaps, I had better guard myself against contradiction by saying many species do. Trees may frequently be seen covered with them; so that from a short distance they look like some strange fruit clustering on the branches. Other kinds choose thickly leaved trees for their habitations; and these can only be seen when one stands directly under the huge boughs.

The bat tribe, or genus, affords a curious study, even without going farther abroad in the land than the Amazon river. The species are so numerous, the individuals so multitudinous, and they differ so widely in appearance and characteristics, that it is not going too far to say they are the most curious of all mammals. Everybody would see, and admit, this, if their size were great: size is such an important factor in attracting the human attention. A mouse with a trunk an inch long would be *merely funny;* but an elephant with one six feet in length is *very remarkable!* So a collection of bats' heads the size of those of men and oxen would be a Chamber of Horrors that would rob that in Baker Street of a great part of its attraction. For I do not think the heads and features of any other genus of the animal world differ so much as those of the bats; and I am sure none other can show such a series of grotesque and marvellous variations of facial form. They have been called "horrid," and "fearful"; and that by evolving naturalists, who ought to have known better. I remember that great man (he was a great man, and a good one too), Charles Waterton, was very angry with a person to whom he was showing his wonders, for calling one of his big frogs, or toads, "a horrid creature": and I agree with him. There is not a living thing on the face of the earth that is not wonderful and beautiful in its way, though sometimes terrible—man alone is vile; but then he is such a rascal—I mean the average specimen of him.

Compare the fox's head of some of the fruit-bats

(hence called "flying foxes") with the enormously wide mouth and thick lips of the Malayan naked-bat, *Chiromeles torquata*. Could any features show a wider, a more wonderful divergence; not only of appearance, but of actual structure also? I ought not, perhaps, to cite these two bats as samples of their marvellous variations: for neither is of American habitat: and it was scarcely necessary to go so far afield as India and Malaya for examples. The singular nose appendages of the South American bats make them remarkable enough. I refer to the "nose-leaves, spear-heads, etc.," which, according to some people, make these creatures "hideous"; and which certainly give them a very curious, not to say grotesque, appearance. In reality the vampire is one of the most innocent-looking of the family; and the fruit-vampire a ferocious-visaged species; but all alike are harmless in general. They are ghost-like, weird-looking creatures, which do not seem to belong to this world: consequently they are regarded with awe; and often, I regret to say, with abhorrence, by the people of all countries. Considering that they are so numerous on the Amazon, and are a never-failing nightly sight on all parts of its course, it is surprising that the Indians regard them as *birds* of ill omen. Amongst all the tribes on the upper waters of the great river they are called "devil birds." It is useless to endeavour to persuade these people that bats are not birds, but mammals: their pee-ai-men will not have it; and of course his parishioners dare not contradict him. Your red man, copper man, black man—call him what you will—is as much priest-ridden, and priest-permeated, if I may coin a term, as any civilized bigot.

These curious nose-leaves, or appendages, of the bat are said by naturalists to be a provision of Nature to enable the creature to avoid obstacles during its rapid flight. The organ is said to be highly sensitive, and capable of warning the bat of its near approach to anything in its way, such as a twig, or another bat. As the appendage must have a use, I think it is very probable that this is a correct explanation of the employment to which the animal puts it. I should imagine, too, that it enables some species to detect the near proximity of the insects on which they prey. Bats have, possibly, an additional sense in these organs; and they are certainly furnished with extremely sensitive auditory organs.

Concerning the eyes of bats: everybody knows that they are popularly supposed to be blind, or nearly so: but in reality, is the bat of defective vision? I am disposed to doubt that it is. The eyes of all the American bats are small compared with the other organs of the animals; but they are exceedingly bright and piercing. All the species that I am acquainted with have coal-black eyes.

The eyes of nocturnal animals afford another curious and interesting study. They vary enormously in size and in appearance; but not much, it would seem, in power. Everyone knows the peculiar look of a cat's eyes. They are all alike, so far as American species are concerned; and it is pretty certain that they see equally well by day or by night. I wonder if this is the case with snakes. I fancy that it is, though I could obtain no conclusive proof of it—most serpents being ugly customers to deal with in the dark. There is just a similar contraction of the pupil to what looks like a liquid slit, when it is steadily regarded, in both animals; and both are very sharp-sighted within certain limits: that is they see well by daylight and dusk up to about 100 yards. After dark, cats see well: about serpents I cannot write with so much assurance; but I have seen them suddenly appear, making straight for a camp fire, as if attracted by the light: and it was quite a common occurrence to find small ones under blankets and rugs when we slept on the ground; fires being always kept in through the night, no matter how hot the climate. The use of a fire at night in the wilds can only be understood by those who have had occasion to learn it.

The eyes of cats and snakes are of normal size compared with their bulk of body: those of bats are not so, being relatively much too small. Cats and snakes can certainly see well in the day-time; bats cannot. But it is singular that some nocturnal creatures which have enormous eyes are almost, if not quite, blind by day. The tartius of another hemisphere may be cited as an instance; and the owl also. Some of the American owls are absolutely helpless if surprised by daylight. But I will trespass no further on these subjects. Owls are not numerous on the Amazon; but there are some curious ones which will probably be described in due course.

CHAPTER XIII

A VOYAGE UP THE PURUS

THE Purus must now be described. In the case of such a river as the Amazon it is necessary to consider all, or, at any rate, most, of its great tributaries. To neglect to do so, and confine attention to the main stream, would be to describe the body only and disregard the limbs. Besides, it is really the tributaries that are the chief characteristic of the Amazon. Of the nine largest subsidiary rivers which feed the greater stream, six take their rise in the Andes; and these alone could find water enough to supply a continent: in fact, the Purus, Madeira, Yapura and Rio Negro, with their secondary streams, exceed in extent all the rivers of Australia put together; and contain vastly more water. It is really these large tributaries that create the Amazon, and sustain it. Deprived of the enormous quantity of water they pour into it, the main river would speedily dwindle to a comparatively meagre stream.

I have already stated all I know about the upper reaches of the Purus. In the later months of 1884 I ascended this river from its mouth; and at that time, at any rate, only one or two Englishmen had been there before me. I thought at the time that I was the first man of my nation who had navigated its waters; but

I heard afterwards, on my return to Obydos, that an Englishman had been there before me. I supposed that this was Mr. Bates; but learned at a later date that it was a Mr. Chandless, who was there twenty years before me. I have also heard some account of his discoveries; but have not had the advantage of seeing his book. Of this matter, more presently.

My outfit for the exploration of this great river consisted of a rotten old fishing-boat of Portuguese build; two men and two large dogs. The dogs played no unimportant part in the little journey: for being large and fierce animals, of a breed formerly used to hunt down slaves, they kept the wandering Indians in awe; and on several occasions prevented my being robbed, and possibly murdered.

I am convinced that the Purus drains the very flattest country of the Amazon valley. It is the most tortuous of all its tributaries; and is full of looping reaches of more or less great length; so that my boat having sometimes traversed twenty, thirty and even fifty miles, in as many hours, would yet be within four or five miles of the country we had seen one or two days previously. We seldom got more than a mile an hour out of the old boat: for breezes were singularly rare on these inland waters; and often we made no perceptible progress; and were compelled to resort to the use of sweeps (large oars) to get any way on the *Firefly*, as I called my old tub—she was originally named the *Santa Maria;* and must have been, at bottom, a tough old girl, or she would never have survived the strain that was put upon her before her adventures finally closed.

Taking a general view of the Purus: the current is

everywhere slow, and often imperceptible. The country on all sides of it is extensively inundated; and in many places there are expansions that, in Norfolk, would be termed "broads." Perhaps I should call them lakes; but I prefer not to, for a reason given presently. There is no part of the river that I have seen that does not run through a forest that is evidently of enormous extent and density; and is further remarkable for the size and height of its trees.

From the centre of some of the broads the forest looks like a distant hedge; but generally the water is evidently only a flood on the low banks, and the trees stand in it. The course of the river is always traceable. At this time there was a good deal of rain: therefore, it is possible that in the dry season trees now standing in three or four feet of water were on dry ground. Here and there little islands of forest growth appeared in the midst of the broads, the water round them being, generally, shallow enough to permit one to leave the boat and walk ashore. In the channel the water is forty to fifty feet deep some distance up the course; and in some reaches even deeper.

There are a great number of islands in the bed of the Purus. They are of all sizes, from a few square yards of sandy mud to forest-covered tracts of twenty square miles area. All the larger islands were covered with trees; but these had been washed out of many of the smaller ones. The islands are quite distinct from the flooded tracts. On those which were treeless were a multitude of caymans, river tortoises, jabiru storks, egrets and ducks; which were so tame as to convince us that they were seldom disturbed. As many as we wanted for food fell easy victims to our guns. The sly-looking caymans waited until we were within five or six yards of them, and then slipped off into the water, and disappeared; though they were lurking in all parts of the river in such great numbers that they were a continual source of danger. We were often afraid to bathe; and all three of us had some narrow escapes. On one occasion José Najas would have been seized if he had not chanced to have an axe in his hands, with which he gave the reptile a tremendous blow, nearly severing the upper jaw, and killing the creature instantly, which was far more than a bullet through the head would do. We had to shoot several which made attacks on us; but as a careful expenditure of ammunition was necessary we soon resorted to axes, and a large double-edged scythe, mounted on a pole, as weapons of defence. The scythe was one of my favourite tools. I seldom wandered about the woods, or swamps, without having it in my hands; and I feared to face nothing when armed with it. I never had to defend myself against a puma or jaguar; but I am certain that I could easily have cut these animals to pieces with it. I have often destroyed large and dangerous serpents with it. One slash, and a twelve or fourteen feet boa would lie in two quivering halves, unable to move an inch. It was as a defence against snakes that I first adopted this formidable weapon. In the thick forests of the Amazonian region there dwells the dreadful cooanaradi, or cooanacooki (its two most common native names), called a bushmaster in Guiana, the largest poisonous snake in the world. It is usually about ten feet long; but is often much larger. One that I cut to pieces was at least fourteen feet in length. The great danger with these huge venomous creatures is that their disposition is quite different from that of the majority of snakes. The rattlesnake, the moccasin, and all the small harmless serpents, will glide quietly away if they have the chance to do so; while the huge anaconda and the boa lie apathetic until actually disturbed: but the horrible cooanaradi, beautiful as a rainbow to look upon, and evil as a fiend, will go out of its way to make a fierce attack on one; and knows no fear. It is, therefore, more dreaded than all the other venomous snakes put together. Against such a creature some more effective weapon than a gun is desirable; for, besides the difficulty of hitting a quickly moving snake, a bullet will not always stop one. A cut with a scythe, and the business is done: for no snake lying in halves ever yet lifted its venomous head to hiss or bite. The scythe is also very useful for cutting through thickets, tangled vines and grass, and similar obstacles. Against the caymans it was not altogether an effective weapon. Their horny hides turned its edge; and the point would not penetrate: so the axe was the favourite instrument of attack against them. Hard as their skins are, they are not so tough as is popularly supposed. A heavy axe, or a common lead bullet, will penetrate them easily enough: but caymans are rather tenacious of life.

The mouths of the Purus form a delta fifty miles wide. I do not know how many channels there are; but there are five main, or large, ones, only two of which appear on the maps. I believe the first reached from the mouth of the Amazon, that is the most easterly one, is the largest; but I have not been through the others. At this point it cuts through sand-banks ; and the Amazon seems to be about three miles wide where its great tributary joins it. Although hundreds of ships must pass these mouths every year, none appeared to ever enter it (in 1884), so little is the heart of the country opened up ; but we met with plenty of evidence that boat expeditions frequently ascended the Purus : and there were indications on the banks that attempts at settlements had been made.

Caymans abound, not only throughout the course of the Purus, but also in the main stream of the Amazon ; and particularly in the delta I have mentioned : but in the Amazon they are shy of showing themselves in the day-time ; and if they ever cross the river in its wider parts, probably do so only in the depths of night. They lurk under the wooded banks, where there are quiet and well-shaded bays and recesses. Deep pools in such situations are always dangerous spots ; almost every one of them being favourite lurking-places of these reptiles. " They are not what you may call handsome varmints," said a Yankee friend of mine, " but the cusses have fine open countenances." I should advise visitors to this interesting region not to place too much confidence in their seductive smiles. Accidents are pretty frequent. I met one man at Parentin who had lost a leg ; and he was fortunate : as a rule, the cayman makes sure of the entire carcass. There is not a town or village on the Amazon that I called at that had not some harrowing tale to tell of the boldness and ferocity of these creatures. They are said to often rush at people walking along the banks of the river, and carry them off. Boatmen frequently lose their lives : and caymans have been killed in the streets of some of the small riverside towns, where they have been found wandering at night—in search of food, it is believed. For there is such a multitude of these creatures that they must often find it difficult to obtain sufficient prey.

On shore they cannot run very fast; and they have some difficulty in turning at a sharp angle. They do not, as a rule, wander far from a river or large pool, except in swamps. They like their meat "gamy"; and when they have secured a victim they carry it to some quiet lurking-place, push it into a hole, or under the submerged roots of a big tree, and wait until it is nearly rotten. They then rend it to pieces, and enjoy their feast. This I have learned by actual observation of their movements and habits. I write in the plural number: for though one only may capture a monkey, a paca, a deer or a man, several join together in devouring it. About a week elapses between the death and the devouring of the prey: I have several times watched carcasses for that time; on one occasion that of a negro, or half-breed.

The feast is a lively scene. There are always several caymans in one pool—perhaps twenty or more. One having decided, I suppose, that the joint is done to a turn, commences operations by rending off a limb. Immediately out dart the others, and each one struggles and wriggles to obtain a mouthful. They do not actually fight; but they snap at one another, and crawl over each other; and altogether seem to display as much temper and animosity as other wild animals in similar circumstances. During the heat of the day, caymans assemble on some sand, or mud, bank, generally in mid-stream, and sun themselves. They lie perfectly quiet, huddled together, and lying over one another, like a herd of pigs.

About 100 miles from its mouth, the Purus suddenly deepens, as a result, probably, of its being joined by three considerable streams; and, also, by an underground spring of great volume and force. At this point I found depths of sixty feet; and, at one spot, of over eighty feet. Twenty miles higher up the water suddenly shoals to forty feet: and after that the depth is variable. I never found less than twenty feet until we had reached, as I suppose, 800 miles from the mouth: that is 150 miles in a direct line to the Amazon. For the Purus doubles its length, at least, by its turns and bends. It penetrates the country fully 800 miles in a straight line: but its actual course is not less than 1600 miles, and may well be 2000. I have passed over five-sixths of its course; and am writing with tolerable certainty when I say that the whole course of this great river is through an almost boundless forest. Across country it is: westward, 200 miles to the Rio Jurua, and 700 miles to the base of the Andes: eastward, 150 miles to the Madeira, 400 miles to the Rio Juruena, and 1000 miles to the Rio Araguay; a total stretch of 1900 miles, which was, in 1884, practically an unbroken forest south of the Amazon: for the few clearings that had been made could only be compared to a flea-bite on the back of an elephant. And, so far as I know, the conditions have not much altered since that date. They certainly have not so far as concerns the millions of square miles which form the heart of the forest.

During the ascent to the point I have indicated (800

miles) there could scarcely be said to be banks to the river. Where they were not underwater, they showed only a few inches of alluvial mould, only occasionally as much as three feet above the surface of the water. Tall trees, so high that birds perched near the tops of them were quite out of gun-shot, stood in the water, and as far inland as we could see; and at night-time, if it was too dark to proceed, we moored to one of these trees well out from the shore. But though the trees were so tall the diameter of the trunks was not remarkable. Few of them were as much as eighteen feet in circumference, though fully 200 feet high. The forest, of which they formed a part, was impenetrable in this district; and thickly matted with huge creepers and masses of pendent moss similar to the Spanish moss which is so characteristic a feature of the swamps of Florida and South Georgia. So closely matted was this vegetation that I spent days of search without being able to see as far as 100 yards into the interior of the forest.

The flowers and orchids of this region were magnificent; and the birds most gorgeous, and so numerous that I could almost fancy the country was an enchanted land. Mammals, on the other hand, were singularly scarce; and human life, and its signs, altogether lacking. There were monkeys in the trees, for we heard them; but saw only a few. At night we sometimes heard the cries of a jaguar; and a curious barking noise, which was not that of a dog, nor of any other animal with which any of us was acquainted. It may have been the cry of some species of howler-monkey; but I never succeeded in finding the animal which uttered it.

There were probably several species of night-jar here,

judging from the variety of their calls and weird noises ; but generally the quietude of the night, especially in the early hours of the morning, was only exceeded by the death-like silence of midday. The sense of solitude was awful ; and told heavily on my two men. Even I, who am so constituted that I should certainly make a good hermit, felt it acutely. I had to resort to special means to keep up the spirits of my two followers (men used to gay lives) and prevent them from breaking down. We tried concerts ; but were not in sufficient force to keep these up. So I resorted to evening readings, and the first laugh I succeeded in provoking from my companions was when I tried to imitate the vagaries of Mr. Mantalini. "The ha'penny be demned" became a frequent expression from the lips of one of my men when he wished to show his contempt of trifles.

At some distant period there have been settlements on the banks of the Purus. Where the timber has once been cleared is always easily perceptible, even though the spot has been abandoned so long that the trees have attained to as great a height, and thick a growth, as those of the surrounding forest. It is difficult to describe the difference of appearance : the trees are of the same species as those which originally occupied the ground ; but look fresher, cleaner of trunk, and have less moss upon them than those in the primeval forest.

What these settlements were I cannot tell, as I am not sufficiently versed in the history of the Spaniards and Portuguese colonists of South America. Some of them are marked on the maps as "Site of Florenças," "Old Mura Mission," "San Jacobo" and "Site of Boa Vista" ; but there are many others which are nameless ;

and which seem to be abandoned settlements of a great age: though there were indications in a few places that very recent attempts had been made to establish river-side towns. For instance, about twenty miles above the site of Boa Vista there are a number of ruined buildings, with wharves and a pier. There must have been settlers here at a recent period: for much of the masonry was new, though disintegrated by the growth of vegetation. It is simply astonishing how quickly trees and creeping plants will ruin masonry in this country, unless they are persistently cut down. They cannot be rooted out of the soil: at any rate, if they are, they immediately invade it again; and grow so rapidly that a path cut one month will be completely blocked the next, unless it receives constant attention. There was a house on the site I am describing which was occupied by a tree, the roots of which were in the earth by the side of one of the doors. The door was pushed back and off its hinges; and one huge branch had forced its way out of a small window, splitting the masonry to the base of the house, and lifting up the roof. Other branches had ramified all over the place; and, assisted by trailers, and several other kinds of plants, occupied the whole house, so that it was impossible to pass from room to room. There were other similar instances in the same place; and some of the buildings were so enveloped in masses of creeping plants that we did not, at first, perceive that they en-shrouded houses. Probably less than a dozen years previously this settlement had been inhabited. That a tree should grow twenty or thirty feet high in a dozen years is not remarkable in this country. I have known one increase in height six feet in a single year; but it is the trailing and creeping plants that are most rapid in growth; and the power of these vines is enormous. They will force out the side of a building, lift it bodily from its foundation, tear down strong walls; and completely bury houses. The "hedger and ditcher" is a useful man on farms in a temperate climate: here he is positively necessary at all seasons of the year.

It was probably the extensive inundations that led to the abandonment of all these settlements, ancient and modern, the country in their neighbourhood being underwater for an immense distance on all sides. There are, of course, many dry tracts; but, no doubt, all, in turn, become flooded. I suppose that settlers, encouraged by the apparently drier character of some spots, have established themselves, believing that the tracts were permanently above the floods. All may have gone well for a year or two: then an exceptionally wet season would cause a great rise of the river. The higher grounds (higher by a few inches only) would be covered by water; the settlers' works would be ruined, their stock lost; there would be no immediate prospects of natural drainage of the land; artificial drainage would be out of the question; "yellow-jack," or swamp-fever, would come on the scene; and the remnant of the poor adventurers would have no alternative but to bolt, and try for better fortune elsewhere. This is the probable history in brief of the whole of the settlements, past and present, on the Purus.

These abandoned settlements consist of small towns, villages and single plantations; and there was clear evidence that attempts had been made to cultivate coffee, cocoa, tobacco, sugar and several kinds of grain.

Wild rice was growing in the shallow water of the river; and odd plants of maize, and cultivated trees and shrubs were found growing, though the fields had been invaded by the wild growths of the forest, which had overrun, and crowded out, the plants of civilization.

Some of the old settlements were scarcely discernable; and some probably quite so, and were passed without discovery. Whether we actually saw the sites of Florença, the Mura Mission and San Jacobo I cannot say; there were so many ruins at the spots indicated by the maps, and all about the neighbourhood. I found the remains of a small church with branches of trees growing through every window, as well as through the roof. What remained of the masonry was kept up only by the support of the vegetation: there was no spire, and all the iron and woodwork had rotted away, or been removed. There was a curious old belfry; but of bells there was not a trace.

There were other remains in the neighbourhood of this church; and some mounds that may have been graves; and a very considerable area of ground had been cleared at some distant date. Nothing was found that threw any light on the name, or nature, of the settlement that had once occupied this ancient clearing.

Not far from this spot, but four miles inland from the river, I, on a subsequent occasion, discovered a very curious iron cross, which was so overgrown by the forest jungle that it could not be seen; and if I had not actually stumbled against it I should not have discovered it. It had been mounted on a stone base; but the roots of shrubs had pushed all these out of place, and they were so encrusted with mosses and lichens that it was not until

I had scraped some of them clean that I discovered they were granite. It is impossible to conjecture from whence these stones came. There is no granitic formation on the Purus, nor within hundreds of miles of it that I know of.

The cross itself was a very handsome one, set in a circle of filigree work; but it was so much decayed with rust that it fell to pieces the moment an attempt was made to remove it. In this neighbourhood there were a few traces of other works of European hands; but the ground appeared never to have been cleared.

Several times we discovered roughly made huts in the midst of small clearings; with heaps of chips, an old kettle and a ladder, all indications that the river was frequently visited by parties of civilized men: and one night, when we had ascended the river about 500 miles, a curious incident occurred.

My two men were sleeping on shore near a fire, while I lay under the half-deck of the boat with the dogs at my feet. The boat was moored close to the shore; so that I could step to the bank by means of a plank.

In the middle of the night the dogs set up a furious barking; and thinking that Indians were about to attack us, I immediately sprang up, and shouted to my men to stand by their arms. To my amazement I saw a bright light coming down the river, evidently shining from the bows of a boat. When she got abreast of us the men in her raised a loud shout, showing that there were at least half a dozen of them. We answered the shout; and my followers made some enquiries in Portuguese, and also in the lingua franca, which is largely used on the

Amazon; but there was no reply. The light went slowly on until it disappeared behind a bend of the river.

From what we afterwards discovered I have no doubt that this was a party of bird-hunters, seeking skins for the European market.

CHAPTER XIV

CONTINUATION OF THE VOYAGE ON THE PURUS

WE experienced some very uncomfortable weather while we were on the Purus. There were several heavy thunderstorms, with a really terrific downpour of rain. It fell " in sheets," as the sailors say ; and greatly interfered with the navigation of the boat : and what was worse it continued for days at a time. After a deluge in the morning, which would fill a bucket placed in the open in a few minutes, it would settle down into a steady fall, which made us all wretched—dogs included. About midnight it would clear up for a few hours, and permit us to enjoy the splendid moonlight. The early morning was dull, foggy and close : about ten o'clock the heavens were rent with ear-splitting thunder ; and the torrential rain recommenced. The blinding lightning struck several trees close to us, splitting one huge trunk right down ; so that part of it fell, with a great splash, into the water not fifty yards ahead of us : and for safety's sake we went out into mid-stream, where we had no shelter, and momentarily expected the boat itself to be struck and sunk.

These tremendous storms frighten all creatures, birds, beasts and reptiles, which rush to cover, the monkeys screaming and chattering, the birds uttering alarm notes ; but during the height of the storm not a living creature of any kind can be seen or heard.

As we continued the ascent of the river it became more tortuous; so that, on the upper reaches, it was rarely possible to see a mile ahead; and the current was quite imperceptible. In some of the broad shallows formed by the bends, the surface of the water was covered by acres of large lilies with leaves six or seven feet across, upon which the water-fowl ran as over a paved road. Here the jacana, or spur-winged water-hen (I think it is a rail), marches with stately tread, holding up daintily each long-toed foot as it takes its measured step. It is a slender-bodied, long-billed and long-legged, as well as long-toed bird; and always walks with slow and stately mien. I have never seen it run, and it flies very ungracefully and badly—in fact it can hardly fly at all; and it is very difficult to force it to take wing. It does not swim particularly well either; but it is a wonderful diver, and travels long distances under water.

On the Purus there is also a large and very beautiful green water-hen, with blue reflections on its plumage. Seen in the bright sunlight this bird has a superb appearance.

While on the upper reaches of the river I shot, or saw, at least five other species of water-hens and rails, all but one of which are found on the main stream of the Amazon, and over a wide area of the valley it drains. The exception was a little dark brown rail with pretty markings of a light shade. It has the curious habit, for a rail, of sitting on the branches of trees a few feet above the surface of the river, and suddenly dropping into the water, apparently to capture its prey. This, I ascertained, consisted of river flies, beetles and crustaceans.

Through opening one of these birds I was led to search for a curious fresh-water crustacean—a river shrimp, flea or crab—I cannot say which. The little creature is of beautiful and delicate formation, but so intricate in general appearance that it is not possible to intelligibly describe it with pen alone. It is about an inch in total length, of a pinkish colour, thickly sprinkled with brown specks, and is very active in the water. It does not seem to be abundant; as I could only find a few.

The rails and water-hens are very numerous. Unless it was raining heavily, one could scarcely look across the river without seeing a dozen or twenty of different kinds; not flocking together, but scattered here and there. None of the birds of this family appear to flock together, though a great many may be found within a short distance of one another.

Ducks appeared in flocks—sometimes of scores, often of hundreds of individuals. The muscovy-duck was very numerous, and often fell a victim to our guns, its size and palatableness making it a welcome addition to our fare. For not all American wild ducks are worth powder and shot. Many of them are dry and flavourless things: and in North America I have had a dozen of them offered to me in exchange for a pound of salt pork. Pork in Canada and the Northern States is, or was, what beef is in England, the standard meat: and in my time pork and molasses was the equivalent of beef and mustard. Molasses was Yankee lingo for "treacle" or "golden syrup"; and I remember a little girl, newly arrived in the land of Stars and Stripes, being sent to the store for treacle. "Tell yer ma I don't know what it is." Back came the little girl; for "golden syrup" this time. Still Sam was puzzled, till suddenly a bright revelation occurred to his mind; and he dabbed a pound of soft soap into the little girl's pot.

In every part of the region this work treats of whole genera of interesting creatures must be passed over. Only a few of the more splendid birds of the Purus can be noticed here. The blue heron and the egret are two of the most common of the water-fowl; and the jabiru-stork is the largest, and most majestic, of this class of birds; which give one of its most prominent features to the river scenery on the Purus.

The common green parrot of the country is also a very abundant bird on the Purus, perhaps more so than in any other part of South America. It is an entirely green bird, and goes in flocks of sixty or seventy; and, as with all birds of gregarious habits, these small flights occasionally join together in one huge flock, apparently for the purpose of visiting a distant feeding-ground. For parrots, macaws and, I suppose, all birds now and then leave their ordinary neighbourhood for a time, and proceed to some far-off country. The scarlet macaw, the blue and yellow, and the variegated all do so; and I have seen at least 2000 scarlet macaws on one tree. The herons, the ducks, the plovers, the toucans, and hundreds of kinds of other birds, large and small, all occasionally assemble in very great numbers.

There are other birds, solitary, or at most going in twos and threes, in general, which, also, forsake their usual haunts entirely, but without previously assembling in flocks. If there are any birds which are stationary, and never forsake their usual homes, it is birds of the rail and the water-hen kinds: but I suspect that even these sometimes seek new waters: for I have known them suddenly arrive at a pool where there had not been any for many months previously: and these emigrants always arrived in the night-time. It is curious that though I have several times known streams and ponds to be thus furnished with new-comer rails and water-hens, I have never once noted the reverse of this, and found that this class of bird had forsaken its usual haunts. The conclusion I draw is, that when waters are over-stocked, the superfluous inhabitants seek a new home.

In a former chapter I described a remarkable tree, the trunk of which was twisted and convoluted in a curious way, and not the trunk only, but the branches displayed the same strange characteristic. Looking over some old notes, I have just found the following remarks by the late Rev. J. G. Wood, which it seems clear refer to the same tree. The difference in name is accounted for by the circumstance that Wood's tree was a Guiana specimen; the Indians of every locality having a different name for a particular object.

Describing my tree in the presence of a person who had resided in Guiana, he said it must be the silk-cotton tree. This I denied, the silk-cotton being well known to me. It is a splendid example of arboreal growth, resembling a huge oak, with a gnarled trunk of immense dimensions (I have known specimens exceed twenty feet in diameter, without measuring any portion of their great buttresses), but it is quite a different tree from the woorah. The person referred to, not satisfied with my account, wrote to the reverend gentleman to ask if he knew the tree; and I saw the reply and transcribed it. I quote Wood's own words. "The tree referred to . . . must be the paddle tree; so called because the Indians make canoe-paddles from its wood. *Aspedospermum excelsum* is a most strange-looking tree. It runs to a considerable height, and the outline of the trunk is most remarkable, bearing a curious resemblance to the clustered pillars found in some of our old cathedrals. Indeed, the section of the trunk looks very much like a piece of one of those intricate puzzle-maps and pictures which used to be found in the toy-shops. As the wood is soft while fresh, an Indian, when he has to make a new paddle, splits off one of the 'flutes,' as these buttresses are called, trims it carefully into shape, and then hands it over to the women, who paint it in divers patterns of black and red. The paddle-wood tree is called by the natives yorari, or massara. When dry the wood is very light, very elastic, very hard and very strong. This oddly shaped tree averages sixty or seventy feet in height, and five feet in diameter. A good section of it is in the Technological Museum of the Crystal Palace."

The woorah may not be precisely the same species as Wood's "paddle tree," or it may grow to a much larger size on the Purus and the Upper Amazon: for while I agree that the average height is sixty or seventy feet,

I have seen many specimens of ten to twelve feet diameter. The wild-pepper vine, or capsicum, is very fond of climbing up and around its trunk and branches: and it is in every respect a very picturesque and pleasing tree.

I return to the birds of the Purus. I do not know if any of those "collectors" who are held in pay by museums have made the Amazon and its tributaries the scene of their operations since my visit; but in 1884–5 there were many species of birds in this region of which I could find no trace or description in books or museums. Amongst them there were three varieties of macaws on the Purus alone, all large and handsome birds, of which the only perceptible difference was in the colours of their plumage. Indeed, all the macaws in Guiana and Brazil appear to be nearly alike in *size* and quite so in *habits*, and to differ in plumage only. What slight variation there is in dimensions is nearly entirely in the length of the tail.

The bird I call the variegated macaw is a living rainbow, its feathers being tinted red, green, blue, yellow and several other hues, arranged beautifully, but so intricately that I cannot venture on a description of it. There is a green species on the upper river which differs from the green kind of other parts; but this is probably only a local variety. Of the third species I saw only one small flock of about thirty birds. It has a scarlet head and shoulders, with the same colour on the lower back and tail; the rest of the body and the wings being mixed green and blue, with a few black markings.

All the macaws live on wild grain, fruits and nuts,

with caterpillars and chrysalides, of which they devour a very considerable number. I have watched them searching the trunks of trees, like woodpeckers, for these delicacies, and tearing up the bark to find their hiding-places. They often descend in immense numbers and destroy the cultivated grain; and they are always difficult of approach within gun-shot; for it is useless to shoot at them at a greater distance than forty yards—they are as tough as leather, and will carry away your pellets as though they loved them. I have picked up wounded birds that appeared to be riddled; and in a few days they would be all right, and as lively as crickets. All parrots seem to be equally tenacious of life.

The assertion of the naturalist Bates that the blue and red macaw "goes in pairs" is incorrect. The whole of the macaws and parrots of the Amazonian region associate in flocks, large or small; and keep well together. They are all of them sly birds, and vicious, in spite of their lively dispositions; and a trapped wild bird will always bite savagely if it gets a chance of doing so; but young ones taken from the nest show an attachment to those who rear them. All the species are correctly described as breeding in trees; but the only nest I ever saw or heard of consisted of wood, or decayed bark, rent to minute pieces by the parent birds. This, however, forms a soft and snug bed. The number of young varies from one to four, two being the normal number. This is the result I found after examining about 100 nests. I need not say that it differs from the invariable assertion that macaws lay only two, or at most three, eggs. I cannot say if different species lay varying numbers—I think it is exceedingly improbable that they do so: and from what I have noted of the breeding habits of birds in general, I am convinced that the first clutches of eggs deposited by a hen are below the normal number laid by the species, as are, also, those in the clutches of very old birds. Macaws breed three or four times a year: and this circumstance may also influence the number in a brood, the birds being naturally exhausted towards the end of the season; which, with them and other American parrots, seems to last about eight months.

During the middle of the day, macaws, like all other inhabitants of the Great Forest, are as silent as death; but in early morning and in the evening they create a frightful hubbub. Those who have heard a thousand macaws screaming in concert will never forget it, especially if they are troubled with nerves. Fire a gun at them, and the noise is redoubled. They rise from their trees screaming as if in anger, and hovering just over the tops, they create a noise which can only be compared to that of a Bedlam. You may shoot again and again, but they will not be frightened away; and you will never kill one with small shot.

Amongst other curious birds seen several times on the Purus, and frequently on parts of the Amazon itself, was the sun-bittern, one of those curious creatures which are a puzzle "to systematic naturalists"; and no wonder: for there can be no system in natural history without numerous exceptions. I forget if the "sun-bittern" has been allotted a "genus to itself"; and I have never learned why it *is* called a sun-*bittern*. It certainly is not like a bittern, but resembles a large woodcock. The Spaniards called it a sun-bird because when the wings are spread open there appears on each of them a large black spot which their fanciful brains thought to resemble the greater light which rules the day. The idea is about as correct and reasonable as that which fancied it could discern the twelve apostles in the stigma of a " passion-flower " ; but, there, I do not know that the superstitious and exaggerating Latins were any sillier than the " schizognathous-palate, holorhinal-skull " gentlemen.

The sun-bird—or bittern—is, in my opinion, a very beautifully marked creature, though its feathers are only various shades of chocolate-brown, lighter tint, and black. It has a long beak, legs of moderate length, and is about the size of a bantam fowl. It is known by a variety of names in various localities of South America ; and also in natural history books. In the latter, it was once the sun-*heron ;* and is sometimes a " fly-catcher," and often a " butterfly-bird " ; but recent discoveries having found it minus the schizognathous-slit, I believe it has not yet got beyond the puzzle-stage with the systematists. We will call it a sun-bird, its commonest designation on the Amazon. It is certainly a most extraordinary creature, even if we consider no other of its characteristics than its curious antics. In life it is continually on the move ; yet it seldom flies, and never very far at a time : for though the wings appear large enough for the bird, they are peculiarly shaped, and evidently weak ; and their action is similar to that of a butterfly's wings : that is, the bird flutters along instead of progressing by measured strokes ; hence one of its colloquial names. A common motion of the bird is to raise the wings above the back and stretch them outwards and upwards so as to display all the beautiful markings. It also flaps them together, but without noise, trails them on the ground; and makes a great display of them in other ways. The bird hops round in a circle, jumps straight up a foot or two, and turns completely over as it descends. In fact, the sun-bird not only differs completely from every other avian in the region, but has antics and habits that no other known bird indulges in. It darts about, snapping its long bill at the flies, hundreds of which it destroys, though the bulk of its food consists of worms, grubs, snails and fresh-water crustacea; and it is itself a fine-flavoured bird; though, apparently from prejudice, it is seldom placed on the table of South Americans.

The sun-bird is not gregarious, but is widely scattered about, and over a great variety of ground. It is found on the outskirts of the forests, but not in the interior of thick woods: it frequents open ground, often in very dry situations; but its favourite resorts are along the wooded banks of rivers and brooks. It utters a variety of cries, all of them peculiar to itself; and none of them very loud. Like snipes and woodcock, it is easily killed. Though so large a bird, a single pellet of small size is generally sufficient to kill it; and as it is very tame, and easily approached, it is probably one of those creatures that will soon be exterminated when the land becomes thickly peopled.

Other birds of this region are quite different from those to which the average European is used. The powise is an instance. This large and handsome bird, the crested curassow, *Crax alector*, is often called a turkey by the Portuguese. In size it approximates to that bird ; and is quite as good as food : in fact it has become one of the domesticated fowls of Brazil, its tame nature, and hardiness, making it extremely fit for such a purpose.

In colour the powise is a crow-black, with beautiful reflections of green, steel-blue and crimson. The basal half of the large and strong beak is bright yellow ; and the abdomen pure white. It has a curled crest of stiff feathers; and this, in the hen, is speckled with white spots. The bird is quite common on the Purus, where it is difficult to shoot with a shot-gun, on account of the height of the trees, the tops of which form its favourite perch; though it often descends to the ground, scratching, and searching for insects like a hen. The bulk of its food consists of fruits, seeds and grain. There are two other species of curassows on the Purus; but they are much smaller birds than the powise.

I must not pass by the maroudi, which meets with so frequent mention in Charles Waterton's works. This strange bird, another of the non-classifiable tribe, is, on the Purus, of the white-headed species, *Penelope pipile*, often called the jacatinga by the Portuguese. It has a habit similar to that of the European starling of sitting on some elevated perch, usually a tree, and making a rattling noise by quivering its wings against its sides, uttering a low quickly repeated note at the same time. What the bird is I am unable to conjecture: it is quite abnormal. The Indians eat it; but the bird has at least quasi-protection from the pee-ai-men, who do not look with favour on its destruction, while they do not absolutely forbid it. The creature has one trait in common with its protectors—it is omnivorous, and will devour anything which will pass down its gullet. I have seen them seize rats and frogs, give their prey a sharp rap against a stone or the hard ground, to quieten it, and elevating their heads let the half-dead creature slip gracefully down their throats. They eat large beetles, big spiders, cockroaches, any slimy reptile they find in the ooze of the river, and fruits and grain of all kinds. Not the least remarkable feature in their gastronomic feats is the size of the morsels they can bolt. Often have I thought, "Surely the creature will divide that piece of food before swallowing it!" No! down it went; and apparently without any exertion on the part of the bird.

One day, about 400 miles up the Purus, a flamingo flew almost over the boat. I put a charge of No. 4 shot under its wing at about thirty yards range; and this sufficed to kill it. The body fell into the water; it fluttered a little before it died; but did not sink. Hardly had it been picked up, when a dozen caymans appeared, poking up their ugly snouts and looking round in evident anticipation of finding something good; and they followed the boat some distance. Did these creatures hear the splash, or sniff their prey?

The flamingo was a beautiful scarlet creature, which, when stretched out to its full length, measured nearly seven feet from the tip of the bill to the extremity of the feet. Only a few of these birds were seen in the Amazonian valley. On one occasion only were they met with on the Amazon itself, when I saw five of them standing in water which was so shallow that it only covered their feet. The flamingo presents an extraordinary sight when asleep, standing on one long slender leg, which appears to be of the same size throughout, so that the creature looks like a large bird stuck on the top of a long, thin stick.

CHAPTER XV

CONCLUSION OF THE VOYAGE ON THE PURUS

NO account of the river Amazon would be satisfactory if the tapir were not noticed; and I feel the more justified in recording what I know about it that there seems to be no modern and reliable history of the animal accessible. The most recent "popular natural history" that I have seen copies, word for word, the accounts given in a work published twenty years ago; and this last work has to rely largely on such ancient writers as Humboldt and Schomburgk; men not over-reliable, and not very close observers of what they did see, especially the first-named traveller.

The Amazonian tapir may be compared in size to a small ox; and weighs, I should think (for I have never actually seen one in the scales), about 400 pounds. It is a thick-set, heavily built animal, with a remarkably piggish external appearance, especially when lying down. The hide is half an inch thick when freshly stripped off, and much more in some places; but it is not particularly tough, and knife, spear or arrow will penetrate it easily enough; nor is the animal very tenacious of life. A single rifle bullet, of small size, drops it at once, and a comparatively small wound with arrow, or dart, will disable it; and it speedily dies, though it is full of blood.

The skin is very smooth and tightly drawn on the animal, and is of a blackish brown hue, and sparsely covered with coarse hair. As a rule it is encased in mud, and its true colour is only seen when the animal is dead and cleaned; or when it emerges from a prolonged bath, or in very wet weather.

It is eminently a fluvial animal. I have never seen any of them except in the immediate neighbourhood of large rivers. They do not even visit lakes and pools, except some of those forest-surrounded lakes which form the head-waters of many of the affluents of the Purus and Madeira.

The usual haunt of the tapir is amongst dense reed patches, and in the swamps; and they eschew dry forest land. They are abroad at all hours of the day and night, and are amongst the most solitary in habit of all American mammals. I have never seen more than two together—the cow and her calf, and the male pursuing the female. The male is never with the cow when she has a young one—one is the normal birth; but Indians have told me that occasionally she has two, which is probable; indeed almost certain: for I know of no animal whatever producing one at a birth which does not occasionally bear two or more.

The young tapir is marked with broken longitudinal stripes, which are sometimes quite white, but more often of a buff colour. These gradually disappear, and are unobservable when the young animal is about half-grown. It is a very remarkable circumstance; and is in this, and similar cases in other animals, some evidence of a provision of nature for the protection of the young animal. On the other hand, the young of several beasts of prey have birth-marks of the "protective" kind; and yet these animals need no protection: for one beast, or bird, of prey never attacks another for the purpose of feeding on it. Many so-called naturalists, and travellers, have told quite a different tale: in plain terms I do not believe one of them. No man could possibly have had more experience than I have had—very few so much. I do not record it in boastfulness: but it is impossible for a man to spend the best part of his life in the wilds, on the constant watch to gain a knowledge of the creatures of forest, mountain and plain, and fail to see an incident said to be common: and I say that no flesh-eating animal will feed off the carcass of another beast of prey. They fight one another, slay one another, contend over slain prey—feed on one another—never. I have never seen the remotest proof of such a proceeding. There are omnivorous animals, like the bear, which devour anything, including flesh; but these will not touch the carcass of a puma, a wolf, or any such creature. Pumas, jaguars and wolves will devour dogs—that is *domestic* dogs, which are not strictly beasts of prey: and wolves will feed on those of their number that are shot down by the hunter (they never slay one another); but this is the nearest approach to thief robbing thief that I have ever met with amongst wild animals. Domestic dogs will not touch the carcasses of beasts of prey, or of wild dogs or wolves. Isolated cases have occurred amongst the captives in menageries, etc., but animals in cages are like sailors on rafts; sometimes driven to mad acts by unnatural surroundings.

I cannot say if the tapir is numerous—I have formed the opinion that it is not. Has it many enemies?

Probably it has. It is a very valuable meat-producing creature in a country which affords few large animals fit for food; and, consequently, the Indians are constantly on the watch for it. It is easily overtaken, and destroyed without trouble or danger. The yarns about its turning on its enemies and defending itself are excellent—so are those about the phœnix: and the two stories have one thing in common.

The tapir is one of the most timid and harmless creatures, of its size, on earth: and when it finds itself discovered it bolts. Headed off, or cornered, as it often is by bands of Indians hunting together, it becomes frightened out of its wits, falls on its front knees, trembles and can do nothing but roar and grunt. I suppose that we do not all hear alike, any more than we see alike; but I hardly know what is meant by the "whistling sound" the tapir is said to emit. Its voice consists of: first, a kind of squeal, which, though something like that of a horse when it is fighting, or expressing displeasure with another, is peculiar to the tapir: second, a snuffling sound, usually uttered when it is surprised, or suspicious of danger: third, a grunt very similar to that of a pig; and used chiefly when it is feeding or wandering about aimlessly: fourth, a low bellow, indicative of fright and anger. If the tapir ever utters any other sound, I have not heard it.

It is a habit of the tapir to lie in mud surrounded by reeds. Sometimes it reclines on its side, and sometimes on its knees, like an ox. When it thinks itself quite secure, and free from observation, it rolls over on its back in apparent enjoyment; and kicks its legs as we may see a horse do when given its liberty in a field.

It seems to be an animal of a joyous disposition: and on farms and plantations young ones are occasionally kept as pets. They never display any vice, and never attempt to regain their liberty; and are quite as tame and tractable as cattle and horses. I never heard of their breeding in captivity.

As is well known, they swim with ease and rapidity; but it does not seem to be so well established that they run along the bottoms of rivers. They do so, however; for I have witnessed them doing so on several occasions, and at widely distanced places. They cannot, however, remain long under water; and when they come to the surface to breathe at the expiration of about a minute, nearly another minute elapses before they can sink again. Consequently escape from their pursuers is impossible. The Indians do not follow them in canoes; but boldly plunge into the water after them. I am not sure that the Indian can swim as fast as the tapir; but numbers deprive the solitary animal of all chance of escape. On shore the tapir is not a fleet animal; and the Indian is a match for it in a forest race; these strange people being able to run and rush about in thick forest, swamp and reed-bed every whit as well as a wild animal.

There were tapirs on the Purus; and perhaps the best way of estimating their numbers is to note their footmarks and resting-places. Judging from these signs I should say that there are not many, even in this almost undisturbed region, as it certainly was in 1886. On the main stream of the Amazon they are decidedly scarce; the traffic having frightened them into the quieter tributaries.

A supply of food being a pressing need with us, as with the native roamers of the forest, we were ever on the look-out for creatures which should afford us a means of replenishing our store; yet in the whole course of my journey only five of these animals fell to my rifle; and but two more were secured by my followers. I have seen a few killed by the Indians; and I have permitted three or four to escape which I might have destroyed. As a rule, when watching the habits of the tapirs I had to do so through a spy-glass from a distance which precluded my doing them any hurt: for they are so shy and timid that they soon detect the presence of any watcher stationed near them.

Of course I made many attempts to penetrate into the interior of the country; but with very little success. In most places the forest growth is so dense that it is absolutely impossible for any large ground animal to force its way through it. I have used axe and scythe for hours, cutting away creepers, bushes and tangled herbage; only to find, after clearing away the blocking growth for a few yards, that the human body could not be forced between the massive trunks of the trees. Supposing this ground to be occupied by settlers, as occupied it must be some day, the land will have to be cleared as the people advance. There cannot possibly be a preliminary survey of the country, except along the rivers and smaller water-courses. I sincerely hope that no attempt will be made to burn the timber off the land. I do not think that such an attempt would be successful, the forest and underlying soil is generally so moist; but if once a forest fire were fairly started in this region, the conflagration would be awful! No successful endeavour to stop, or control, it could be made: it would have to be permitted to burn itself out: and thousands of square miles of the grandest timber growth on earth, and millions of living creatures, would inevitably perish: perhaps whole species be wiped out. It would be a world's catastrophe if this splendid forest and its denizens were to be destroyed. No forest fires ever do occur in the valley of the Amazon: I have strong hope, therefore, that it is not possible to kindle them.

The tributaries of the Purus, like those of the Amazon itself, are innumerable—I mean those which have sufficient water in them to float a boat; and by means of these the country can be penetrated in all directions. It is everywhere an unbroken forest; and at least two-thirds of it consists of swamp. The rivulets and brooks which empty themselves into the Purus nearly all take their rise in pools, small lakes and swamps, which are only very slightly raised above the surface of the river. Consequently the currents of all are very sluggish, almost imperceptible, and the beds of the smaller ones choked by a dense growth of reeds and larger vegetation: in particular there is a tree like the banyan (perhaps it is a species of banyan) which drops roots, or root-branches, to the ground, and into the streams, sometimes completely arching them. In the Purus we often took the boat under a tree of this description for shelter at the side of the river, mooring to one of the drooping roots; until one evening a jaguar was seen (and shot) in the branches above us. We took the hint; especially as venomous snakes also sought a refuge in these fine trees.

I had a small canoe of my own make on board; and in this I used to take excursions; on one occasion ascending a river about 100 miles, as far as I could go. On this excursion I was absent from the *Firefly* (my large boat) three entire days and nights. During this time I never had a fair sleep, never saw the sky, and worked at the paddle almost incessantly. Huge creepers, as well as the roots of the tree just now described, descended into the water; great masses of moss trailed downwards, hanging like shrouds; for not a breath of air disturbed the silent reaches of this stream. Trunks of fallen trees lay across it, some of which I could paddle under; on to others I climbed to lift the canoe over. The moss had a faded, withered appearance, and the lower branches of the trees and bushes were leafless, and full of decayed vegetation washed thither by floods. Occasionally I saw a small flower, or orchid; and these were all of very pale hue—white or greenish. At the sides of the river there was a thick growth of canes or reeds, which afforded lurking-places to a good many unpleasant creatures, caymans in particular, and large snakes ten or twelve feet long. Here, also, was a kind of bull-frog, quite as large as that found in North America; and water-lizards, or iguanas, a yard long.

The height of the trees I could only conjecture: the vault of dead branches and trailing vine-stems above my head was from fifty or sixty to a hundred feet high. Above this was a mass of foliage that shut out the view of everything, never once affording a glimpse of the sky, nor a ray of the sun. The prevailing gloom was so great that all objects were only dimly seen; and in some spots it was almost dark. Indeed, often, ahead, it appeared to be quite so, and the way looked like a black tunnel. The sense of confinement, and the prevailing gloom, played on my nerves; and I was sometimes nearly afraid to proceed, or to enter some forbidding opening in the mass of weird trailers.

This river was never more than seventy yards wide, though it was, throughout nearly the whole length of its course, nearly twenty feet deep. There was no ripple on any part of its surface, and long stretches of it were stagnant, and covered with a grey scum. There were no giant water-lilies here, although these plants are abundant on the Amazon and the Purus; where there is not only a white one, but also a yellow and a blue kind. Masses of weed choked the water in the shallows near the bank, and sometimes reached the surface in the deeper parts: and the forest on both sides formed an impenetrable wall.

I was nervous of the caymans, some of which gave me a good deal of unwelcome attention. I had more than twenty round the canoe sometimes, apparently meditating an attack; and when I wished to rest, or try to sleep, I used to climb up some twenty or thirty feet into one of the trees which overhung the water; and passing a strap round a stout branch secured it to my arm, to prevent accidents, and thus endeavoured to obtain rest. I did not, however, get beyond the dozing stage at any time during the three days.

I was hardly able to distinguish between night and day, except when it was absolutely dark; at which time it was, of course, impossible to proceed, though I sometimes endeavoured to do so by the light of a lantern suspended at the bows of my tiny craft, which was so small that it would not hold a second person with safety. The light attracted such numbers of caymans that I was obliged to give up its use. I tried a shot or two at these pests; but this had little effect. I killed a couple of the caymans; which did not seem to perturb the others in the least: so it would seem that *fear* is the outcome of intelligence: for there are no more doltish creatures in existence than the alligator tribe.

As this canoe journey (partly described in a previous work) has provoked some comment, I may remark that there is no doubt that I paddled more than 200 miles in the seventy-four or seventy-five hours I was absent from the boat. I see nothing remarkable in the feat; and I offered to wager my challenger (a book-naturalist) that I would canoe 300 miles in seventy hours on any English river he chose to select. He very wisely buttoned his breeches-pockets, and said no more.

I had several strange experiences during this little journey, amongst them, on the third day, I was startled by a sudden rushing, rattling sound, and the fall of a great quantity of dead branches, leaves, etc., and amongst them a few large hail-stones as big as pigeons' eggs. That the leafy canopy above was able to resist the battering of this tremendous storm, is proof how dense and thick it was. Several birds, and a monkey, killed by the hailstones, fell into the water; and, of course, many must have been killed which I did not see. In this way I learned how the multitude of caymans below may get a portion of their food—for hail-storms are frequent in this region.

Living creatures of the higher orders were very scarce on this river. I heard parrots and macaws screaming; and sometimes troops of monkeys came down to look at me. These animals were tamer here than in any other part of America I have visited; and I was actually glad of their presence, so awful was the sense of loneliness in this solitary place. Once or twice these monkeys ventured within twenty yards of me; a tameness that is unique in my experiences of wild simians.

Birds, generally, were very scarce; but I shot a beautiful light green water-hen with a metallic gleam on its plumage. Small birds were practically absent, as were all the long-legged waders of the stork and heron families.

I saw shoals of small fish; and, near the mouth of this affluent, discovered a vast number of eels spread on the leaves of partially submerged water-plants. They were in an exhausted state, and covered with a thick viscid slime. I thought their condition was due to some stage of the reproductive process; but the learned in this matter shake their heads; and insist that eels must go to the sea before they can become family men—I mean, fish—and that having performed this necessary function they straightway die.

A noted naturalist has said that "reams of paper have been spoiled in discussing the breeding habits of eels." Possibly. But have those habits been really discovered? Naturalists may wriggle like eels, but they will not be able to slip away from the fact that many of their theories, and, what is worse, their assertions, are simply guesses. I have met with some evidence that eels which cannot reach the sea, breed: and I know, certainly, that the celebrated electric-eel of South America never visits the sea. In fact, it is seldom found even in rivers, though it is plentiful in the swamps and small lakes on the courses of the Purus and its tributaries. The exhausted eels I have mentioned, many hundreds in number, were all small; but in the Purus we caught some which were six feet long.

Fish are very abundant in the Amazon, and all the rivers which are included in its system. I am not a great fisherman; but my two followers spent most of their spare time handling the rod and line; and they could give popular names to many members of their catches. One, the "devil-fish," was a monstrous little wretch. Though weighing only a quarter of a pound or less, it boldly attacks the human bather; and a shoal of them seem to be capable of doing serious injury to a naked man. The Indians and the negroes, as well as the whites, dread them, and say they not only bite pieces out of the legs and bodies of people they find bathing in the rivers, but act as a sort of fresh-water fish-wolf, hounding and devouring any creature they find wounded or in distress. I cannot confirm these stories from my own observations; but I do not disbelieve them.

The fish is the well-known *Serrasalmus piraya*, called by the Indians, and one of my men, "the piree," a name which I find spelled "perai" by some naturalists. It is quite a small fish, similar to a roach in shape and appearance of the body; but the head is round, and a fishy caricature of that of a pug-dog. The teeth are very strong and sharp; and, affixed to a piece of stick, are used by the Indians as a rasp or scraper.

Some of the fish in the Purus are very large, exceeding twenty pounds in weight, and, superficially, resemble chub, bream and carp: and there was a monstrous-looking creature with a head like a cat-fish; and a body thirty to forty inches long. This was one of the few Purus fish which had much flavour in it. The "tiger-fish" has a spotted skin; but there is another kind with brown stripes which would much better fit the name. There is, also, a well-flavoured fish with a long snout, and a long thin body, something resembling a gar-pike, which never took our baited-hooks; but a few were caught in nets, the largest of which was forty inches long.

Two hundred miles up the Purus the stream was quite a mile broad; and a hundred miles higher it was often that width, and still averaged 1200 yards. The depth was sometimes ninety feet; and, with the exception of a few spots, forty to sixty feet. There were great expansions resembling lakes up to 600 miles from the mouth; and islands everywhere, and also some large mud-banks underwater, which are covered with weeds, and are a danger to the navigation of the stream. We grounded several times, and lost much time in getting off, as three men were too few to properly handle the boat when she was in difficulties.

The Mr. Chandless (of whom and his book, if he published one, I know nothing) mentioned in a former chapter is said to have found the Indians on this river in a very primitive state: in fact, they were compared by him to the people of the stone-age.

They are certainly few in number, and the tribes are much scattered. This may be owing to the swampy condition of the country; much of which could not be permanently inhabited, even by "stone-age men." All the South American Indians are in a low estate, as regards civilization; and in general intelligence, and knowledge of the arts of savage life, are much the inferiors of the Red Men of the North. Like some other primitive people they have, however, in one or two instances, displayed a marvellous power of invention. The blow-pipe, like the boomerang of the Australian savage, may have been an accidental discovery in the first place, but the perfection to which it has been brought could only be the outcome of the brains of a genius.

In general disposition the Indians are peaceable and kind-hearted. They are "lazy beggars" until want makes them active; but there is nothing murderous about them; and a traveller going amongst them is well, and hospitably, treated. They never did me the least hurt; but, on the contrary, were generally the first men to lend me a hand when I was in trouble or difficulty.

We had been on the Purus some time before any Indians were seen. One evening we had just cast anchor for the night, about 100 yards from the left bank, when George Maccara called my attention to a man on shore, who was hiding behind a tree, and watching us. He had not a rag of clothing on his body, and was holding a heavy bludgeon in his hand. As soon as he saw that he was discovered he disappeared like a shadow.

After darkness set in the dogs became so restless that I knew that Indians must be lurking on the river's bank; and as we could not know what their disposition towards us might be, we moved the *Firefly* out into the middle of the stream, cast the dogs loose, and kept a careful watch until daylight.

Early in the morning we thought we could see some dusky figures gliding to and fro amongst the trees near the brink of the river; and as it was important that we should be on good terms with these children of the wild, Jose Najas and I landed in the canoe, taking no visible arms with us, though I had my pistols in my pocket.

At this point of the river the bank was six feet high, and there was a slight rise in the ground, the country being more open than any we had yet seen on the Purus. Large trees grew thickly together; but there was no undergrowth except brown grass, and we could move about freely.

Except a few impressions of naked footmarks there were no signs of Indians; and we walked slowly about, or lay under the trees, for two hours before any of them appeared. By and by three men showed themselves out of the forest, but seemed afraid to advance: so waving a white handkerchief, a signal of peace I hoped they would understand, I advanced alone to meet them. They permitted me to walk right up to them, when others began to appear, until nineteen men and boys stood round me. I spoke kindly to them, and they jabbered to me incessantly, neither side, of course, understanding a word that was uttered, though it was easy to see that the men intended to be friendly.

Several of them appeared to be about sixty years of age, though these were quite as nimble as the boys.

The old men had loin-cloths, or aprons, of plaited grass, about their waists; all the others were completely naked; and the only arms they displayed were tomahawks, or brainers, made of pieces of flaked flint fastened to the end of sticks; not very formidable weapons, I thought.

I had brought a few articles with me which I hoped would please them; amongst other things, two or three clasp-knives. Evidently they knew the use of steel knives, and were anxious to possess them; but the springs puzzled them. However, they soon learned the trick of the arrangement, and were greatly pleased with their presents. A pair of scissors was not so well appreciated until I showed the use of them by snipping off a lock of hair from one fellow's head. Then there was great amusement, each one striving to clip his comrade's hair.

We became such good friends that we could not part; and they tried, in a friendly manner, to prevent our return to the boat in mid-stream. Finding that I was determined to go back, all except two of the boys entered the water, and swam round the canoe till we reached the *Firefly*. Nothing that they saw on board our little vessel pleased them more than the dogs, which were wild to be at them. I feared an accident, as they would tease these ferocious animals, which had been trained to hate men of colour; and, in fact, one of the Indians did get severely bitten; but this in no measure lessened his admiration of the dogs: and most of these men showed large scars on their bodies, which proved that they were used to severe accidents, received, I suppose, while hunting, or fighting with other Indians.

Our visitors remained to breakfast, drinking hot cocoa with great relish, a circumstance which astonished me; and eating sugar and salt with avidity. They put large pinches of salt in the palms of their hands, and then clapped it into their mouths; and wanted more than we could spare them. They ate up all our spare game, but did not care for any kind of flour food; and later in the day expressed nausea at tea.

When we weighed anchor, and proceeded up-stream, they lent willing hands at the sweeps (the river was too deep for the use of poles) and worked them well, going several miles with us—to the limit of their territory, I suppose; for by and by they wished us to stop, and expressed a disinclination to go farther. I went on, however, and they all swam ashore except four, who remained all night, sleeping in the body of the boat. At daybreak several other Indians, strangers to us, came on board, and held a long conversation with the four who had been with us all night. They showed that they wanted food by putting their fingers in their mouths. I could ill afford to grant their request, but not knowing how hard pressed they might be I fed them; and, like the men of yesterday, they earned their bread by working at the sweeps. They evinced great aptitude for this kind of work; and soon handled the sweeps very skilfully.

Like the Indians of the previous day they showed a disinclination to go beyond a certain distance; and on finding that they could not induce me to stop, they left, one or two at a time, until in the early afternoon they had all swum ashore. The last we saw of them was a number of them standing on the river bank waving their hands, and shouting for us to go back.

We did not anchor until long after sunset, the moon being about the full; and we could see by the reflections of fires above the tree-tops that there were many other Indians about; but none of them showed themselves.

From this point there was a gradual change in the appearance of the river. The banks were higher, and its width more contracted, though it was still very deep; and often broken into several channels by islands lying side by side, sometimes so closely that the arched trees formed a complete canopy over the waterway. Some of the quiet reaches were covered with a splendid lily—the *Victoria regia*—with leaves six and even seven feet across; and so thick and strong that a large otter, weighing at least fifty pounds, mounted one and rested on it without breaking it, or causing it to be submerged. In this region the flowers of this plant are of a pale pinkish hue, like blush roses; and the under sides of the huge leaves are crimson coloured. They are favourite resting-places of some kinds of water-fowl, such as the jacana, and all the rails; and I have seen a flock of snowy egrets perched on a patch of them; and land birds, also, often resort to them in great numbers. Some of these we shot for food, and trapped others; but in spite of such supplies, we were often so short of fresh meat or fowl that we resorted to hooking the caymans, several of which were killed for food. The flesh has a musty taste, and cannot be recommended; but it was useful as a makeshift. The Indians eat it; but even these people, who are never fastidious in the matter of viands, only resort to it when nothing better is to be had. If surprise is felt that there should be a scarcity of food in a country where birds are so numerous, I must point out that the expenditure of powder and shot had to be curtailed, and a lack of ammunition would have been a serious matter to us; and it is astonishing how quickly stores of all kinds disappear when there is a daily drain on them. To trap many birds, or animals, necessitates that the trapper should be stationary.

As the river became narrower and shallower, there was a very perceptible rise of the country on both sides of it; and the difficulties of navigation increased considerably. The bed of the river was full of sunken trees, which were a source of much danger to us; and several times holes were knocked in the bottom and sides of the old *Firefly*, and we had to "pipe all hands to save ship." Fortunately we succeeded in beaching her before she sank; and the damage was soon repaired; but as there is no tide in the Purus, and the boat was heavy, it gave us much trouble to warp her off the mud after such beachings, to say nothing of the strain to the old craft herself.

As we reached a region where the ground was higher and drier, the number of large animals met with was greater; though the forests of the Amazon are not the places to seek big game. Jaguars are plentiful enough; pumas are occasionally met with; tapirs are scarce; and the small deer of the country not very numerous. In fact, considering how sparsely peopled the country is, and how little the game is persecuted, it is astonishing that the larger animals are not found in greater numbers.

Take, for instance, the big serpents of this district. They have practically no enemies. No beast preys upon them, or can destroy them; and the Indians have no weapons that are effective against them. The cayman is about the only creature that can master a big boa, or anaconda; and he does so by surprising them as they lie partly submerged in the water at the brink of the river; a favourite position of these serpents.

All things considered, one would expect giant boas and anacondas to be numerous; but they are not. Even the smaller ones are difficult to find; and one may search for months without finding a boa twelve feet long, or an anaconda of thirty feet. Yet it is certain that these repulsive creatures much exceed these sizes. I have seen preserved remains of anacondas that must have been nearly, if not quite, forty feet in length, though I have never seen a living animal of this kind that exceeded twenty-three or twenty-four feet. Thirty feet is, I believe, the maximum length allowed by the professors for the anaconda; but these gentlemen have not seen everything under the sun.

The usual run of boas is eight to twelve feet; but I shot one which measured sixteen feet to the inch. Such a monster could be very formidable; though the only authentic account of a big serpent attacking a man that I have heard was the case of an attendant in a United States menagerie who was attacked by one sixteen feet long, and very nearly killed. It was said that a dozen men had great difficulty in compelling the creature to relax its coils. This snake was described as a "python": it was probably an anaconda.

On the Purus we saw several jaguars every week, and sometimes two or three a day. They were seldom interfered with by us, as I was not there as an animal exterminator; but their abundance may have had some bearing on the scarcity of deer. When we reached what I may call the dry forest region, monkeys were noticed to be more numerous than they were on the lower bends of the river; and a day or two after we parted from our Indian friends, we witnessed a band of them mobbing a jaguar in a very laughable way, though there was probably a tragedy behind the fun. Noticing a great commotion amongst these lively animals, we ran into the bank to learn the cause of it; and discovered a large jaguar stretched on the bough of a tree which overhung the water. Troops of monkeys were descending from the tree-tops and leaping and dashing around him with marvellous, but ludicrous, agility, taking care, however, to keep well out of reach of his murderous paws. They yelled, screamed, and, according to George, *swore* at him in no measured terms. He had probably excited their ire by robbing them of a companion.

On our approach the jaguar leapt lightly to a lower branch, and from thence dropped into the water and swam to an island in the river, where he disappeared amongst the jungle. Both jaguars and pumas take readily to the water; but the jaguarondi, the lynx (of the north), the ocelot, and the smaller cats do not. Possibly, in an extremity, some of them would do so, though I doubt it. Some funny people think that all animals not only *can*, but *do*, swim. They are mistaken. So far as I know, all animals *float*, when put into the water; but lots of them drown in the act of *attempting to swim* as rapidly as they would do if they were actually held under the water. The domestic cat, and the domestic mouse, drown in this way. The mouse cannot swim twenty feet, nor the cat more than thirty or forty yards: and in spite of direct contradiction, and that from what is considered to be high authority, I repeat an assertion that I have made on a previous occasion, and insist that American monkeys cannot swim; though possibly, like men, they may be *taught* to do so.

There are four kinds of monkeys on the upper reaches of the Purus. The species which we found lecturing the jaguar was a black spider-monkey with a bright pink face. There is another kind of black spider-monkey in this region, distinguished by its dusky face. These two species (like all others in Brazilian forests) keep apart very strictly. If they happen to meet in the same tree their relations are strained, to say the least of it. The third species is a howling-dervish amongst monkeys; and my word may be taken for it that he thoroughly understands his business. The fourth monkey is a pretty little marmoset, not larger than a European squirrel. The first three kinds go in troops of the usual number, sixty or seventy, ranging, sometimes, to double that number: the marmoset appeared to be in small parties of five or six; but it is extremely difficult to learn much about so small an animal in a vast forest where most of the trees are at least 150 feet high, and bushy in proportion. If five are seen, possibly there are fifty more higher up the trunk. All American monkeys are shy; and if watched remain still; or, at most, occasionally peep from amongst the leaves; and show their disapprobation of impertinent intrusion by a voluble chattering, or a surly snarl: though these monkeys are not bad-tempered animals. As to their throwing sticks, fruit, etc., at travellers: I agree with Waterton that it is pure nonsense. To avoid recurring to the subject, in this place I may mention that monkeys on the Purus seem to be more or less localized. One species seldom occupied more than 100 to 150 miles linear of territory; and the monkeys near the mouth of the river are quite different from those about the head-waters. At the farthest point we reached, marmosets were more numerous in both species and numbers.

The first deer seen were also found in this region; and the country had a park-like appearance. Accompanied by one of my men, I took a long walk into the interior. There was scarcely any swamp in this district, and we could move about amongst the trees with ease. Mahogany and the silk-cotton were very common; and there were a number of new species of trees which I had noticed in another part of the Amazonian valley. The cinchona was quite common; but there were no moras here.

Parrots and macaws of new kinds occupied the trees; but the monkeys were not seen in this comparatively open forest. The macaws were green and red, and green and black, with some dark blue on the back and tail. There were also several flocks of the blue and yellow kind common in Guiana and along the north bank of the Amazon: so this bird has probably a greater range than any other macaw.

Animal life was unusually prevalent in this park-like country. Here we met with the great ant-eater, and saw a number of sloths in the trees; and also porcupines curled round the branches, a common attitude with them when they wish to rest or sleep. These Brazilian tree-porcupines are very different animals from those of Europe. They have long, lean bodies, and a prehensile tail, by which, like the monkeys, they cling to the branches when climbing or descending a tree. They have quills like those of a hedgehog—" specialized hairs," I suppose I should call them; and they stink worse than a foumart; and are thus doubly "protected."

Charles Waterton knew this porcupine well, and he scouted the theory of " protective odours." What he has to say on the subject is so scathing—so crushing—that I must ask pardon for the digression and repeat it.

" Many of the weasel tribe have the power of emitting a very disagreeable odour from the posterior part of the body. We are gravely informed in the ' American Biography of Birds ' that the polecat has this faculty ' given him by Nature as a defence.' And pray, at what old granny's fireside in the United States has the writer of this picked up such an important piece of information? How comes the polecat to be aware that the emitted contents of its glands, inoffensive to itself, should be offensive to all its pursuers? I say *inoffensive* to itself because I cannot believe that our Creator would condemn an unoffending animal to produce its own punishment by means of a smell which never leaves it." [He might have asked what enemies the polecat, or any other beast of prey, has; and why it needs special protection. What does the rabbit think of the polecat's odour? Does it warn him to bolt to his hole?]

"Although this odour from individuals of the weasel tribe is very distressing to *our* nasal sensibilities, it by no means follows that the scent should have a similar effect upon those of all other animals. For example, the smell from purulent carrion is certainly very disagreeable to us bipeds; still it cannot prove so to the dog—for, in lieu of avoiding it, this quadruped never loses an opportunity of rolling in it. If the polecat has had the fetid gland 'given to it by Nature as a defence,' then must Nature have given a sweet one to the civet for its destruction; seeing that, whilst we shun the one on account of its insupportable stench, we pursue and kill the last in order to obtain its sweet perfume. Now, as both of these animals are of the same family, I cannot help remarking, with Sterne, in the case of the 'poor negro girl,' that Nature has put one of this tribe sadly over the head of the others, if the North American theory be sound.

"Again, if Nature has given this abominable stench to the polecat as a defence, she has cruelly neglected our former invader, the Hanoverian rat. The polecat is not much exposed to destruction, as its movements are chiefly nocturnal, and, in general, it is apt to shun the haunts of men. But our Hanoverian, having a most inordinate appetite for the good things of this world, is ever on the stir, in the very midst of its enemies, to satisfy the craving of its greedy stomach; and it will cater for itself the four-and-twenty hours throughout. Hence your housekeeper complains that it will try its tooth on primest Stilton in broad daylight, and that it will have its whiskers in the creambowl, even whilst the dairymaid is gone upstairs with butter for the breakfast-table. Still, my darling Hanoverian has nothing but an ordinary set of teeth wherewith to protect itself, although exposed to ten times more danger than the foumart, which last has a fetid gland given it by Nature 'as a defence'—in addition, I may add, to vast muscular strength, and to two full rows of sharp, and well assorted, teeth."

Quite true, Squire Waterton. You might have added that the chief and real defence of polecat and "darling Hanoverian" is their shrewdness and cunning; and further enquired, if the stenches of the foumart and skunk are protective, what is that of the deer in rutting season? and of the unwashed negro in all seasons?

The unsavoury odour of the tree-porcupine does not affect the savouriness of its flesh, which is well known, and well relished, by all men in South America, red, black, white and copper-coloured; and did its "protective odour" save it from our camp-fire on this occasion? Did it!

I need say very little more on this subject, which may not have much interest to the majority of readers; but it is well to note that there are a great many creatures which have exceedingly strong, and, to human nostrils, intensely offensive odours, which cannot possibly be protective, because they are possessed by the *males only;* and in many cases at the breeding season, and at *no other* time. I need instance no others than the male goat, and the deer tribes generally. As a matter of fact, most wild animals have strong scents of some kind; and I heard Mr. Fox complain bitterly that his odour brought all the hounds and idle red-coated gentry in the village after his tail. "But," I remarked, "the scientists say 'animal odours are protective.'" "Protective be blowed!" he snapped. "The scents of Mr. Bunny and old Puss were given them that I might follow 'em up sharp: and they know all about odours when I nip 'em across the loins." So we see authorities differ!

About six miles from the river we came to a lake nine or ten miles long, and five broad, with several well-wooded small islands in it; and a number of tall palm trees growing on its shores—altogether an enchanting spot; though the footprints of jaguars were very numerous in the mud and soft soil: for this great cat is eminently a water animal; and is said by Darwin, and some other naturalists, to catch fish habitually, though I have seen it do so on one occasion only.

Here and there were traces of Indians, also, in the form of fire-places where they had cooked and eaten fish and birds; and some small animal of the cavy genus. At one spot were three hive-shaped huts, where a party had slept on heaps of grass.

On our way back to the boat we passed a tree in which at least a thousand bats were hanging by their feet head downwards. Two of these were knocked down and captured alive; and several others killed that I might dissect them. They were of the fruit-eating, large vampire species; and none that I handled exceeded thirty inches in expanse of wing. They were not, therefore, so large as those described in a previous chapter; and the conclusions I came to here, and noted down at the time, seem to have been rather hasty. It must be remembered that this voyage up the Purus took place on my first arrival in the country; and before I had the experiences in Peru, Ecuador, etc., already narrated. I thought at this time that the great vampire never touched animal food; I have since modified that opinion, though the great bat found in the interior of Ecuador may be another species.

No traces of insects were found in the stomachs of those killed on the Purus; and those in the trees were seen to be feeding on fruits of various kinds. Of the two captured, one soon fretted itself to death; and the other was released to save it from a similar painful fate.

There were more jaguars in this district than in any other ever visited by me; and there can be little doubt that this region is the head-quarters of the animal. The islands in the lake were their favourite haunts; and on one morning alone eleven of them were seen to swim ashore from one of the lake islands. Though there were Indians not far off, and apparently visiting this spot very frequently, the animals and birds were surprisingly tame: one large jaguar passed within twenty yards of us in so listless a manner that I think it must have been gorged with food. It entered the lake and swam slowly to its lair in one of the islands.

In addition to jaguars, there are a very few pumas in this district; and an abundance of smaller wild cats, of at least three species, the jaguarondi being one. They were all so shy that I did not succeed in learning much about their habits.

Deer were found to be plentiful in the forest, and they came down to the lake to drink every night; and though it is considered unsportsmanlike, I believe, to shoot *over water*, our needs must plead the excuse for several of them biting the dust at this spot. The slaughter attracted the attention of some of the huge caymans which occupied the lake; and at evening I was a witness of one of these reptiles seizing a deer and pulling it under water. The caymans do not, however, seem to attack the jaguar when in the water. I have heard stories that they do; but I never saw anything of the kind, nor met with an Indian who had. Possibly such a thing does occasionally happen.

I am compelled to revert to the "protective odour" nonsense, by noting that when the wind set towards us we could always tell if deer were near us by the nauseous stench which reached us, apparently from a full half-mile distance, even when thick forest intervened between us and the animals. This intimation of their presence led to the death of at least a dozen of them: I must leave the acute scientist to decide whether or not the noses of jaguars and Indians are as good as mine! Across the lake the scent was perceptible when the deer were at least four miles away, and could only be seen through a glass.

The deer of this region vary greatly in size. The largest are long-bodied, ungraceful-looking animals of about 100 pounds weight. Higher up the Purus there is a very small species, which, I believe, was seen in other places, and mistaken for a cavy; very little notice being taken of it on account of its small size. It is not bigger than a fox-terrier; and I have known George, one of my followers, pick clean at dinner the bones of a specimen of this deer. There is an intermediate species, weighing fifty or sixty pounds; and others were met with locally. They are all much alike in appearance and habits—differing in size only. The males have short, thin, spike-like horns, which are never forked, hooked or branched. A freaky old girl is Dame Nature. She provides the male deer with a stinking gland (or a pair of them, to be strictly correct) and with horns, and leaves the females without these useful, or dangerous (which ?), appendages; but in the closely allied antelopes, both males and females have horns, and neither of them "protective odours." Why is this ?

I am afraid of becoming tiresome with my natural history notes. There are so many curious creatures on and about the Purus that it is simply impossible to notice them all. Most of the characteristic animals of Brazil are more or less plentiful on this great tributary of the Amazon, itself a mighty river. Capivaras were afterwards found to be roaming round the lake in small herds of forty or fifty. These are simply giant guinea-pigs weighing 100 to 120 pounds in fine specimens. They are eaten by Indians, and other people, under press of circumstances; but the meat is dry, without fat, and flavourless. It is a great lover of water, spending much of its time in swimming, or rolling, in muddy shallows: and is never found in dry districts.

The agouti, an allied animal, not much exceeding a wild rabbit in size, is found in all the forests, wet and dry, but is so coarse of flesh that it is not worth a charge of shot.

We spent some time at this spot, daily coming across country to the lake, a distance of about six miles from the boat on the Purus; and sometimes I camped alone for the night on its shores. During this sojourn we had several interviews with the Indians, who were not, however, so genially disposed as those farther down the river. For the first time we saw some of their women and children, who were not permitted to approach us. The inference was that some of those white people who occasionally frequent the Purus had not treated them well. They seemed to me to be a miserable race; but I shall have more to say about them presently.

As we advanced up the river there was a very decided rise of the surface of the ground; the river narrowed much, and we now had a perceptible, but not a strong, current. Generally the banks were clothed with thick forest; but here and there we saw small savannahs (park-like grass country) with only a few trees scattered over them. The ground became undulating, and finally hilly; and in this part the deer were very numerous; but always appearing in very small parties—never in great herds.

About two months after entering the river we arrived at a point marked on the maps as the Barrier of Caiauarite. It is formed of a number of shelving rocks extending across the river, beyond which it was impossible to take the *Firefly*. But the river at this point is still a great stream, fully half a mile wide, and at least twelve feet deep in mid-channel.

During excursions inland we came to hills of elevation. One ridge culminated in a point which I thought was about 800 feet above the surface of the river; and other hills were seen much farther inland; but owing to the dense forest our view of the country was much restricted; and I determined to make a few more exploring voyages in the canoe, the number of tributaries, large and small, on this, as on the lower reaches of the river, being very great.

I do not intend to give an account of my adventures on these little journeys, in one of which I nearly lost my boat; but merely to describe the country and its productions.

CHAPTER XVI

THE COUNTRY BETWEEN THE PURUS, THE MADEIRA AND THE TAPAJOS

THE Madeira is the largest of all the Amazonian tributaries; and there are many towns and settlements on it. This was a chief reason why I did not ascend it in my boat; my tastes leading me to choose the wildest and most savage parts of the country for investigation. But I know a great deal of the river; and of its headwaters, which take their rise in Bolivia. There are reasons why I should not describe these rivers in detail. There is not, in my opinion, a more beautiful object on earth than a lordly tropical forest; and I am of a temperament well suited to a lone and solitary existence. I hate a town, and thoroughly abhor a city. I have never seen the inside of a London, a New York or a 'Frisco theatre; and though a passionate lover of music, I can almost count on my fingers the great concerts I have heard. I went a few times to the Opera House at Rio; and during temporary visits to this, my native land, I have visited such places as the Crystal Palace and the Albert Hall. The Silences of the Wild never preyed on my nerves, and endangered my reason, as they did those of my companions. I can always fall back on my mind and find amusement in thought and the contemplation of the marvels and beauties of nature.

But constituted thus, I am still conscious that there is a great monotony in such a mighty forest as that of Matto Grosso. The variations in it are great; but the distances are so vast, one is so long in reaching a change, that the monotony of sight must necessarily cause weariness to an ordinary eye. Much more must descriptions be monotonous. Forest is forest; and here for hundreds of miles one part of it is so much like another that a change in the colour of a flower, or a variation in a species of bird, is a welcome relief to the eye.

This being so, it will be recognized that it is not desirable to follow the courses of all the great tributaries of the Amazon from their sources to their mouths. It is better to dwell on those changes in character which are distinctive of the various streams. This I hope and think will be admitted.

Let it be noted, then, that though the Purus, as far as the Barrier of Caiauarite, appears to run through one of the flattest plains on earth, the country northwards and eastwards beyond these rapids makes a decided rise: and though the ground between the Purus and the still larger river, Madeira, is level, and mostly a swamp, the wider tract between the last stream and the Tapajos (which is scarcely inferior to the Purus in length, size and importance) is a tableland of some elevation with a decided slope towards the Madeira.

This tableland is from 150 to 300 miles in breadth, and like the moist plains of the Purus is covered with an almost unbroken forest. Beyond the Tapajos there is another rise of the ground, forming a valley through which this river flows until it joins the Amazon. Then comes a tremendous stretch of country, fully 500 miles broad in its central part, which is tolerably level, but with some variations of ground, and a shallow valley, watered by the Xingu, a river which is, probably, with its windings and great bends, well over a thousand miles in length. The eastward boundary of this region is formed by the valley of the Araguay, the last of the great tributaries of the Amazon on its south, or right, bank.

All this vast stretch of country is covered with a dense forest, which, in most places, is absolutely impenetrable; and covering a country which, at this moment, is not half so well known as the most remote regions of Central Africa. In fact there is not an accurate map of the country extant. The rivers and their tributaries have been ascended; and the courses roughly laid down; and a few officials and private travellers have made attempts to explore the country; and have brought home descriptions and delineations, which, so far as I knew them, proved to be very confusing; and which I could not at all rely on for my guidance.

To say that I know this vast country would be a matter for laughter, and justly lay me open to the charge of boastfulness. One man could not possibly explore so tremendous a stretch of country: no one man can have more than a general—a very general—knowledge of its features. For my present purpose of writing a monograph of the majestic river which gives a title to this book, I have read and reread every note I have of my experiences in this region. I have corrected, and recorrected, every sentence I have ever written on the subject; and made the most careful calculations I could: and I am convinced that in the course of my career in

South America, which was one of constant and never-flagging work, I travelled, in boat and canoe, at least 20,000 miles on the waters of the Amazon and its tributaries alone. Therefore, I say, that generally, my sketches of the trend and characteristic features of the Amazonian system may be relied on; and the particular descriptions of districts and regions are absolutely faithful. The point on which I fail is one which it was not in my power to control. I lacked means, and the scientific training which would have enabled me to make the most of my observations, and render them of real value. As it is, I can do little more than give rough sketches and interesting descriptions of what I saw and experienced.

Now it is to be observed that what the Portuguese call Matto Grosso (Great Forest) is a large province in the south of the region I have indicated, and it is bounded by Para on the north, and Amazonas on the north-west; but the boundaries of these provinces are not demarked, and cannot be at present: I am not sure that it would be correct even to say that they are provisionally fixed. The whole region is one vast forest—that important fact cannot be too frequently repeated. There are hundreds of miles on each of the rivers that have been recently mentioned, the Purus, the Madeira, the Tapajos and the Xingu which, even at this hour, have not a white man's dwelling of any sort on their banks. I have spoken of travelling 20,000 miles on the rivers, great and small, of this system. At *this hour* it would be quite easy to take a boat or canoe *double that distance* on the waters of the Amazon and its tributaries, and not see a town, village, hacienda, or even hut of the meanest description occupied by a man of any other race than the aboriginal Indian. There are at least a million square miles in the centre of this forest which have never seen the permanent habitation of a man of European origin; and thousands upon thousands of these miles have never felt the tread of his foot, or, indeed, of that of any man; and if it is asked how I can assert this with so much assurance, my reply is, because it is impossible to penetrate the forest of this remarkable region. I have tried my utmost to do so, and failed: the Indians have also tried to penetrate it and been unable to get 100 yards amongst the trees. I have heard scores of them say so. And where an Indian cannot roam, must be impervious to any large animal.

I do not think there is a similar forest to Matto Grosso in any other part of the globe. The trees literally are matted together, forming a forest wall, which is as firm a barrier as one of masonry could be. It is not possible to say what may be in the interior of this dense growth; but it is a reasonable inference that it is, if I may use the phrase, solid throughout. I have travelled about 180 miles along the outskirts of such a district, and been unable to penetrate anywhere, or by any means, except the water-courses. These I have ascended as far as possible, finding the forest on each side as dense as on the outskirts. The brooks in such a tract run through tunnels of herbage, and can never be ascended many yards. Even the rivulets (streams twenty to thirty yards wide) can never be navigated by a small boat more than a mile or two: the beds are soon found to be choked with trees and shrubs growing in the water, as well as with reeds, or canes.

I have found the trees in such a district growing so

close together that I could not pass my hand between the trunks; and often with the stems touching, if not actually grown together. Above, the branches are intertwined in grand confusion; and probably no creatures except birds, monkeys, snakes and insects inhabit these dense tracts.

Unwilling to be balked, I have made almost superhuman exertions to gain the interior of such a forest as that I have just described. It ought to have been pretty clear that where an Indian had failed a white man would not succeed; and so it proved. I put in practice a performance I first tried on the Trombetas: viz. I climbed *up* the trees until the branches were tolerably clear, and then stepped from bough to bough. On this occasion several Indians accompanied me; but the method of progression was too laborious, and too dangerous, to be pursued far, and there was nothing to be seen except branches of trees and a few toucans, which were much upset by this strange invasion of their realm. We advanced, perhaps, half a mile in this aerial fashion; when even the Indians became apprehensive that they would be unable to find their way back: so we returned. The rate of progress I found to be less than half a mile per hour, though the branches were so thick that if an accident had happened and a man had lost his footing I do not think he could possibly have fallen far enough to hurt himself much.

Such tracts as this are led up to gradually by ground that is not so thickly timbered. They are usually found in regions that lie between two great rivers, and are only pierced by the smaller streams. Consequently they are generally found on ground that is tolerably dry, though there are many impenetrable stretches of wood on the Purus, the Madeira and other large tributaries on the south bank of the Amazon, as well as some on the north.

Again, some of the penetrable tracts of Matto Grosso are only so at great expense of time and trouble. I have exerted myself for days and weeks at a time without travelling farther than four or five miles a day on an average; and sometimes not nearly so much if the ground was a swamp. Huge trees must be walked round; and though this may seem a trifle to mention, when every few yards you meet a forest giant with buttresses, and huge twisted roots, stretching over ninety or a hundred feet of ground you will find that it *trebles* the distance you actually walk. Then one sinks into the slimy mud and water up to the knees; there are creepers, and pendent masses of moss, to be forced through, and other difficulties which, common, I dare say, to all tropical forests, are found here in excess of what is usual. There can be no more completely isolated spots on earth than these forest recesses. Men, Indians and escaped negro slaves, fugitives from justice and bandits, have haunted some of these hiding-places for many years; and defied police and soldiers to the ends of their lives, dying in comparative peace at last. Of course this has happened in districts not too remote from civilization; but I was shown one spot in the forest on the Tapajos, more than 100 miles from Guri, where some of these outcasts, numbering, it was said, more than 500, established themselves and founded what they termed "a city"; clearing the forest, and enslaving two whole tribes of Indians. They built halls, a theatre and a church! and private dwellings which were said to have been palatial in their magnificence: and, indeed, as I saw, must have been buildings of considerable architectural achievement. Here the rogues might have lived in peace, turned honest and industrious men; and, with the aid of their church and their priests, died in the odour of sanctity. But unfortunately for them they could not agree amongst themselves; and, instead of tilling the ground, took to fighting; and, as all tax-payers know, war being an expensive game, each side took to more and more extensive raids on their distant neighbours in search of the necessary gilded sinews for martial purposes; and at length provoked reprisals and extermination! So Santo Paulo, as they termed their den, and even the church of "Our Lady of a Thousand Mercies" (or successful robberies), were committed to the flames.

But some lonely individuals have lived extraordinary lives in the solitudes of the primeval forest; and I regret that the scheme of this book does not admit of my recounting some of them.

CHAPTER XVII

THE COUNTRY BETWEEN THE TAPAJOS AND THE ARAGUAY

I HAVE remarked that though, generally, there is a certain monotony in the description of the great rivers which run through Matto Grosso, there is also a marked difference in the head-waters of some of them. For instance the rivers which join together to form the Madeira are very widely spread, draining a great part of Bolivia, and extending so great a distance into the heart of the continent that this great tributary of the Amazon is probably the second river in length in the whole of South America. There is here the usual multiplicity, and consequent confusion, of names; but if we take the Guapay as the main stream, as I think it is, the course of the Madeira, including windings, is more than 2000 miles in length. Although Matto Grosso crosses the Bolivian frontier, and extends some distance into that country, I consider it is here out of the confines of the Amazonian valley, and must not, therefore, deal with it in this book. But I may say that the Guapore runs at the foot of a secondary range of forest-clad mountains, from the heights and slopes of which it receives many small tributaries, on one of which stands the provincial capital of Matto Grosso, formerly called Villa Bella, or Beautiful View, a name common enough in all countries, but peculiarly well chosen at this spot, where there is some of the most pleasing scenery I have ever viewed: and this is a strong assertion.

In this region there are a great number of small, and very charming, waterfalls; but when we get below San Jose, a small frontier town, the real rapids and falls of the Madeira begin to be met with in earnest. Between this town and the Rio Jacare there are a great number of torrents and falls, some of them of grand dimensions. I have never counted them, and I have forgotten the names and dimensions of many; but altogether, including the great rapids, some of which may be classed as falls in the rainy season, there cannot be fewer than 150 of them. Those, so far as I remember, which are worthy of particular mention are San Thomaso, Antonio, Barbo, Sangravelho, Paredao, Indiena, Girau, Balsamao and Campo Bello. But there are fifty others equally beautiful; besides the less attractive rapids.

The head-waters of the Tapajos also spread out in a fan-shaped radiation, and afford many beauties to the artistic eye, though they mostly rise in springs buried in the very heart of the Great Forest. I must hurry past these, and also the upper waters of the Xingu, and get farther east to the neighbourhood of Rio Araguay, the last of the great tributaries of the Amazon on its southern bank.

I think I have stated that I commenced my exploration of the Amazon in the summer of 1884. By May, 1885, I had traversed that river to the foot of the Andes, going as far as boat and canoe could take me: I had been up and down several of the great tributaries, and not a few of the small ones; and was still jogging along on the outskirts of Matto Grosso. I had been back to Para, buried one of my followers, who died of exhaustion, and got rid of the *Firefly* just before she ceased to be of some little value as *firewood;* and in the latter part of the month I have named I could have been found encamped near the source of the Rio Fresco, which is a tributary of the Xingu, but is less than 100 miles westward of the Araguay, and about the same distance from the little town of Lara, which is actually on the last-named river.

I had purchased mules and engaged servants farther down the Araguay, and was now on the point of surveying a fresh, and quite different, portion of Brazil; but that portion has an eminent bearing on the Amazon valley.

The Rio Fresco is about 150 miles long, running its whole course through forest land: but there is a difference in the character of the country here. It is a tableland of some elevation, with a moderate slope to the Xingu. The spot we camped on was the westward verge of the Araguay valley, which differs altogether from the valleys of the other great tributaries of the Amazon.

Our halting-place was a small savannah, enclosed by giant trees on all sides. Small openings, grass-covered and meadow-like, are frequently found in this part of the forest, as they are in Guiana, and the whole of the east side of Matto Grosso. They are never very extensive—can never be designated plains, or llanos; and are sometimes only two or three acres in extent. They are invariably called "savannahs" by both Spaniards and Portuguese: this word meaning "a little sheet," i.e. of land.

Photo Underwood & Underwood

FALLS ON THE AMAZON BELOW TABATINGA

What causes these openings I cannot say; but I have noticed that here and there in the forest there are patches of dead trees, which have perished in a body without any perceptible reason. These patches seem to correspond in size to the savannahs—they are from three or four to a hundred acres in extent—rarely, however, so large as the last-named area: and I suppose that when the dead trees are utterly decayed and gone to dust, their former sites are marked by these little forest meadows. They are "fairy rings" to the tired traveller—a relief to eye and body

My party now consisted of George Maccara, one of the most faithful companions it was ever my good fortune to travel with, two Indians, a negro, seven mules and a dog—one of the large animals which had been up the Purus with us—the other had gone where all dogs, and all men, go in time.

I must transcribe the description of the negro from a former work (I have the publisher's kind permission to do so): for I cannot possibly improve on what I have there said.

"The negro was a deplorable specimen of mankind. Never, in all my experience in the slave States of America, have I come across a fellow-creature in whom the attributes of manhood were so effectually, and so terribly, stamped out. He had been born a slave, and bred a slave, until his freedom was purchased on the conditions of the 1871 Emancipation Law; and was now getting his daily bread in the best way he could—that is by doing any odd jobs, or other work, that he could find.

His back was a horrifying sight. In the course of his

life as a slave he had received thousands of lashes; and his flesh was corrugated, from his neck downwards, with white ridges, the cicatrices of his wounds. His stories of beatings, starvations and tortures were terrible to listen to; yet in spite of all the torments he had endured he was still a man of herculean strength. He was engaged by me to manage the mules, in which kind of work he was an adept. I am rather partial to negro servants. Properly treated, they are generally useful and industrious men. This man, from long subjection to his task-masters, had acquired much of the cringing nature of a dog. When orders were given to him he appeared to be subject to nervous trepidation; and if spoken to at all sharply, he sprang about as if his life depended upon the immediate performance of the directions he had received. At meals, in the forest, I need hardly say we could not indulge in the decorum usually observed at a well-ordered table; but our custom was to sit on the ground round the cooking-pot and help ourselves in a rough-and-ready fashion. Yet this poor negro was afraid to eat in my presence, even in this unconventional way; and the nervous discomfort it caused him to take his humble fare in the sight of me, his master, was so great that I was fain to permit him to take his food back amongst his mules, where he could not be seen. He did not know his age—he appeared to be forty-five or fifty years. He had been married five times. Four of his wives had been sold away from him: the fifth had died owing to ill-usage from his brutal master. He had been compelled to marry (if marriage it could be called) at the command of his owner, for a similar reason to that of all stock owners—for the increase of wealth—a negro and an ox being much the same thing in a slave-owning country. His ignorance was so great that he hardly remembered how many children he was the father of; but he used to cry when he narrated the circumstances under which his first-born son had been taken from him. Some of his children had been sold away from him, and were lost for all time: others he knew the whereabouts of, as they were still slaves; and he was saving every penny he could earn to purchase the freedom of a favourite son.

"Among the devilish cruelties to which he had been subjected was that of being hung up by his wrists for twenty-four hours (a day and a night): the dreadful marks still remaining on his arms told a tale which could not be misunderstood. He was unconscious during the latter part of this terrible punishment. I think it scarcely necessary to notice the assertions of some writers who have denied that the torture of slaves was general, or at any rate frequent, in Brazil. I have never met anybody who really knew much about the country who was of that opinion. The ill-usage, and systematic torture, of slaves was general in former days; and I have been in districts where one could hardly go into a town, however small, without meeting negroes who were blind, or maimed, as a result of their owners' brutality. They were always branded, like cattle, with a hot iron; and I never met a party of them so marked with their owners' name, or distinctive mark, without remembering the words of one of our Jolly Jack Tars when ashore on leave. Horrified at some brutalities he saw committed on a slave, and being told when he interfered by the poor wretch's tormentors to mind his own business, he turned to his companion in honest indignation and exclaimed: 'I say, Bill; if the devil doesn't get them fellows I don't see the use of having a devil.'"

To finish with my negro. I afterwards placed a narrative of his case before an American Liberation Society, with the result that four of his children, two boys and two girls, were traced; and their freedom secured, as, also, was that of two of the women he had been compelled to live with. Some difficulty arose, on religious grounds, about the latter part of the transaction; but I got the then Emperor of Brazil (who treated me in a most friendly way at all times) to intervene; with the result that old Thomas married an elderly woman, the mother of three of his children; and the whole family was sent to Liberia. The second woman was otherwise provided for. Old Thomas was found to have amassed 800 dollars in the twelve years he had been free, every cent of which was destined to help buy his adored boy's freedom. At the time of the lad's liberation he was about eighteen years of age.

Snakes were very abundant in the forest near our camping-place; and I was much amused by the movements of some whip-snakes which darted about the bushes and low trees with amazing rapidity and gracefulness. They were about forty inches long, of a bright green colour, and not thicker than a clothes-line; and so active that I found great difficulty in capturing one. It was venomous, but in what degree I do not know.

Another little snake of this region is of a light drab colour, and not more than a foot long. Its eye is of an intense brightness; and the creature is said to be able to fascinate small birds, so that they cannot escape from it. I do not know what truth there is in this story, but it is very widely spread; and implicitly believed by people of all classes. Some Brazilian gentlemen assured me that they had seen small birds, including humming-birds, paralysed by its steady gaze. I was not so fortunate myself as to see anything of the kind; but, of course, the story may be true, especially as the Indians believe it. I have great faith in the powers of observation of these men. The Indians call this snake the tarangabos; but the Brazilians often name it the "enchanter." I was greatly interested in this little serpent because I immediately recognized it as of the same species as one preserved in spirits which was given to me by a sailor when I was a boy. This was afterwards (about 1859 or 1860) given to a naval surgeon, Dr. Macwilliam, who, I understood, in turn, presented it to the museum of the Royal College of Surgeons. So, perhaps, the systematists will look it up, and enlighten us on its points of interest. If it has gone to the dust-hole—well, that is where the legs and head of the curious dodo, and Captain Cook's moa, went!

Tree-porcupines, sloths, agoutis, capivaras and ant-bears, or eaters (they are called by both names), are all numerous at this spot; as well as macaws, toucans and monkeys; and generally, most of the animals of Central Brazil, which I have already mentioned. There are deer and tapirs also, but this spot is within reach of hunting parties from some of the towns on the rivers Tocantins and Araguay; and consequently, they have probably undergone a considerable reduction of numbers.

I shall select only a few creatures for description in

this place. The large otter of the Amazon, and most of its great tributaries, the largest species of the genus, I believe, was not seen in this region. It is replaced, to use the approved phrase, by a much smaller species, with a rich brown coat, and a length from snout to extremity of tail of about thirty inches, or three feet in fine specimens; while the large otter of the Amazon averages five feet, and six feet in large individuals.

Concerning unusual size in animals, I may say that all kinds have individual variations, dependent, it would seem, on various causes—locality, abundance of food, and some others. Old males are generally of great development; and I have noticed the *average* size of many mammals and birds to be from ten to twenty per cent greater in some districts than it is in others. I am not going to write an essay on abnormal development in animals; but I may mention that there are certain classes of creatures which occasionally develop in individual cases what may almost be called monsters.

I instance serpents. The boa, the anaconda, and some others in favourable situations, attain to an altogether unusual size. I cannot say what the maximum may be: it is not under forty feet for the anaconda. According to some *celebrated men* it is fifty per cent more than this for pythons. Captain Burton, for one, gives a graphic account of a terrible adventure with one which proved to be nearly sixty feet long; and three years ago those wicked newspapers reported that the gentlemen engaged in delimiting the Bolivian boundaries had shot one sixty-five feet long; and reported another destroyed by a second party as eighty feet long! I wrote to one of the best-known naturalists of the present day and asked what he thought of these stories—could he throw any light on them, the Sir Richard Burton yarn in particular? But mum was the word: he had not even the courtesy to acknowledge my letter. It is some consolation to know that the gentleman I am referring to agrees with me regarding the anaconda, and admits a possible forty-feet reptile of this class.

As a rule, the mammals and birds show nothing extraordinary in individual development; the puma, and, in a lesser degree, the jaguar, are exceptions; but fishes and arachnids show very common instances of it. Some of the spiders of this region, though usually of no monstrous size, are occasionally seen at least five inches in length of body, and with a spread of legs approximating a foot. They appear to be of the common bird-eating variety; but whenever I have come across such huge specimens I have invariably turned them out of holes under the roots of trees, crevices of rocks, and similar situations; and they have never appeared to be so active as the smaller ones, which average three inches of body, and seven inches spread of legs. I have thought that perhaps these very large spiders are those which have attained a great age, and have crept away to die.

Coming back to the otters: one of the handsomest of those found in South America is common on the Fresco. This is the Demerara otter, *Cheironectes Yapock*. It is a beautiful little animal of a light grey colour with black markings so disposed that the creature looks as if it had been seized with a smutty hand. It has more the appearance of a rat than of an otter; and is a fierce little animal, capable of inflicting a very ugly bite. Anxious to obtain a specimen alive, I dug one out of its burrow, which was fully thirty feet long, and had several branches which had to be stopped to prevent the animal's escape. My dog fully entered into the fun of these otter excavations; but the little animals showed fight, even to this huge member of the canine order, and inflicted several severe bites on Mike, until he learned the knack of seizing them.

Another animal not hitherto mentioned is the peccary, or American native pig. Most persons have heard of this animal; and probably know something of its general appearance and habits; so I need only say that I quite agree with the usual accounts of its viciousness and irritable temper: in fact, I have a profound respect (*almost* amounting to fear) for this little devil—for that is what he is. I think I might screw my courage up to the sticking place, in the case of one or, perhaps, two, of these pestiferous little wretches; but face forty or fifty of them!

Whenever I met peccaries in the forest, I lost no time in getting over the way: and if it is thought I am rather bald and am revealing a weakness that might have been covered, I have only to say *you* have not seen peccaries on the rampage. It is positively awful to witness such rage and wickedness in so small an animal: and if I am a coward in this matter, I lack courage in a very goodly band; for I have seen the boldest trappers out West change countenance at the sight of peccaries; and seen them "run like mad to tree" at sound of those gnashing tusks. What makes the courage run out like water is the knowledge that there is *absolutely no defence* against these ugly little fiends. The very beasts of prey know that; and my lord, the jaguar, if ever he does seize a peccary (which I very much doubt) only does so when he can surprise a solitary pig, and rush to tree with it at once.

Amongst other things I am a bit of a hedge-surgeon, and one day a poor Indian was brought to me—I was going to say, in pieces. He had blow-piped a peccary, and the peccary's relatives had cut up rough about it, as he might have known they would; and his legs and the lower part of his body hung in ribbons. Do anything for him? There was not a man in the Faculty that could have kept him alive six hours. This is not a solitary case: I once helped to gather up the fragments of a white hunter who had tried conclusions with a herd of these brutes, contrary to the advice of his friends. When the peccaries had done with him there was nothing but rags and bones left. Two of his mates came up in time to interfere, and shot several of the peccaries; but they had to make a rush for trees; and the animals got at the legs of one man before he could swing himself clear of the ground, and made him a hopeless cripple for life. I have heard scores of yarns about these animals, in which life or limb was lost, some of them, I dare say, exaggerated; but the majority true enough.

I have shot peccaries; even when standing on the ground. Fortunately for me I was under cover at the time; and these little pigs have not good sight. You may see them standing quite still, their snouts raised to the level of their backs and all pointing the same way, apparently listening. Suddenly away they rush, full charge and all together; and if *you* happen to be their objective, let us hope you have lived a decent, godly life: for you will have no time to pray now. You place your back against some support, determined to fight it out. You fire your second barrel, and roll one of the enemies over; up goes the butt of your gun and you brain another; you may even, if you are a lanky-bodied, desperate creature, full of pluck and muscle, earth a third: you will do no more. Peccaries' tusks cut like razors. You may have on the stoutest leather stockings man can walk in: they will be no more protection to your legs than rotten muslin. In two seconds they will fly into rags, and your flesh will go with them. The rest will soon be over; you will not suffer long—on this side of the Styx, at any rate.

This is an exaggerated picture? I have no doubt many persons will think so. But why should I stretch the truth? What is gained by so doing? When I was new to the southern States of America, self-sufficient and rash, I made up my mind that the peccary stories I heard were silly, and I went out to see for myself. I *saw*: and I had a more fortunate escape than my rashness deserved; but I am not going to tell that story. I have met other fortunate ones who have by chance escaped from an open battle with peccaries; and they were all of *one opinion*—that they had experienced fools' luck; and had better take the lesson to heart.

Now I have had the courage to state what no man before me has had the boldness to say plainly—that the peccary is the most dangerous and most determined enemy man has amongst wild beasts. The habits of this animal, and of the banded, or white-collared, variety have been laid down by one or two persons whom, it would seem, the scientists have decided to accept as authorities, for no particular reason except that they are, or were (for I think one, at least, of them is dead), men of social position.

Social position is, no doubt, a very good and pleasant thing, and to be treated with high respect; but, in common with systematic science, and theory which is not systematic, it stands open to criticism; and the assertion that the white-collared peccary differs in habits from the common kind, and is a harmless animal, is not correct: neither is it true that any peccary can be approached with safety. Both varieties are irascible little animals, and seem to know instinctively that man cannot stand against their numbers. Two or three of them could not do a man much hurt, if he stood on his defence; it is the combined attack that is fatal to him.

The habits of both kinds of peccaries are similar. They herd in droves, which are usually from forty to seventy strong. Occasionally one sees more than a hundred of them together; but this is not usual. They are eminently forest dwellers; and are never seen in open country. When feeding they scatter, and on coming up with a drove the hunter may not see more than two or three. If he keeps quiet they may not notice him, and will pass quietly on: for they are dull of both sight and hearing. If they do get suspicious, and make an attack, one high-pitched grunt brings the whole band rushing together like mad furies. They squeal and grunt defiance, at the same time gnashing their tusks with a loud rasping sound. They are light-limbed, and as active as dogs, or wolves, though I have never seen them actually leap from the ground.

Pigs in every respect, they are clean-living, and do not wallow in the mire like the common hog. They seem to prefer the drier parts of the forest; but do occasionally frequent swamps, and run through mud and shallow water. Possibly they swim across rivers and streams; but I have never seen them do so; and the only animal food I have known them devour was snakes. In attacking these they evince their usual boldness and pluck, or blindness to danger. Rattlesnakes, moccasins and coral-snakes, some of which are six or seven feet long, and poisonous in the first degree, have no chance whatever with a peccary. Perhaps the animal is impervious to the venom. The usual diet of peccaries is fruits, nuts, seeds, roots, grain and vegetation of many different kinds. I have never seen them touch filth, such as the common hog rejoices in; and the Indians say they will devour mice, small birds and pieces of flesh; but nothing that is tainted.

Peccaries are never met with singly, or in pairs, as is stated in every natural history I have seen; and the assertion that there are half a dozen different species is simply fudge. There are two species only: and these, like every other animal under the sun, form local varieties in some districts.

This information will show that, notwithstanding the dangerous character of the animal, I have watched it pretty closely. I used to have a platform placed in a tree in districts where these, and other animals which I wished to study, were abundant. Peccary meat, I should mention, is very good, though lean, and I have shot many of these little animals from the safety of a tree-perch. On one occasion I was surrounded by a herd forty-nine in number. As I was completely concealed, twenty feet above the ground, the pigs could not see me; and it was rare fun to witness their fury, and the manner in which they rushed about in search of their unseen foe. They evidently could not tell, by hearing, from whence the shooting came, for they never once looked up, and yet they associated the tree with their concealed enemy: for they rushed round and round the trunk tearing the bark, and rooting up the earth.

When I have shot pigs in this manner the herd, after a prolonged search for their aggressor, have generally run off, leaving three or four of their number dead for the benefit of my larder; but on this occasion they showed a determined intention of waiting until they had discovered their enemy.

I had shot four of their number, all that was wanted for food: and, lighting a cigar, sat down on my boards to wait until the patience of the survivors was exhausted, expecting that they would retire in about an hour. But no; they ran about squealing and gnashing their tusks for so long a time that I feared my meat would be spoiled. For the peccary is afflicted with a "protective odour," though there is not an animal on earth that dares to touch it: and if the gland from which the offensive smell is emitted is not removed before the carcass becomes cold, the flesh of the entire animal is uneatable. So when my cigar was finished I became impatient. Two hours elapsed, and still my friends below were whetting their tusks and their courage. Some of them were laid down to rest, but kept up their angry grunts and threatening rattle of the tusks: so

I shot four more, as the first lot were spoiled; and again waited. I soon discovered that it was of no use, however, and that the fiery little wretches below would have to be peppered in right good earnest. So I opened an exterminating fire; and it was not until I had killed thirty-eight that the eleven survivors saw fit to take themselves off; and it was some time longer before I was satisfied that they were really gone, and I might venture to leave my lofty perch.

The European wild boar uses its tusks to rip one up; the peccary reverses this operation and tears downward; but do not imagine that the victim gains anything by this difference in the method of attack. The tusks of the peccary, though smaller than those of the hog, and often invisible while the animal is alive, are as strong as steel and as sharp as a knife; and inflict the most ghastly wounds.

When the Indians hunt in bands they often surround herds of peccaries; and numbers giving the men courage, they sometimes kill the greater part of them; but wounds received in the fight are often fatal, and always terrible. I saw one man who had a cicatrice extending from his thigh to his shoulder. The injury was received whilst he was lying on the ground, after being knocked down by the rush of the herd. Some of the nerves had been destroyed, so that he was partially paralysed on that side.

The two species of peccary keep separate from each other; but overlap, and often occupy the same forest. In other instances only the one species or the other inhabits a district, and there are local varieties, as I have mentioned, and these last are always the sole kind found in their particular region. In fact, the peccary, as all, or nearly all, other animals, bears out my theory that species (that is variations from *original types*) are the outcome of locality, and not of " natural " or any other kind of " selection."

CHAPTER XVIII

THE VALLEYS OF THE ARAGUAY AND THE TOCANTINS

LIKE all the other great rivers of the Amazon valley the Araguay bears several names on different parts of its course. The upper four-fifths of its length is divided into two great branches, running nearly parallel to each other at no greater distance than 100 miles. They are divided by a picturesque, and very beautiful, range of mountains, the Cordillera Grande, about 800 miles in length; but continued, after a short break, into the very centre of Brazil. This range gives many short tributaries to both branches of the great river. The stream to the east is much the shorter and narrower branch, but is better known and more used than the western stream, and gives its name to the last fifth of the course which joins the Amazon.

It will be noted that two great rivers, running parallel to each other at no great distance, and divided by a ridge of high mountains, is a not uncommon feature of South American landscapes.

I have already described certain spots as the most beautiful I have seen in all my wanderings; but I am not sure that I have not done the "Great Ridge" an injustice. These mountains, of course, are no rivals of the majestic Andes; but for quiet, serene beauty, and marvellous effect of outline, they are matchless. They offer no lofty peaks to strike the eye with amazement: on the very highest summits of the range the traveller may stand in his loose pioneer's shirt, experience no sense of chilliness—suffer no difficulty of breathing. His range of vision will take in no huge rocks, remarkable for their snow-capped baldness; no mighty craters unique for size and grandeur as in the Andes; but will roam over rugged forest-clad rocks, graceful here in feathery foliage, picturesque there in jagged abruptness. Trees, magnificent in blossom and richly coloured foliage, clothe the mountain slope, and bend in pendent gracefulness over precipices that are an elegant adjunct to the scenery rather than an awe-inspiring feature to the eye accustomed to the terrible declivities of the Ecuador Andes.

The Cordillera Grande stretches due north and south; and is remarkable for the great number of brooks and rivulets which rise on its slopes. These, of course, have very short currents: there are, perhaps, twenty-five streams on the east side, exceeding forty miles in length, emptying themselves into the Tocantins; but the head-waters of this great river form a huge network of streams. On the west there are probably twenty rivulets of forty miles, and upwards, in length, running into the Araguay. On this side there is one river, the Aves, with a course of about 120 miles, having a north-west trend until it joins the Araguay. This river Aves runs through a rocky defile which is a soul's delight from end to end. I defy any man, not a born brute, to pass through this valley without a cheerful joy at his heart, as he witnesses the continual, and wonderful, change of beauty at every turn of his route.

An adequate description of this spot, with pen alone, is impossible. The valley is narrow, often a cañon, the rocks are broken and rugged past thought, and the stream often noisy and turbulent, now and then broken into rapids, cascades and falls; but there is not a gloomy or forbidding spot in the whole valley. Sometimes the rocks are so high that the rays of the sun do not reach the bottom of the gully for one half-hour per day; but all is so ethereal here, the light so strong, though mellow, the atmosphere so clear, that one never feels imprisoned as he must do in some of the vast crevices of the Andes.

Every part of the valley, and the rocks above and around it, are clothed with foliage, dense yet graceful, amongst which palms and tree-ferns hold a prominent place. Feathery canes and graceful drooping and climbing plants half hide the rugged rocks; and the whole shows a rich profusion of blossom that is not surpassed for glorious colour and curious shapes in any other part of the continent. There we saw the bright yellow trumpet-flower in its greatest perfection. Some of the blooms were so large that we men could wear them as hats, in imitation of the Indian women and children. Other curious flowers were a purplish, tubular blossom, four inches long, something like a huge fuchsia, and a large white star-shaped flower six inches across the disc. But it was not in size that the greatest, or most curious, beauties existed. There was a plant bearing clusters of brilliant coral-red blossoms that was a glorious sight in itself: and a creeper covering acres of the sheer rocks with masses of snow-white bloom. These are but a few of the floral wonders of the district; and I pause not to describe the remarkable growths of passion-flowers, and of flowering grasses that added their beauties to the more prominent blossoms of size and masses.

Those persons who delight in fanciful shapes in rocks, in Turk's heads and old men's faces, in cathedral spires and devil's chimney-pots, would revel here. We exhausted half the objects on earth, I think, in comparing them to the strange and remarkable shapes these rocks had weathered into. There were caves here, also, some of which were too deep and extensive for us to spare time to even attempt to explore. Others took more the form of grottos, festooned in trailing plants, ferns, feather-palms and flowers that for perfection of form, and richness of hue, might have been transplanted from the gardens of paradise. Alas! that I must spoil this picture by admitting that the serpent of Eden lurks here. In some parts of the valley venomous species of these horrible reptiles swarmed in so great numbers that we had to walk cautiously to avoid treading on them. As a rule, all snakes glide away on the approach of man; but none of them appear to be very acute of hearing, and there is danger of stepping on sleeping members of this extensive family—widely spread, and very numerous, in South America, at any rate. Snakes were the one drawback in this glorious valley.

Birds, especially humming-birds, parrots, macaws and toucans, were the chief feature in the animal life of this place. The humming-birds were especially magnificent; but I can give no specific names—at any rate with certainty—there are so many local varieties of these glorious little creatures. Besides a common green species, about the size of the English wren, there is here a green-backed, lily-white breasted variety with a purple throat and crest, a true "living gem" when seen in the brilliant light of the sun, with a hundred fire-like reflections scintillating from the plumage of its little body, which is not larger than that of a blue-tit. Viewed hovering, and darting about in the brightness of this heavenly region, humming-birds seem much more richly tinted than the poor little specimens one finds in a museum. It made my heart ache, and my spirits sink, when I saw the collection in the British Museum. "This, then, is what death does for the most beautiful of God's feathered creatures," I involuntarily exclaimed —no, muttered—as I viewed the cases of poor little faded bodies. "Splendid examples of the taxidermist's art." No doubt. "And fine samples of the scientific systematist's arrangement." Also, no doubt. But having seen these beautiful little jewels of life fluttering in their native element, in their native climate, can you wonder, my dear fellows of the systematizing classes, that I say, "Would to God that the people who come to your musty museums could see these precious things as I have seen them"? But hold! I think I have said something, near the beginning of this book, about taking the lives of these charming creatures for the benefit of museum directors. So I did; at the rate of about five shillings per body, which scarcely paid the carriage and customs dues. There is a Nemesis in these bird-murders sometimes.

Yellow, white and red are very uncommon colours in the plumage of humming-birds in Matto Grosso; but there is one in this valley with a red crest, or patch of scarlet, on the crown of the head. It has also a bright red band across the wings, with brilliant topaz on the tail and tail-coverts. It seems to be scarce, as only two specimens were seen.

Trogons, motmots and kingfishers were among the other remarkable birds found in the valley. The motmots are notable for their racket tails, artificially produced ; so it is said. The authority on which this curious habit is declared to be common to all the motmots, some twenty-five species, appears to be good. Gentlemen holding responsible positions at the British Museum, and the Zoo, will tell you that the bird has been seen to nip away the webs of the two central feathers of the tail, leaving a racket-shaped patch at the end of each bare shaft. The whole school of professional naturalists believe this to be a fact ; but we need engage our attention only with those persons who have had an opportunity of studying the bird in its native haunts. The late Charles Waterton "stoutly maintained that the bird did not produce this peculiarity of plumage by its own act ; but insisted that it was natural to it." Waterton, like other people, might make a mistake ; though mistakes, with him, were very rare. "Where can I confirm the story ?" I have asked. "By watching the bird in its native haunts," was the reply. Just so. I have done this, and have never seen the bird nipping its tail, or doing anything of the kind. It is very surprising that I have never met with a motmot with a perfect tail. Surely the bird *must let the web grow before it can shear it off*. But this is precisely what it does not seem to do. With what object does the bird thus mutilate itself ? And note : that the operation must be repeated after every moult. Well ! there are a good many things some of us poor sinful mortals cannot comprehend. Why do dear little cupids go about stark naked? Why do the angels, who have no shame, require raiment of white? And why does the motmot disfigure its tail? I should like to further enquire why the domestic mouse smells like the sole of an old shoe; but I think I have discovered that. The delightful odour is intended to give pleasure to Mrs. Housekeeper, and to protect little Miss Mouse from the unwelcome attentions of Thomas Tabby Esquire.

One more bird I must mention. In the valley of the Aves the cock-of-the-rock is unusually abundant. I had seen this bird in Peru; but it is not an inhabitant of the dense forest. It is a bird of exceedingly bright-coloured, and attractive, plumage, yet it loves to display itself in open situations, where it seems to be able to well maintain itself, in spite of potential enemies. Perhaps the hawks and wild cats know that all is not gold that glitters, and have reasons of their own for leaving it alone.

This bird, called a manakin by some naturalists, and a chatterer by others, is the size of a jackdaw, and is remarkable for several peculiarities not noticeable in many other birds—if any. In the first place the feathers are so loosely attached to its skin that many of them fall off, however carefully the bird is handled. Whenever I shot one a cloud of its feathers flew out. The plumage is a very bright orange colour in the male, with a rich purple crest. The hens are not so brilliant, being of a canary-green hue. But these colours fade after death with great rapidity, and soon become a dirty cream tint. The bird, therefore, cannot be seen in museums as it appears when alive.

It is a very lively creature; and, according to some describers of it, has regular "dancing-places," which it visits so frequently that the herbage is worn away from the ground. I think we shall find a pinch of salt agree with this assertion. However, a "lizard's body, lean and long, a fish's head, a serpent's tongue": it may be true, although I have never seen anything of the kind: and I have never been invited to a birds' "dancing-party," though I have frequently solicited the honour of being permitted to be present at one.

All the short streams previously referred to have rapid currents, with frequent cascades, leaps and falls, some of which are precipitated from a very considerable height, though they are of no great volume. One stream very vividly recurs to my memory. It is a series of cascades which, throughout its entire course, are only partially visible through thickets of flowering shrubs, and arches of overhanging trees festooned together with the most lovely of climbing plants.

At one point it disappears, with a hoarse roar, into a hole in the rock, which seems to be a deep tunnel in the heart of the mountain: for the same stream reappears three or four miles lower down, shooting out with so much force that a space, or recess, is left by means of which a person can pass right under the fall, in a similar way to that which is done under Niagara. From this point the torrent drops about 200 feet into a bosky dell, where it again disappears, this time into a dense forest growing on broken, rocky ground, which we found so difficult of access that we did not penetrate it farther than a few miles.

In this district the babble of meandering brooks, and

rushing torrents, is incessant. The deep roar of heavy falls mingles with the cheerful rippling of rock-impeded rapids; and these sounds are heard in various pitches and modulations, according to the distance of the flowing water from the spot where the listener stands. "Under the greenwood tree Who loves to lie with me, And turn his merry note Unto the sweet bird's throat." These words frequently recurred to me while in this paradise of Brazil, as it justly deserves to be named: and, tired with the strenuous exertion of many months of toil, I lay here longer, perhaps, than I was justified in doing. The greenwood tree was represented by some of the finest specimens on earth, though the foliage was not always green. One great tree, for instance, had leaves of a decided puce colour; another showed a great mass of orange-red leaves, the exact hue of the cock-of-the-rock's plumage; but I never saw the bird amongst its branches. Perhaps the protective tint was so perfect that my blind eye could not detect it.

And the "sweet bird's throat!" Early morning is the time for bird sound in this region: though many of them repeat their performances in the evening. I cannot say that there are many songsters in this country; but there are a few that make singular sounds, and a few more that can produce sweet ones. Columbus, in a long letter (preserved, I believe, in the Municipal Library at Genoa), narrating the discoveries on his first voyage, speaks of the delightful songs of birds on Watling's Island, and particularly mentions the nightingale. As was pointed out in after days, there are no nightingales in the New World; but it is rather singular that if I had not been well assured of that fact I should have thought I heard this charming bird in the gorge of the Aves. Late into the night a series of delightfully varied notes was poured from the tree-tops, so like those of the nightingale that a mistake on the part of a listener would certainly have been excusable. I have not the least idea what bird produces these sweet songs. It was never heard in the day-time; and to discover a bird amidst the foliage of a bushy tree 150 feet high would be a task for a wizard.

I believe that some writers have reported that the humming-bird has a pretty song. I have never heard it. The sound that these beautiful little creatures usually make is in singular contrast to their gorgeous plumage, being a high-pitched, rather angry-sounding squeak, varied occasionally by a sharp chirp. Nothing approaching a song from these birds ever reached my ears.

Two or three species of night-jars keep things lively till three or four o'clock in the morning—that is if the howling dervishes do not spoil their efforts by a too boisterous rivalry; but there happened to be no howlers in this favoured valley. Other songsters are few; though we heard a bell-bird tolling on two occasions, at ten o'clock and midnight respectively. Afterwards these birds were heard at various hours between four o'clock afternoon and midnight; and from five to eight in the morning. I have it in my notes that in this region they were never heard in the middle hours of the day; and time after time I have jotted down my observance of the death-like silence which prevails between early morning and early evening.

Other noises of the night indicated that the inhabitants of the forest, generally, were on the move; a curious natural comment on the doctrine that the nocturnal habit is adopted for purposes of safety. I have certainly supported this theory, which seems to be a most natural one: but the fact is that nearly all animals are more or less nocturnal. Birds are the least, and insects the most so. Very few mammals are strictly diurnal: lizards love to run and to bask in the sunshine; but frogs, toads, snakes and our friend "with the fine open countenance" (the cayman) love the hours of darkness: and for a good reason—their deeds are evil enough, even froggy (in this country) often bolting a victim half as big as himself.

The croaking of frogs is one of the characteristic sounds of a Matto Grosso evening; as is the hissing of snakes. Rarely, for the reptile is comparatively scarce, will be heard the bellowing, roaring, grunting—I know not what word to choose to describe the noise—of the anaconda. Perhaps it may be termed a hoarse hiss; but it is a much deeper sound than the voice of any other serpent. It appears to be uttered in anger, and is probably provoked by the too near approach of the jaguar, or some other creature which the snake dislikes. That the anaconda ever attacks the larger cats, or any other animal larger than the deer of the country, I do not believe. No doubt an anaconda could destroy a man; but, as I think I have already noted, I never met with an authenticated instance of its having done so. I may, in any case, safely put the ratio of danger between the large constricting snakes and the small venomous ones at 10,000 to 1! This statement may cause momentary astonishment; but take the official statistics of

India into consideration. As many as 20,000 persons per annum lose their lives through snake-bites: but there are twenty poisonous snakes in South America to one in India—and I am miles within bounds in this statement—and how many persons die of snake-poison in this country? Nobody knows and nobody cares. South America is not a land of statistics and fatherly officials to look after the interests of your precious souls, and still more precious bodies! but here you may do much as you like, and suffer quite what you do not like. So if you choose to get in the way of coocooradi, rattle-snake or coral-snake, and die in consequence, Johnny Portuguese is very sorry, shrugs his shoulders and sends for the nearest priest, who, as you are an infidel, orders you to be buried in the nearest convenient spot, as the lost may not lie in consecrated ground. In a word, judging from what I have seen and heard, I believe the mortality from snake-poison is simply awful. The Indians go about naked, or nearly so; the negroes never wear shoes; and the consequence is that these people move about silently, and therefore are continually treading on snakes which have not heard their approach. As a rule, all snakes, the horrible bushmaster excepted, glide away when they hear a noise.

Often have persons suffering from snake-bites been brought to me. Sometimes I have saved them: generally I have seen them too late to be of service to them. In the case of rattlesnake bites, and a few others, I have found large doses of whisky an effectual antidote. Probably brandy would be equally efficacious; but I have never had the opportunity of administering sufficient quantities: for it must be understood that spirits, unless given in very large doses, are not likely to do much good—in fact the patient must be made blind drunk.

If the bitten person was brought to me speedily, I cut the injured part clean away, or put a heated iron on it—deadly diseases require desperate remedies. I have found spirits of ammonia poured into the wound of great use; and on three occasions I rallied, and saved, persons who had reached the comatose state, by injecting a preparation of strychnine, according to the directions of an American surgeon who was one of the first persons to use this remedy—in the American continent, at any rate.

CHAPTER XIX

THE CORDILLERA GRANDE REGION

AMONGST the more remarkable trees of the valleys of the Araguay and the Tocantins are two or three species of the gutta-percha tribe; and the bullet-wood and cow tree.

The bullet-wood is so called because it is so hard that it is believed it will resist the impact of a musket-ball. It is evidently a species of gutta-percha; for on wounding the trunk, or a branch, a white juice exudes, which speedily condenses into a thick semi-fluid substance which can be rolled into a ball. It does not appear to have a commercial value; and some which I brought to England was looked upon as a curiosity by manufacturers of india-rubber articles, who had not previously seen anything like it. It is called the boorooah tree by the Portuguese, a corruption, I suppose, of "bullet tree." The timber is well known to the merchants. The fruit is like a plum, and the tree is said to bear it only once in five years.

The cow tree may be an allied species: for it, also, gives forth a white juice, which, on being exposed to the air, thickens in some degree. It has the properties of cream; and may be used in tea and coffee as a substitute for cow's milk. It is a delicious-flavoured and highly nutritious substance.

I have not hitherto mentioned the armadillo, one of the most characteristic animals of South America. There were some in this district; and I must say a few things about them, as we shall not meet them again. There may be many in different parts of the Amazonian valley, though I do not think that there are, the nature of the soil not being favourable to them. The armadillo loves dry ground, and is far more often found on plains than in forests. I know the natural histories say that they frequent forests; but I have never seen any signs of them where the trees were growing thickly. In open forests there are a few; but practically they are all armoured-moles. They rarely show above ground; and those who know how difficult it is to dig out of the ground "the little gentleman in black velvet" may guess the trouble one has to surprise an armadillo. They are never found on hard ground, and they burrow so quickly that if one is placed on the soil to race against a man stationed fifty yards away, the armadillo will win: that is it will burrow so quickly that it will be at least a yard deep before the runner can get up to it. I have succeeded in digging them out of the ground; but only rarely, and with the assistance of several other persons. When the animal gets a certain distance beneath the surface of the ground, it tunnels in various directions. The passages must be marked, and a number of men dig down quickly to head the armadillo off. When the animal perceives that its passage will be intercepted, instead of burrowing lower, it shuffles backwards stern foremost. Then is the time to capture it.

The depth of the burrow, in the first place, depends on the size of the armadillo. I have never found any sunk lower than six feet. Then a kind of chamber is made, from which tunnels radiate in all directions; and to an indefinite extent. I have followed some of the passages 170 feet without reaching the end; and I have found that a large number of these animals join together to form quite a labyrinth underground, so that it is not possible to assign any portion of the work to one animal.

None of the species that I am acquainted with are "strictly nocturnal animals." They do not, however, come out of their burrows till evening, except the weather is dull and wet. Heavy rains drown them out; but these are exceptional circumstances. As soon as the sun is well down armadillos come out of their retreats and begin to search for food. This is the time to capture them. As soon as you see one well away from its burrow, rush forward. The animal will at once bury itself. Now you must watch carefully and patiently; surveying the ground all round: for the armadillo cannot turn in a chamberless burrow. Presently it will seek to come forth from its temporary lurking-place; breaking up a fresh opening at a probable distance of twenty feet or less from the first hole. Run forward quickly. The armadillo will have no alternative but to back into its burrow; and as it cannot do this as fast as you can dig, it will soon be in your possession. At any rate, this is the method I have adopted to capture several. I have also used dogs, and the lasso; but it is absolutely necessary that the animal should be surprised in the first place at a distance from its usual retreat, otherwise it will burrow back to its labyrinth, and you will have your trouble for nothing.

The species which inhabit the valleys of the twin rivers which bound the sides of the Cordillera Grande are the giant armadillo, and another kind not identified. The first is a burly, thick-set animal weighing from eighty to 100 pounds, usually about thirty inches in length, but sometimes much longer: this measurement not including a thick, armoured tail of twelve or thirteen inches. The head is small; and, I should think, the tremendous claws are proportionally the largest of any animal in existence. If this animal chose to stand on its defence, its foes would probably have an exciting time of it; but it is as innocent and harmless as a child. You can turn it over, and pull it about just as you think fit: it does nothing but snuffle and grunt, and strive to escape. It is an enormously powerful creature; and you will have much trouble in handling it; but have nothing to fear.

It is said to be insectivorous, naturalists evidently judging by the character of its teeth. It certainly does eat worms, slugs, beetles, and small fry generally; but is nearly omnivorous so far as regards animal food. My negro used to take the offal of any animal we killed and throw it some distance from the camp, instead of burying it as directed. This, in a few minutes, would be completely covered with flies; and beetles would burrow under it. In this climate the whole mass would be a festering, heaving heap of maggots and corruption in an hour or two, and it served as a lure to the armadillos, who assembled round it as soon as evening set in, and devoured the whole loathsome mass. I have also seen the armadillo devour centipedes and scorpions, these venomous things having, apparently, no power to do it hurt. I have never seen it meddle with ants or termites; but it may do so, it being obvious that I could not make myself thoroughly acquainted with all the habits of every animal I met with. The smaller armadillo of this region is singularly like a miniature species of the giant kind, but with a shorter tail, and certainly feeds on termites, as it was seen to burrow into the hills of these insects, some of which, in our neighbourhood, were of a remarkable height.

Sloths there were in this region; and the little ant-eater, *Tamandua tetradactyla*. It does not differ from the great ant-eater in general form; but the tail is not bushy, the fur is parti-coloured—dirty white and dingy black, and the animal is very much less in size than its big relative; and there are some very remarkable differences between the two species. The great ant-eater, for instance, never climbs trees; in fact, it cannot do so under any circumstances. The little ant-eater often does so; and still more remarkable, its tail is prehensile in no uncertain measure—evolution with a vengeance: but with what object? Not to search for its food, which is found on the ground: and why has Nature given it a monkey's tail, and left it in possession of the enormous claws destined to break down the citadels of the termites? Clearly it is simply a freak on the part of Nature; the more marked that the creature is not, as often reported, "mainly of arboreal habits." The fact is that it is more often on the ground than in trees, and never ascends them to any great height! It has the curious habit (curious because there is no discoverable reason for it) of climbing bushes and young trees to a height of ten or twelve feet, and hanging listlessly to a branch by its long tail. There, like a great opossum, it remains pendent for hours at a time, quite motionless, but not asleep. When it wishes to repose it descends to the ground and curls itself up under the shelter of a dense cluster of bushes. Strange that a creature capable of climbing trees, and furnished with a prehensile tail, should sleep upon the ground; but there is no doubt whatever about the fact: and perhaps there is no greater danger in such a situation than in trees, which are infested by two of the most destructive creatures in South America—the jaguar and the anaconda: and though the last is a rare reptile, there are other serpents, more numerous in numbers, and not less dangerous in habit, that make trees none too safe a place of resort for any animal.

Birds, and other creatures, migrate in South America, as they do in all other parts of the world. It therefore happens that a species found in a district by one traveller may be searched for in vain by one visiting the same district at a different season of the year. This remark is suggested by the fact that we found several trees full of pendulous nests similar to those of the cassiques, but no birds of that genus were seen in this region. None of the nests appeared to have been recently occupied; and the birds to which they belonged were probably absent in some other part of the country; and this, I believe, was the case with other species.

During the next month we suffered great privations while exploring the country towards the Xingu. Our corn-flour was quite consumed, and some of our stores accidentally lost in an uninhabited country where it was impossible to replace them. Still, I was anxious to push on into the heart of this region, as I heard at Lara and other places that it was a *terra incognita*. Game there was in this country; but owing to the broken, rugged character of the ground, and the density of the forest, we had great difficulty in finding it and approaching near enough to kill it. For this work the two Indians proved to be invaluable; but their frequent want of success proved that these people, in the wild parts of the country, must often suffer great privations. This indeed they admitted, and said that it was a chief reason why the men of several villages banded together to surround the animals in a tract of the forest, and so ensure their destruction: otherwise they would sometimes starve, individual hunters being quite unable to track down sufficient game for the support of their families.

Reverting to this time, I recall that we had some startling, if not remarkable, adventures. One evening we had just lighted our fire, and begun to cook supper, when a huge jaguar (magnified by our fears, I dare say, and am not too squeamish to admit) dropped into our midst from the branches above our heads. We rolled one over another, and the jaguar gathered himself up and bolted with great celerity—not the only case of mutual fright I have experienced in the wilds.

We looked at one another with curious expressions of countenance: the Indians grunted: the negro said his prayers; and the white portion of the party swore a little, I am afraid; but everybody was thankful, and *brave*, when the danger was past. We all looked into the tree, and carefully examined it, lest the jaguar had left a partner behind: and our nerves were altogether so shaken that nobody was satisfied until we had moved to what was considered a safer spot.

During the month, also, we killed no fewer than five or six anacondas, each of them approximating twenty feet in length. The Indians and the negro feasted on the flesh of these; but George and I were not yet sufficiently starved to stomach such food. I did, indeed, taste anaconda flesh, and found it coarse and stringy, and almost flavourless. What taste there was in it was decidedly fishy.

Travelling due south we crossed several big streams, one of them the river Guapindas: and a few days afterwards the Xingu, by swimming, at a place where it was a quarter of a mile wide, and infested by caymans. Subsequently we were compelled to cross, and recross, it several times, and two of the mules were drowned; and all of us had narrow escapes of a similar fate. But I am not justified in further detailing this part of my experiences in Brazil. I wish simply to reveal the character of the country, and the great difficulties the explorers of it must face. During the period I have mentioned I do not think we ever travelled so much as ten miles in twenty-four hours: frequently we could not have made more than four or five; though all of us worked axe in hand during the hours of daylight. We became so exhausted by privation and want that it was a question of life or death with us to move on as rapidly as possible. One of the remaining mules had to be killed for food; and I was compelled to abandon most of the specimens I had collected on this section of my journey—a circumstance that grieved me much.

A few more words about the Cordillera Grande, an

important part of the Amazonian valley; for it is its easternmost boundary; and I must return to the Upper Amazon, and commence the last section of this book.

I can only guess at the heights of the peaks of this range, or deduce them from barometric observations. One or two of them seem to verge on 7000 feet; and several certainly are at least 6000. Bare rocks crop up here and there; but the range is completely clothed with splendid forests. Its gorges are mere clefts, through which small streams flow; but they are exceedingly picturesque; and, in spite of their comparatively small size, many of them are impassable: indeed, passes over the mountains are not easily found, and do not seem to be so numerous as is usual in ridges of so small an elevation. In a distance of eighty miles we could find only one; and it is certain that there was no other within fifty miles of it.

The bare rocks are generally huge crags split, rent, torn by weather, or natural convulsions, and often presenting great flat, cliff-like faces of 100 to 400 feet in height, so perpendicular and smooth that not even a blade of grass can find a roothold on them. They form a beautiful variation of the landscape, and contrast to the dense tropical forest which surrounds their bases. From the valleys below one can look up and see the clear-cut forms of these rocks silhouetted against the sky, a glorious sight on a bright night when the moon gives a light that is not even dreamt of in our hard northern hemisphere.

The whole of the mountains on the eastern side of Matto Grosso abound with caves, a feature which, so far as I know, is almost absent from the Andes. I do not know that any of these caves are very remarkable for size or depth—none of them are such natural wonders as those of Kentucky—but they afford some strange and interesting features. In the northern part of the Cordillera, the portions of the range with which we are mostly concerned, they are small; but one which I entered and explored ran *upwards* into the heart of the mountains a distance of about four miles. It appeared to have been formed by the splitting and reclosing of two enormous rocks in some remote age: for there is no sign of modern volcanic action.

Water, no doubt, rushes down this channel after heavy rains; and I should imagine that a person would be in great danger if he were caught by a storm-burst when at the far end.

Of course, artificial light is necessary to enable one to explore this cave, and a much stronger one than that of a lantern is desirable. I had no better light, however, and this enabled me to see only that the roof was a considerable height above the floor. As far as I could see, the sides of the tunnel were almost perpendicular; but in a few places they bulged, or leaned together, closing the cleft above my head. Twice I was compelled to stoop in order to proceed; and more often my difficulties were increased by deep holes, or fissures, in the floor.

Under foot, the ground was generally composed of rough stones of various sizes; some of them boulders, but the greater quantity large pebbles mixed with sand; all, at this time, dry, or, at most, merely damp, though marks on the sides showed that water percolated through the rocks if it does not actually run in a stream at times. A slimy lichen discoloured the rocks and stones, and I once or twice saw large frogs, or toads, a small lizard and several mice scuttling away from before me. Stalactites of a pendent form hung down, and sometimes almost blocked the way ; but I contrived, as I have said, to push forward about four miles, when I found the passage too narrow to squeeze through. It was then a mere crack, slanting upwards, and not more than eighteen inches wide.

I do not think that the tunnel, or cave, was anywhere more than twenty yards wide : in many places it was scarcely as many inches ; and I had to turn sideways to squeeze through. No doubt it had been wider ; but the stalactic formations had encroached very much, and would, no doubt, ultimately fill the entire crevice.

Other caves in these mountains were of the usual form, and of no remarkable size : the largest was, perhaps, a couple of acres in extent, and led to others of much smaller size. All were full of stalactites and stalagmites, showing many curious formations and groups.

CHAPTER XX

HIGH UP THE AMAZON RIVER

THE head-waters of the Amazon have already been described. The matter dealt with in the following letter has also been referred to in an early chapter :

"ADMIRALTY,
"*28th September*, 1912.

"SIR,

"In reply to your letter of the 19th instant, I am commanded by my Lords Commissioners of the Admiralty to inform you that H.M.S. *Pelorus*, a protected cruiser of 2185 tons, sailed in the early part of 1909 up the River Amazon from Para to Iquitos in Peru, 1985 miles from the mouth of the river.

"2. The permission of the Brazilian Government was obtained for this visit.

"3. An account of the cruise, by one of the crew, appeared in the issue of the 'Standard' for the 18th April, 1909.

"I am, sir, your obedient servant,
"O. MURRAY.

"P. FOUNTAIN, Esq,
Rawridge, Ripley, Surrey."

I would remark that if Yquitos, which formerly belonged to Ecuador, and not Peru, is only 1985 miles from the mouth of the Amazon, distances have been exaggerated, and the total length of the river is not so great as is usually represented. I thought Yquitos, or Iquitos, was at least 100 miles farther from the mouth of the river. Altogether the *Pelorus'* reckoning would reduce the total length of the river by 200 or 250 miles. It is not very material; but I deemed it desirable to note the circumstance. The point is that the Amazon is navigable for the lower 2000 miles of its course by ships of fully 3000 tons. For much larger vessels than the *Pelorus* can get as far as Nauta, fifty miles higher up the river than Yquitos. For at these places the depth of water is from sixty to seventy feet. Above Nauta, however, it suddenly shoals, and there are many shallow places and rocks in the bed of the river. Still, vessels of 200 or 300 tons can ascend a long way farther if care is taken in the navigation. I would undertake to carry a vessel of 250 tons nearly up to the first cataract. The question, however, is not how far the river may be actually navigated; but to show that mercantile vessels of heavy tonnage can practically cross the continent, and ship the products of the largest river valley in the world.

It will be observed that the British naval authorities adopt a different spelling of names from that I use. I follow the older maps and navigators; and still more frequently stick to the names *given by the original founders and discoverers*. I do not think that reasonable fault can be found with this method. In the first chapter I have given my reasons for writing Amazons, and not Amazon. The stream is really the "Rio de Amazones." That is what its discoverer called it, as already mentioned. With regard to Yquitos: it is a Spanish word, and the accent is put on the "Y" exactly as it is in our word " eye." Iquitos, therefore, cannot possibly be the correct spelling. It is usual to pronounce the name quickly, and in an abbreviated form thus : 'Ȳ-tōs (both vowels long). On the Amazon " lingua franca," a sort of jargon, is in vogue, and it is largely dominated by " Yankee English." The United States are usurping all the trade, all the style, and all the customs in South America. Their dream is a cluster of American republics which shall oust all European trade, ways, and influence; and they are making big strides in this direction. Spanish and Portuguese are already much corrupted; and changes of names and spellings are largely due to United States influence. Nobody hears of Rĭo now (the true pronunciation); it is always Rīo—even in the mouth of a Portuguese. Similarly, if in the States you speak of Medĭna, you provoke a broad smile: and, " I s'pose you mean Medī'na ? " If I remember right, last year Mr. Secretary Somebodyorother wanted to reform the orthography of the *American language*, and spell circle with a round O !

Twenty-eight years is a long time in the world's history, and between American and Briton and pushing German I have no doubt there have been considerable developments of commercial matters on the Amazon since 1884.

There were indications of it at that time ; and in the immediate neighbourhoods of the towns and villages, and also up the tributary streams, there were considerable clearings of the forest—clearings which may be divided into old and new. But it must be understood that compared with the whole forest-clad region these inroads on the timber were a series of mere flea-bites.

I am not going to indulge in a calculation of the time the forest would last if a determined effort were made to clear it away. Hundreds of thousands of square miles would have to be *drained* before a tree could be touched; and this would be a job for a gentleman named Hercules! Timber, to be worth transport, must be got cheap, at least until old Time has put another century or two on the world. So the great bulk of the forest is safe for the present.

Another circumstance that will tend to preserve the more distant parts of it is the fact that cleared ground rapidly becomes reafforested without any replanting by the hand of man. Trees grow very rapidly in this country; and though the giants of the forest may take a long time to attain full development, it is not the very largest trees that the timber-merchant seeks with most eagerness. The buttressed cotton-wood, and the huge mora (of which there are several species), for instance, seldom pay for cutting down. The largest trees are seldom free from defects, nor do they yield the firmest and finest timber. Some of the most picturesque trees, therefore, will not be destroyed, even in the neighbourhood of the settlements.

This is proved by what I have termed the old, and the new, clearings. Formerly lumberers went some distance from towns and villages, where the land was mostly owned by private persons, or by Government, and felled the timber at their uncontrolled will. There was no machinery, and no power, not even horse help, as a rule: consequently only such trees were cut as would fall into the water, or could be easily pushed into it. Thus it could scarcely be seen where these fellings had taken place. But, when richer men than the pioneers of the lumber trade in this region saw that there was wealth to be made from the forest growth, they obtained grants and concessions, and erected saw-mills and wharves. In the case of the older works, these were generally temporary erections: and when the forest had been cut down over a fixed area, they were removed to a fresh site. I have examined many of the old clearings; and found that in the space of about twenty years there is a new growth of trees fit for timber purposes. So it will certainly be a very long time before the distant parts of Matto Grosso are invaded.

The worst mischief, at present, is done to trees of particular species—the cinchona for instance. The bark of this tree is very valuable, and ought to be stripped off with care; and only partially, so that the life of the plant should not be destroyed: but irresponsible persons, long prior to 1884, had been in the habit of searching the forests, as far as they could penetrate, for the cinchona and the rubber trees. The cinchona they cut down to strip off the bark: the rubber they bled to death in their greed to obtain as much of the valuable substance as possible.

The opinion that the trees yielding these products are only found in the highlands of Peru, Guiana, etc., is an incorrect one. They were formerly very plentiful in the accessible parts of the forests bordering the Amazon, and still are so in the remote districts on both sides of the river; and in all parts where the ground is not a swamp.

In 1884 there was not a yard of railway within hundreds of miles of either bank of the Amazon, and I am not aware that this state of the country has since been altered. There were no great towns in the interior of Brazil or the neighbouring states to warrant the tremendous outlay which is usually necessary in this country for the making of railways. I gave some attention to the matter when on the Amazon; and heard the opinions of both American (U.S.) and English engineers. We could find no place at all, away from the immediate vicinity of the cleared grounds around the towns, where a line could be made for less than £5000 English per linear mile. In many places double this amount would not cover the cost. Sufficient local labour could not be found; and the cost of clearing the ground alone would be enormous. In a stretch of fifty miles of forest ground lying between Olivenca and Matura it was found that 150 bridges, viaducts, and culverts would have to be constructed; 10,000,000 trees felled and about 800 square miles of swamp made firm, or embanked! Where would the capital come from? and, if found, what would the return be? It occurred to me at the time, and I have seen no reason to alter the opinion, that centuries must elapse before an extensive system of railways will be needed, or can be constructed, in Central Brazil. I suppose, to-day, it would be quite easy to find six or eight tracts in the valley of the Amazon, varying from 100 to 400 *miles square* (*not* square miles) which do not contain a single white inhabitant. The whole continent is sparsely populated: Central Brazil particularly so. The population is concentrated on the water-ways, and is little more than *two* per square mile for the whole country; and it is to her extensive and magnificent rivers that Brazil must long look for her means of internal transit. In no country in the world are there so few hamlets and isolated dwellings of the farm and plantation class; and in no land are peasants so few. Brazil is a country of: 1. Rich men. 2. Comparatively rich men. 3. Proud beggars. 4. Miserable abjects.

The third class are what are (or used to be) called "mean whites" in the southern States of the North. They live anyhow, and by any means—except work. The great mass of half-breeds may be placed with them; and some of these are soldiers or sailors; the true whites being altogether too exalted personages to hold any military rank under that of commissioned officer. I do not wish to say anything unkind against a nation in whose land I have sojourned, and received some hospitality; but it is a fact that Brazil suffers severely from lack of the mechanic and labourer classes. The slaves have now died out—there are no negroes in the country who are not nominally free—and for all practical purposes, really so: and the black is not nearly so numerous in South America as he is in the States. He is not in sufficient numbers to till the soil and harvest the crops; and the proud beggars will not condescend to do work of any kind, unless drinking, stabbing, making love, and card-playing be counted works.

So Brazil has more than once endeavoured to people her waste lands with emigrants; and Russians, Germans, and a few Irish and English have come hither "to better themselves." These unfortunate people were promptly sent into the interior of the country; and then found themselves compelled to do the work of the emancipated

Photo Underwood & Underwood

A FREIGHT TRAIN IN GUAYAQUIL. A TYPICAL SCENE IN THE LARGE CITIES OF AMAZON VALLEY

slaves—or starve. Pay they seldom got, and thousands have died miserable deaths of semi-starvation and the diseases engendered of improper and insufficient food. In fact, these European emigrants have over and over again been subjected to the position of slaves; and whole bands have met the fate of extermination through ill-usage and starvation. If enquiry is made: "Where were the respective consuls of these people?" that is precisely what I have repeatedly asked! So far as England is concerned, various notices and cautions have been inserted in the public papers; but ought not something more than this to be done?

Let me add my caution. There is a Government in this land, and I believe it is honestly striving to do its duty: but Brazil is pretty much about the size of Europe. In the interior there are about one policeman and two soldiers to a hundred thousand miles of territory. There are no railways, and you may walk a thousand miles in any direction before you come to a made road. The proprietor of a large estate of any kind—owner of from a hundred to a thousand square miles of land, is a little god in his way—and *in yours*. He does what he likes, and if you do not like it, take my advice and clear out. In no country is it a safe game to oppose arrogant wealth—in this it is a positively dangerous one. You will certainly get no justice: but in all probability you will get a good broad knife between your blade-bones, placed there by a gentleman of class No. 8, who knows the exact position of your liver, and of the effect of a deep stab therein. The Señor Portuguese resembles the devil in two points: he is superlatively polite, and fiendishly vindictive. So beware!

The current of the Amazon is ponderous, not rapid. In the upper parts of the Ucayali and Marañon it is turbulent, boisterous, full of rapids, cascades, and falls, as already described. Nauta is situated at the junction of the Ucayali and the main stream; but notwithstanding the tremendous body of water discharged by the great tributary the meeting of the two currents causes no particular commotion, no noticeable impact on the opposite bank; but the force must be very powerful; for a huge quantity of sedimentary deposit is brought down by the Ucayali, yet it is all swept away—there is no formation of mud, or sand-banks, or of islands, as there is at the embouchures of the Javari, Jurua, Purus, Rio Negro, Madeira, the Tapajos, and the Xingu: all of them sluggish streams on their upper reaches; and some of them throughout their entire courses. This is a proof that the Ucayali has a swifter and stronger stream than the other rivers just mentioned; and also that the current of the Amazon itself must be very powerful; yet one would hardly think so, judging from superficial appearances. It will be remembered that the Amazon is seventy feet deep just below Nauta; a very great depth, indeed, for any river; and it is the only stream in the world which can show anything like such a depth, and volume of water, 2000 miles from its mouth. In fact, the Amazon is an exemplification throughout the whole of its main course of the adage that "still waters run deep." Below Nauta the main channel is nowhere less than seventy feet deep; and, with some variations, it gradually increases in depth till, below the junction of the Rio Negro, it is never less than 200 feet!

By main channel I mean the deepest part: for the

river is often so broad, even in its upper parts, that a boat, or small vessel, may drift, or sail, along either bank for days and yet never be within a mile of the chief or central current; though, by the by, the current is not always in the centre of the river, or even near it. There are places where the deepest soundings, and the strongest currents, are not a quarter of a mile from the bank, though the river may be two or three miles broad. No doubt the *Pelorus* made a systematic series of soundings; I cannot pretend to have done that; but I have plumbed every mile of it, and examined it from bank to bank, with the results I here give. Notices of unusual depths, and of shoal places, must be given as we reach them; but I may remark here that the Amazon is unusually clear of deep holes; though there are many shallows with deep currents on either side of them.

Below Puca-allpa, which is about twelve miles farther down the stream than Yquitos, there is a vast stretch, which is one of the straightest parts of the Amazon. For nearly 200 miles there is no great bend in the course of the river, which is, all this way, of considerable width. Just below Pevas there is a reach of twenty miles in extent; and beyond Pernate, looking straight forward, the stretch and breadth of water are so great that one could easily believe he was looking out to sea.

On these great reaches a boat allowed to drift will keep near the centre of the river, and drop downstream at the rate of about a mile an hour, though there is no perceptible current on the surface. When a stiff breeze is blowing, or a storm raging, the water is so much disturbed that a small craft, such as the *Firefly* (which had a tonnage of nearly twenty), rolls and rocks as if it were well out to sea. On some of the broads I have seen waves rise apparently about three feet, making it impossible to launch a canoe, and dangerous to use a small row-boat.

There are a few small islands in these reaches which call for no particular notice; but some of them which are very low and denuded of timber—sand-banks, in fact—are much resorted to by Amazon river tortoises, which are, I believe, a distinct species; and are, in any case, of gigantic size, some of them measuring not much under a yard in length; and weighing, I should think, at least 200 pounds: in fact, they rival sea-turtle in dimensions.

Hundreds of them were seen lying on the mud and sand; and they were of all sizes from tiny things a few inches across to giants of thirty-three inches, the length of the biggest captured by us. They love to repose exposed to the blazing hot sun, and apparently asleep; but on the approach of a boat they slip into the water with an ease and speed one would scarcely believe such ungainly creatures could possess: and they swim with great activity; not on the surface of the water, but well beneath it. I have seen them at as great depths as the eye can penetrate the water, which may be forty or fifty feet where it is clear and undisturbed. Very few come near the surface—six or eight feet beneath it, perhaps: and these, on seeing me watching them from the branch of a tree, hanging over from the shore thirty feet or more, changed direction at right angles, and darted away as rapidly as fish could do. They are much persecuted by Indians, and, indeed, all classes and races of men; which, I suppose, accounts for their great shyness. The Indians along the shore destroy great numbers of them; and also their eggs by the thousand. The tortoises are generally surprised at night-time when they land on the sand-banks after feeding, the Indians lying in wait for them. The eggs are beaten up into a batter; and this, on being placed over a slow fire, gives up a great quantity of oil, which is much relished by the native rovers of the forest. The flesh of the tortoise, cut into strips and steaks, is boiled or toasted. In the case of old animals it is tough and flavourless; but younger ones are passable. The flesh is not, however, to be compared to that of the turtle, and there is never much fat on it. The Indians often keep it a full day before eating it; which is tantamount, in this climate, to rendering it "gamy": and I found that this method made it more palatable.

The tortoise feeds chiefly on river-weed; but it also eats grass and leaves on the banks. It is said to resort to favourite sand-banks to deposit its eggs, which are left to be hatched by the heat of the sun. They are deposited in layers at a depth of about eighteen inches; but I could not ascertain how many each female lays. The Indians do not seem to trouble their heads about such details; and it is difficult to make them understand numbers above ten or twelve. Generally, if they wish to say 20, 100, or 1000 they use a word importing a great number. Small numbers they indicate by holding up their fingers. Indians who have been bred and brought up near towns or settlements learn to count greater numbers, but it is rare to find one who can express a greater number than 100, except in general terms.

This tortoise is remarkable for its flatness of form: it is much the flattest tortoise, or turtle, I have seen, a very fine specimen not being more than ten inches high when drawn within its shell. Both shell and reptile seem to be heavier than in the sea-turtle. Formerly banks were completely covered with these creatures; but at the time of which I am writing, the numbers were beginning to show signs of the constant persecution to which they are subjected; and particularly of the enormous quantity of their eggs which are yearly destroyed.

I do not know that the cayman molests these tortoises; but it is a fact that the two reptiles are never seen on the same bank, or in the immediate neighbourhood of each other. In describing the Purus, I have wondered where caymans could obtain a constant and sufficient supply of food. On the Amazon I have heard the Indians say that this last-named reptile captures large fishes. I have not, myself, seen anything of the kind; but the Indian accounts are probably reliable. I have formed the opinion that the children of the wild are truthful and accurate when describing the creatures and objects with which they are surrounded and come into daily contact with; though I have no doubt, where their personal interests are concerned, they can, like Jones of Westoria Street, and Lazarus of Eastend Alley, tell a "crack" or two: this is, I believe, the cautious Scottish way of putting it.

On the north bank of the Amazon, between Yquitos and the mouth of the Ica, a distance of about 800 miles, there are a considerable number of towns, villages, and ranches which appear to be in a prosperous condition.

Some of these are miles inland from the river-bank ; and there are roads, or what in England we should call bridle-paths, leading some distance into the interior. All these, I believe, are maintained and kept open by private enterprise—no light, or inexpensive, work in a country "where you may stand and see the vegetation grow." The assertion has been made, and it is not devoid of truth; for there are plants here which I have proved by careful measurements will grow thirty-six inches in twenty-four hours! In fact, the growth and development of many of the herbal wonders of this region are so extraordinary and amazing that I have often imagined the line between animal and vegetable life is not so broad as is usually thought; especially when the habits of some plants are considered. For instance, there is a "fly-trap," or carnivorous shrub, in this region, which I frequently saw on cultivated, or cleared, ground, but never in the forest ; and which may have been imported here by human, or animal, agency—that I cannot say : but I have seen flies and butterflies of considerable size alight on this plant. Instantly the prickly-edged, hairy-surfaced leaf has closed on the unfortunate insects. Interested beyond measure in the development of the tragedy, I have put aside all other work and considerations to watch the end of this curious plant-action. In about two hours' time the leaf would begin to slowly unfold ; and another hour would elapse before it was fully open. The body of the fly, beetle, or spider would be completely consumed, only the wings, legs, and elytra remaining, and these broken and rent as if they had passed through the mandibles of a bird or lizard. The wings of butterflies would be crushed into minute fragments; and even the hard elytra of beetles broken into very small pieces.

I tried a number of experiments with this strange plant. A plump caterpillar was greatly enjoyed, and was very speedily consumed, the leaf beginning to reopen soon after an hour had elapsed, and scarcely any ejecta remaining. Some caterpillars and spiders are very lively and active, and I thought ought to be able to escape from the leaf; but they could not do so, although the action of the trap was anything but sudden or spring-like. I noticed that the spiders drew in their legs as if injured or in pain; and I came to the conclusion that the plant was poisonous. Upon putting my finger on a leaf I found that this was the case. The hairs with which its surface was covered gave quite a sharp sting, which, however, did not cause persistent irritation, for the moment I removed the finger the pain ceased. The leaf which I had touched seemed to be disturbed. It partly closed, slightly reopened, wavered a little, closing and unclosing; and then remained fixed in a partially closed state. Some hours afterwards, however, it was spread wide open, waiting for a victim.

Next I tried what a fat cockroach could do. I have a particular aversion to cockroaches, chiefly I think because they are so aggressive with their protective odour, inflicting it on everything eatable and drinkable that they can get at; so I was not sorry to discover that even this strong and evil-smelling creature could not escape the toils of Venus' love-trap (is it love-trap, or fly-trap?). He got his head and fore-quarters out, it is true; but the leaf closed on his fat and succulent rear parts, and he took his fate very quietly—paralysed or rendered comatose, I suppose. When Venus had done with him there was very little of him left besides head and whiskers.

A scorpion, an inch and a half long, had a better fate than he deserved. He contrived to get out of the trap very easily; but he did not seem to have admired his experiences. After he had made three or four escapes he seemed rather sickly: so I kept him, thinking he would die of Venus' poison; but he did not: so next day, as he appeared quite lively, and in a very aggressive mood, I let him go; to make a meal off some poor inoffensive worm, or grub, we may make pretty sure.

I have called this plant a Venus' fly-trap; but it was a very different growth from the plant commonly so called. Its great spike-protected leaves were four inches long, and one and a half wide; and it was of shrub-like growth and more than four feet high.

Along these reaches of the river is a sort of borderland. Peru and Ecuador are peopled by the descendants of Spaniards, Brazil by those of Portuguese—one race, in the opinion of persons best qualified to judge; but it is as great an insult to a Portuguese to tell him he is of the same stock as the Spaniard, as it is to compare a Japanese with John Chinaman. But in this region the two peoples are in close relationship, and as is usually the case in similar circumstances all the world over, they agree better in close proximity to each other than they do when a thousand miles apart. There are Portuguese in this quarter of Ecuador (or Peru as it now is), and Spaniards settled over the border of Brazil; and these people of both nationalities I found more amicable and hospitable than in any other parts of their countries:

not that I wish to make any kind of attack on the people of either country. Everywhere I met *some* persons who were mostly kindly disposed—and everywhere there are some churls, even in Merry England. Only, in a book of this description, it is desirable to state just exactly what were the experiences of a sojourner in the country—mine were decidedly mixed.

But one of the pleasantest episodes of my life on the Amazon is connected with a Spanish family in this region. They occupied a rancho on the little river Yano, Chimnath or Lerote, about twenty miles from the town of the last name, and sixteen from the north bank of the Amazon.

The Señor and his charming wife and daughters were unconventional people, who, exceedingly happy in their own family life (not by any means a common thing in this part of the world), seemed to have no other desire towards a stranger but to make him as happy and comfortable as themselves. I met the Señor by accident; and our friendly relations commenced at once, on the instant; and he induced me to remain a whole fortnight lying off the little private wharf, where the produce of his estate was put on board the lighters which conveyed it to Olivenca, the port at which it was usually shipped. My friend grew both coffee and cocoa very extensively, and had the largest plantation of bananas I have ever seen, all of which went to the United States; the trade in this fruit with England not then being so extensive as it is at the present time.

I resided at the house during this fortnight, and obtained a much-needed rest. My host was one of those amiable characters who are ever ready to enter into all the tastes and pursuits of their friends; and we were soon botanizing and specimen hunting together; and it was here that I first saw and studied the web-spinning, bird-eating spider, which is the one, I suppose, referred to by Madame Marian, a French lady, as long ago as 1720. It is not one of the largest of the bird-eating, or rather, killing, class, being about two inches in length of body, and three and a half inches the longest legs. It is very quick and nimble; and, I should think, very venomous, since its victims seem to be paralysed the moment it bites them. Birds are not its chief food; and it cannot master those which are as large as the English sparrow, and seems to be afraid of them. I have seen birds as big as starlings and sparrows break through the web, and escape before the spider attacked them; and others it has itself cut loose and let go. But very small ones, such as the gem-bird, ant-bird, and humming-bird, are often captured and destroyed, the spider sucking every drop of blood and moisture from the tiny bodies of its victims, and dropping the little carcasses, shapeless masses, except for wings and legs, clear of the web, where what remains of them is soon demolished by ants and beetles.

The web is not spread vertically, but horizontally, between two bushes, or tufts of herbage, so that birds darting upwards are prevented from rising. They do not seem to have sense to fly away laterally, or downwards, but keep bobbing upwards in an endeavour to break through the web, with the result that they become more and more entangled. Meanwhile the spider, on the first shake of his snare, rushes from his lurking-place on the *top* side and hangs partly over the edge to watch.

As soon as he sees that his prey is too much entangled to offer resistance, he darts upon it, burying his ugly fangs amongst its feathers, and with a quiver the little victim subsides into quietude, and, let us hope, a painless death. The bird-slayer proceeds much as does a common spider with a fly. He commences his feast on that part of the web where the prey was captured; but he soon spins a strong line or two around it, and holding these with his two hindmost legs, drags it to the lower side of his lurking-den, which is placed under the shelter of a leaf, or broad bough. Here he finishes his meal, and immediately cuts the remains loose, letting them drop to the ground beneath where we may see a whole heap of insects' wings, elytra, etc. For this spider preys largely on beetles and flies of all descriptions which are not too small to be worth its attention. At night-time many beetles, some of them quite large creatures, take wing, and go forth for an airing, some of them never to return to their accustomed hiding-places: for they are preyed on by a host of nocturnal birds and other animals abroad for protective purposes, or in search of a supper; and amongst others by this spider. Cockroaches fly about much at night-time; and I noticed from the remains under the webs that many of them find their way into the poisonous maw of this bird-trapping spider.

The web is closely woven like that of the house-spider, is of a very light grey colour and remarkably strong. I placed my hand under one or two, and found I had to use considerable exertion to break them up; and several portions stuck to my fingers so pertinaciously that I could not get rid of them without some trouble.

This spider is quite distinct from the ordinary bird-killing species, of which there are several varieties. The largest is a tremendous creature, with legs spreading, as I have already mentioned, over a foot of surface—laterally at any rate. It, also, is an active creature, capable of running and rushing about with so great activity that the details of its structure cannot be seen; and to the unaccustomed eyes it might be mistaken for a small animal. It can jump upwards from the ground a distance of at least a foot, and forwards three times that length. I have also seen it spring backwards several inches; and when it pauses, or moves slowly, it holds up its nippers in a threatening attitude; and seems prepared to show fight. Its colour is a deep black; but other kinds, or species, are grey, and some incline to a brown tint; while several, though apparently closely related to the bird-killers, are evidently too small and weak to capture such large prey. All these spiders, however, can master and carry, at a running pace, prey which weighs double their own weight. The large race—the true bird-killer—lives entirely, I think, on birds; at any rate, these form its chief food. It is a hunting-spider; and young, unfledged birds are those which form the bulk of its prey; though I have seen it suddenly leap upon old birds from the shelter of clusters of leaves. It likewise spins, or rather lines, with a silk-like web, dens under roots, boughs of trees, and in the crevices of rocks, from which it springs out upon any birds which come within range.

These spiders are so repulsive-looking that I have never cared to handle them; but I have held them down with a stick while I examined them; and have captured several, and kept them for a time. They would eat blood, and gorge themselves to so great an extent that they became torpid, and apparently slept for twenty-four hours; then they again became lively, and ready for another meal. They would not touch dead birds which I put into the cage; and the blood of large mammals seemed to upset them, though they took it eagerly. Live birds they literally rushed upon, and one of them took a mouse without hesitation, but seemed to have some difficulty in mastering it. I watched carefully whenever I had an opportunity, but never saw these spiders, in a wild state, attack mice, or any other small mammal. I found one running quickly with a bird the size of a thrush in its mandibles; which circumstance is a good illustration of its size and strength.

Their legs are very thick and strong, and give the animal the appearance of a crab. Those which I kept in confinement were so quarrelsome that they had to be separated. If I kept them long without food, their bodies diminished in size but not their legs, and they became gaunt and exceedingly irascible creatures. Those which I killed and stuffed shrank and warped out of shape; and those which were preserved in spirits lost their natural colours.

These spiders are most numerous in the thick forests growing between the river Ucayali and the Madeira. I never saw any in the countries westward of the Ucayali, nor in any mountainous district; they are inhabitants of thickly wooded, level country, and of Matto Grosso in particular. They do not seem to extend into the northern parts of South America: at least, I never saw any there. I think, however, the web-spinning species may extend its habitat a considerable distance northwards in the central parts of the continent; though there, and in some other parts of South America, it is replaced by a large species which is not a bird-eater.

I do not know the specific denomination of this spider, because I cannot find that it is figured, or preserved, anywhere in England; but its native name, on the upper Amazon, is teeteeroo; and among some tribes lower down the stream, pernon. But I have half a dozen other names jotted down, the languages of the Indians being quite different in parts of the country which are not even widely sundered.

The habits of the teeteeroo are those of a hunter; but a peculiarity of this species is that it is a carrion feeder. If a beetle, or a cockroach, be crushed and thrown down where these arachnids abound, one is pretty sure to be found in the morning feeding on the carcass. They also eat dead worms, slugs, and grubs: and I believe that in this case the term "eat" is the correct one: they actually devour the soft parts of the creatures I have named, and do not merely suck the juices. But they cannot of themselves kill beetles and cockroaches; and I have never succeeded in getting them to touch blood, meat, or dead or living birds; and when I enclosed one with a large centipede, this creature made short work with the spider; and had it doubled up and half eaten in a few minutes.

The body of a fine specimen of the teeteeroo (or titiru may be a better spelling of the word) is about an inch and a half in length; but the spread of the long and rather slender legs is tremendous, being quite eight inches. As may be imagined, the speed with which the creature can run is very great; and this faculty is, no doubt, more highly protective than colouring it pink, blue, or green could be!

The birds alluded to in my description of these spiders are American warblers; but, as is often the case in the creatures I have to incidentally mention, I cannot specifically identify them. I fully acknowledge any kindness I have received at the hands of naturalists and museum officials; but I have noticed that these gentlemen meet my suggestions that my creatures may be new species, or at least not known in England, with a pitying smile, and a decided, "*I don't* think so: *you* must be mistaken." It might be worth while to enquire what became of the Emperor of Brazil's collection of birds, reptiles, and insects. He received, from my hands, a great many specimens which were entirely new; and which, so far as I can ascertain, have never been seen in Europe.

CHAPTER XXI

ANOTHER FIVE HUNDRED MILES DOWN STREAM

SOON after passing Marco, a small town a little way back from the south bank, the Amazon makes a turn direct to the north, and for something under fifty miles the course is slightly serpentine. I could discover no adequate reason for this sudden change of direction. It is probably caused by a slight inclination of the land toward the north. Just before reaching Olivenca (ten or twelve miles) it sweeps round to due east again; and after a short reach to the north, commences a great bow-shaped bend of 800 miles or more. This is, roughly, the configuration of the river between long. 64° and 70° W. It winds and turns a little; but the bends are never very abrupt; and there are no long reaches. The width of the stream varies greatly in this course; and there are many islands, large and small; and throughout the entire distance, and far beyond it, the north bank of the river has an unbroken series of islands of peculiar formation. They are formed by the rivers joining the Amazon on the north shore being connected by *cross streams;* which, though not a feature confined to this region, is here more extensively developed than in any other part of the world. It means that from just below Tunantins to Ayrao on the Rio Negro, a distance approximating 500 miles, the whole of the north bank of the Amazon is formed of a series of great river-islands. Further down, this peculiar feature is continued on the south bank for another 150 miles; and, thereafter, at intervals, on both banks almost to the embouchure of the mighty stream.

It is not difficult to perceive the reason for this configuration of the country. It is occasioned by the extreme flatness of the land, which prevents the currents of the lesser rivers acquiring sufficient strength to cut their way straight through to the main stream; they consequently take a circular, or cross-country, course, and meeting other rivulets, become confluent with them.

These islands vary in size. There are fifteen large ones, besides those below the confluence of the Rio Negro. They are all of them very low and marshy, and almost without white population. On the whole of them there are only three or four small towns and villages; and from the mouth of the river Jutay to Pesquera near the embouchure of the Rio Negro appeared to our eyes an unbroken line of swampy forest on the north bank of the Amazon; and the south bank was of much the same character, though here and there we saw clusters of towns and villages. Town, in this region, is generally a relative term. It may consist of a few widely spread private houses, intermixed with the hovel-like residences of mean whites and half-breeds. There will be a few general stores in such a place, and perhaps a straggling street or two. A band of Indians is generally hutted on the outskirts of the town; and they live much as gypsies do in Europe. In many of the towns mentioned in these pages there is but a single church, which speaks volumes for the comparative poverty of these collections of houses in a country where priestly religion dominates every place and every class. The rich planters live in lordly haciendas, with what are really small towns of their servants and retainers; and a church and batch of priests of their own. Slavery is abolished—that is to say, no person may purchase fresh slaves; and those blacks who are still in bondage may, if they can, buy their liberty. So in 1884–5 the number of slaves was already greatly reduced; but such free negroes, and not a few *whites*, as had to work for their daily bread, were to all intents and purposes still slaves.

The islands referred to above are, to a great extent, impenetrable on account of the denseness of the forest growths and the moist conditions of the ground. In an extent of 500 miles of river course we actually passed a greater number of merchant ships than we saw individual Indians, the only people who can be said to really people these swampy tracts of land; few of which have a name. The chief of them are Mercicra, about 100 miles by 40; Codaya, 100 by 50; Pesquera, 150 by 100 in the broadest part; and Ile de Tupinambaranas, on the south bank, 150 by 50. Ile de Campinhas, also on the south bank, is smaller. These are the only large ones that I know to possess acknowledged names: though many of the others have local designations; and the Indians appear to know them all by appellations of some kind.

The swamps of the islands form a perfect paradise for caymans, and huge snakes of the boa and anaconda families; though I did not see any of these reptiles which exceeded twenty feet in length. Amongst other curiosities found here, I shot an iguana, or water-monitor, much more than six feet in total length. These enormous lizards are much sought after by all classes in this region; and fetch heavy prices for the tables of the rich. They are certainly delicious eating; and the flesh is as white, and as tender, as that of the cod-fish.

I found it possible, by means of the small streams, to get, in my canoe, well into the heart of some of the swamps: for the water is so deep that it has killed many of the trees, or prevented their growth. There was some danger in these little journeys, on account of the numerous caymans, which were unpleasantly tame. I feared they would upset my tiny craft: for, even when they decided to run, they waited until I was so close before they turned that I momentarily expected some scaly tail to fetch me a blow that would swamp me.

These terrible reptiles are much the largest crocodilians in America. When full grown a cayman measures at least twenty feet in length. I have seen a stuffed specimen which was twenty-five feet long, and several which exceeded twenty-two feet. I have shot one which was the last-named length. No effort seems to be made, by the people of the land, to reduce the numbers of these dangerous reptiles; and they are the most numerous of all land animals throughout the Amazonian valley. For though amphibians, they spend much of their time out of the water. I have sailed past mud-bank after mud-bank, each of which had from sixty to 200 caymans lying asleep upon it; and I have seen as many as 1000 in a single herd. They are so little afraid of a shot that a rifleman may pick off several before the herd takes alarm. They are disposed to be aggressive; and are credited, all along the Amazon, with daring attacks on human beings; such as rushing into the streets of waterside towns, and bearing off men, women, and children. I have mentioned seeing many mutilated persons; but I am disposed to question the likelihood of caymans coming ashore to seize victims. In the first place the streets of Amazonian towns are very narrow—only six to eight feet wide (so built to shade off the sun's rays), and I cannot believe that a cayman could turn in so narrow a space, especially with a victim in its jaws. Again, I have demonstrated many times that a cayman cannot overtake a human being; and supposing it to surprise a decrepit person, it can easily be avoided owing to the difficulty it displays in turning at a sharp angle.

Amongst the weird and loathsome things of these island swamps are slugs eight inches long, and snails as big as a man's fist; there are, also, large earthworms; and a host of creatures one would rather not meet, amongst which undesirable acquaintances the mosquito is neither the least nor the last. I think this is almost the first time I have mentioned this abominable little fly; the truth being that I have written so much about it in former books that I was ashamed to recur to it here, lest I should have the charge made that I was hard up for a subject. The fact is, however, that I never spent a day on the Amazon, or any of its tributaries, in which I was not at some hour, or all hours, of the twenty-four driven to a desperation verging on lunacy by the torments of these hateful pests. I have always been an object of particular persecution on the part of mosquitoes; and have sometimes been reduced to such a pitiable state that I could not see until the swelling of the face had subsided.

I have somewhere read that the mosquito never rises above a certain height; and that, therefore, a high wall, or a thick grove of trees, will keep them back. I do not know where this writer made his observations—it certainly was not in South America, unless he was a blind man. There is nothing under a mile high in this country that they will not get over, or under, or through; and their cursed whining buzz, like the top note of a tuning-fork gone wrong, is the warning, not that they are going to do the deed, but that they *have done it*, as you will speedily discover: for a peculiarity of this detestable thing is that you do not feel the bite until it begins to itch—and such an *itch!*

In the Great Dismal Swamp, and other parts of the southern States, I have seen these flies so thick together that they looked like clouds of dust: here in the forests of Amazonia they were actually in clouds so dense that the lower parts of the tree-trunks could not be seen.

There are three great northern tributaries of the Amazon that I cannot describe here. They are the Putumayo, or Ica; the Caqueta, or Japura; and the Rio Negro. It is with regret that I pass them by, especially as they drain an immense tract of the great Amazonian plain; but there is no help for it. A cursory glance at them would be disappointing; and the country they pass through is so wonderful, so full of changing lights and shades, so to say, that if I attempted to do them even moderate justice I should double the length of this book. But I hope I see a light gleaming through the forest—I trust that the success of this poor effort of mine to give, at least, a dim conception of the majesty of glorious Amazonia may be so far good as to encourage the publishers to consider a companion work on the sister river—the Orinoco.

For the two wonderful streams of South America, the Amazon and the Orinoco, are sisters—*they are linked together* (a natural feature unique in itself—at any rate, on anything approaching so vast a scale) by the Casiquiare: so that a boat entering the mouth of one of these great rivers could proceed to explore two-thirds of the whole South American continent; and if the supposed craft did not draw more than two feet of water, I think I could very easily show that it might traverse at least 100,000 miles of waterways! Could anything on this earth be more wonderful? And what would be seen—what discovered—in the course of such a voyage as this?—a world which it would take many volumes to describe.

There are spots on the Amazon, especially where many small islands in mid-stream cluster together, where the river widens out to the dimension of a lake: indeed such expansions as those at the confluence of the Jurua (ten to sixteen miles when the river is in full flow); opposite the town of Cassara (six to eight miles); and abreast of Coary (sometimes twenty miles), undoubtedly are lakes. The lake of Codaya, really an inundation of the north bank, sixty miles below Coary, is not so broad as the Amazon off the last-named town.

There are many small lakes on both banks which may be described as permanent inundations. They would probably drain away to a great extent if they got an opportunity of doing so: but the climate of Amazonia is as unique as her mighty river. The main stream, right across the continent, is never more than three or four degrees south of the Equator, and at its true mouth right under it; yet the heat is not so great as in other tropical regions; and there is no real rainy season—no marked division of season at all. Rain comes at any time so far as months, or quarters, are concerned; though night-time is nearly always the clearest—moonlight here is anything but a "lesser light" of heaven—it is visible glory. Storms, and torrential rains, usually occur in the afternoons, between three and five o'clock; and often recur day after day for considerable periods of time—weeks, if not months. If there are intervals between these storms they are very short—three or four days at most. There is no dry season. Rain is never long absent from the Amazon valley. Without question, it is the vast forest that fosters the downfall of wet—that controls the climate of Matto Grosso.

The seasons of the valley are wonderfully like those of Europe: that is, the majority of the trees blossom in the same months they do in England, and fructify in autumn—September to December. There are incidental variations, of course. Some trees and shrubs are continuously blooming: others, like the coco shrub, bear fruit several times a year: but, on the whole, May, June, and July are the flowering months, September, October, and November the months when fruits most abound. Creatures which estivate (take a prolonged summer sleep—synonymous with the hibernation of the north) in other parts of South America, do not do so here. The cayman is abroad all the year round; though in Bolivia, and other parts, north and south, it buries itself in mud to pass the "dry season." Iguanas, frogs, toads, snakes, and tortoises, as well as many insects, etc., do the same; but these classes of animals are in full life and vigour at all times in the Amazonian region; and what is as remarkable, they attain their maximum size here: there are no such tortoises, serpents, lizards, and caymans elsewhere as there are in Amazonia.

By the by, I never learned the origin of the word "cayman," which some writers spell "caiman." It is not an existing native name of the creature, which is an alligator. I have many Indian names noted down, that which is most in use, apparently because it has been adopted by the Portuguese, being "yacara." None of them come nearer to "cayman" than this. In some tribes they use the same word to designate a cayman, an iguana, and a small lizard: others use the same word, with a prefix to denote the various species.

It is scarcely necessary to mention that frogs abound in all the marshes and swamps of this region. I do not know that I am justified in making the distinction; but I invariably use the word marsh for open ground, destitute of trees, which is sodden, and partially covered with water. Swamp is inundated forest land. The bull-frog, and other varieties, inhabit both marsh and swamp; and there is in this region the largest tree-frog I have seen. It is of an olive-green hue with black irregular markings, and bright yellow on the lower parts. Several specimens which I captured weighed about six ounces each. They are bright-eyed, but not very active creatures; and as they keep at a great height above the ground are not easy to find, especially as they do not seem to be numerous. I should think this is a bad place for tree-frogs, even when protectively coloured; there are so many snakes in the trees; and other creatures to which a plump frog would be a *bonne bouche*. I may instance the turkey-buzzard, the harpy-eagle, the king-vulture; and some others which love to harbour in the trees of the densest swamps in most of the Amazonian forests. As I have not said much about birds of prey, the condor excepted, this may be a good place to describe a few which ought to be mentioned.

We will take the turkey-buzzard first. A weird bird, of unpleasant appearance and filthy habits, is this avian. I have already insisted that no terrestrial creature, which feeds on living prey, has an enemy other than man. The turkey-buzzard has not even to reckon "order Primates, genus *homo*," a foe: for everywhere in South America it is protected by popular opinion, if not by the law, as a useful scavenger. There is no doubt that it obtained its name from its superficial likeness to a turkey when viewed from a little distance. In one of the good old natural histories, published a hundred years ago, decades before the scientists and evolutionists had begun to chip the shells of their unhatched eggs, it is narrated how a naval officer, a lover of good feeding, serving on board a ship that had long been without a supply of fresh meat, saw some of these birds from the deck of his vessel. Hastening to his captain, he begged for leave to go ashore and secure the valuable prize. The captain granted permission; and the officer, hastening ashore, shot at the lordliest and fattest of the "black gobblers," as he called them. Running up to secure his game—"phew!" He dropped it in disgust, discovering his mistake, and intolerant of its stench at one and the same moment.

That it gives forth a very offensive odour I can vouch

from personal knowledge; and when a flock of them comes between your nobility and the wind, you may perceive this "protection" from a considerable distance. Squire Waterton used to dissect them. Some silly goby in search of a castigation asked the Squire how he could handle "such filthy things." "Why shouldn't I?" demanded the Squire. "Can't you smell how they stink?" "So does an alderman after a City feast," was the cool retort.

I have never, myself, dissected an alderman, not having courage enough to defy the police, legal, and Ward-mote regulations made for the protection and conservation of these civic feasters; to say nothing of my being a victim of that inherent fear of the unknown which most of us dread; and consequently thinking that it must be a dreadful thing to fall into the hands, or jaws, or claws of a "Ward-mote," and the "liverymen" who guard the fearsome beast. But I have no doubt the Squire knew; and that we may take the fact on his authority.

Here, on the Amazon, turkey-buzzards live mostly in the trees; but they seem to know that they have little to dread from man or beast; and are so tame that they may be approached, anywhere, to within a yard or two. They regularly visit the streets of the towns on the river's banks, and rows of them may be seen sitting on the parapets of the houses, which are, so far as I can remember, all flat-roofed. This is in the early morning: for the turkey-buzzards, like all other living creatures in this region, take a siesta during the heat of the day. What becomes of them between ten o'clock and evening-time I do not know. In common with every living creature, except the gnats, and the butterflies, they hide away somewhere; probably in the midst of dense foliage at the tops of the trees: at any rate, they are not discoverable in the middle of the day; nor are the monkeys, the parrots, macaws, and the toucans, or any other living thing of importance, the before-mentioned gnats, or mosquitoes, excepted: and these contrive to make themselves of very great importance, indeed, to people who do not consider bulbous noses and bunged-up eyes inconsiderable trifles.

When the turkey-buzzards are at home—that is when they are gorged to the extent of being unable to swallow any more (and I have often seen them with food hanging from the gapes of their beaks)—their favourite perches are the branches of dead trees, or those which are leafless, and at no great height from the ground. As I have said, you may approach very close to them; but if you get too near, they become restless, eye you with suspicious glances, droop their wings, shuffle along the boughs to get farther away from you, utter a kind of hoarse hiss to show their displeasure; and if they are very full, begin to vomit their food; not, as the "popular" natural historians assert, as a means of intimidation, or offensiveness, but to get rid of a weight which prevents them from rising and flying away. They seem to visit the ground as little as possible, and only for the purpose of feeding, or searching for food. I may have already mentioned my opinions about the sustenance of carrion-feeding creatures; but the subject will bear further consideration. Death reigns over every living creature; and all the excited kickings, ravings, and dogmatic theories of the scientist cannot abolish *that fact*. But what becomes of the billions of living things that perish annually? The evolutionists do not tell us much about this. Darwin saw a guanacos' cemetery somewhere down south; and Sinbad found a nest of elephants' bones: but these are isolated cases. In both North and South America, in the time I roamed about them, five or six large mammals must have died annually on every square mile of wilderness—and this I consider a very moderate calculation. But one of the rarest of sights was that of the carcass of a wild creature which had met a natural death. How are dead wild animals disposed of? Do they form the chief portion of food of the carrion-eating portion of them? Probably they do: for whenever I have shot a large animal, carrion vultures of all sorts have assembled to feast on the offal: and although, as I have said, one beast or bird of prey will not attack another for the purpose of feeding on it, vultures will feast on the putrid carcass of a puma or any other animal without reference to genus or class. That I admit: and I have also seen an animal of the polecat tribe devour the contents of the stomach of a similar mammal which had been ripped open in a contest over prey: but did anybody ever see one hawk strike another; or a tiger devour a lion, or even a jackal? I challenge the whole world of "scientific systematists" to bring *undeniable* evidence of such a thing in wild animals living under normal conditions. These remarks apply to the higher vertebrates only. Fishes and reptiles devour one another without reference to preying habits: in fact, with them the general rule is "all is fish that comes to the net."

The turkey-buzzard, and most other vultures, devour living prey of a sort—the sort being such as requires no rending or tearing: for these birds do not seem to be able to rip flesh from the bones until it is rotten. I have seen vultures devour rats, mice, young birds, dead fish, snakes, frogs, toads, lizards, eels, and young domestic poultry: and a favourite feast with the buzzards is the newly hatched tortoises and alligators, of which they consume thousands, visiting the sand-banks for this purpose. All the small fry enumerated above is devoured just as it is caught, without any preliminary killing that I could observe. No doubt the gastric juices of *Rhinogryphus aura* are highly soporific!

Though all the older naturalists called this bird a buzzard, and the name still sticks to it, it is undoubtedly a vulture. It is clothed, like a croque-mort, in a suit of rusty black. The cadaverous-looking face is turkey-red, and sometimes dirty yellow; for there are several varieties of the bird, which are classed as distinct species; but I have some grounds for believing that they interbreed. The nest is placed in a tree, from twelve to twenty feet above the ground, and is here, on the Amazon, composed of twigs, roots of plants, and stems of creepers, etc., and resembles a large rook's nest, but is of looser construction. The eggs, three in number, are in curious contrast to the bird: for they are beautifully blotched and flecked with various shades, light and dark, of reddish brown. I have seen it stated that the turkey-buzzard does not make a nest, but lays its eggs on the ground. Wherever I have found the bird it was a swamp-haunting and swamp-breeding species; and it does, in any case, make a nest.

Waterton knew this bird well; and held a controversy with Audubon about it, the Frenchman insisting that it found its prey (carrion) by sight. The Squire knew better; but, as is usual, the man of sound knowledge was thrust aside to make room for the ignoramus, whose views have been generally adopted—by the armchair naturalists. The truth, however, cannot be overridden: it is by the sense of smell, not sight, that all vultures find their food. I have placed that beyond even the shadow of doubt; but all I have to say here on the subject is to ask, "How could a carcass be found in an Amazon forest by *sight?* Go and look at the country and then come and tell me it is possible; and I will give you a Caudle lecture that will last you for the remainder of your life.

As to smell. In the north, my party perceived the odour of a burning forest that was afterwards proved to be sixty miles away. Darwin says the scent of the skunk can be easily detected a distance of five miles; and I have known a party of Indians *smell a town* (quite a small one) which was fifteen miles off: so there can be no difficulty about scent and distance: for all the systematists are satisfied that the senses of animals are far more acute than those of man. I believe they are—sometimes.

I have chosen the turkey-buzzard for particular description; but there are other vultures in the Amazonian valley, notably the king-vulture, one of the handsomest of the family: were it not for the condor I should write—*the* handsomest. It is a much larger and bulkier bird than the turkey-buzzard; and may be described as parti-coloured, though the white portions of the plumage are deeply tinged with yellowish, or buff. There are a number of excrescences round the base of the beak, forming a kind of comb, and this, and the naked face and throat, are coloured with brilliant red and blue hues. The bird is remarkable amongst vultures for its bright and expressive eye: and, in fact, it is a condor in general appearance and habits, except that it inhabits forests, and not lofty mountain ranges. It is not a common bird on the Amazon; but is more prevalent farther north, especially along the course of the Orinoco. In some books it is described as a solitary bird. This is a mistake. I know that none of the American vultures are of solitary habits: but the king-vulture is certainly not so gregarious as most of them. This seems to be owing to its restricted numbers: for it is nowhere an abundant bird. Books assert that it spreads north as far as Texas, and other southern States of the north. I can only say that I have not seen it farther north than the south part of Mexico, where it is anything but common.

It spreads rather widely in tracts which it haunts; but there are usually about forty in a flock; and they are as tenacious as rooks in their love of particular trees; always roosting and breeding in the same grove. Like the condors, they make but little nest, and lay two, and often three, eggs, which are light pearl-grey in colour, without spots, and except that they are smaller, greatly resemble those of condors. The nest is a scanty collection of rotten sticks, decayed bark and vine-stems, without any pretence to lining. It is placed in a great fork of a tree, usually where the trunk makes its first bifurcation, some forty to sixty feet above the ground; and the tree selected is always sufficiently large to completely conceal both nest and bird when sitting.

In general habits and food, I could not perceive that the king-vulture differs much from other American members of its genus. They are all fond of taking great circular flights at an immense height above the earth; so that they sometimes appear as mere specks in the sky, and perhaps disappear entirely; but as they utter no cries when on the wing, it is difficult to make sure that this is the case. Like that of the condor, and, indeed, all the vultures, their flight is exceedingly beautiful and graceful. It is not an exaggeration to say that it is majestic. One never sees these birds flying in a straight line, or taking a journey from place to place. They wheel, and perform evolutions, gradually ascending higher and higher, and when they are tired, descending in the same way. I do not believe that any of the American vultures, except, perhaps, the condor, ever go more than a few miles from home. Their flights seem to be chiefly undertaken for amusement; but as their wheelings are over a considerable area of ground it is possible that they are in search of the scent of their prey; I am the more disposed to think that this is a correct surmise, as, when watching them from the boat, I have seen them suddenly descend, and alight on the tree-tops, from whence they rapidly dropped to the ground in twos and threes. These remarks apply to the turkey-buzzards, as well as to the king-vultures. I have never actually proved that there was carrion under the trees where these birds alighted: for on the two or three occasions when I attempted to reach the spot I found the forest quite impenetrable. What I can say, and that positively, is, that the vultures could no more see the ground than I could. Also, I have had the turkey-buzzards come trooping up when I have slain animals in forests so dense that a glimpse of the sky could not be obtained in days of travel.

I have, once or twice, seen the black vulture on the Amazon, viz. near Fonteboa and Cassara, and a few miles above Miranas on the river Jutay; and also on the Madeira, between Borba and Missao: but it is not a common bird in this region. It is the smallest, and least vulture-like, of the American members of the genus; and is called a crow in the United States—a bird which it resembles in general appearance, and the colour of its eggs, which differ entirely from those of other species. The bird is evidently not a true vulture; or is well on in its "evolution"; in which case, where are its *immediate ancestors?* Not in America, I am prepared to assert.

I should mention, perhaps, that the turkey-buzzards not only pick a carcass clean when it is sufficiently decomposed; but carry away the bones likewise; so that I have known the decayed body of a jaguar, a tapir, or a deer completely disappear in the course of one day; and I have seen them toying with the smaller bones on the boughs, and in their nests. They do not seem to be able to carry the larger bones up to their breeding-places; but there are generally some animal remains on the nests; such as smaller bones, hair and fragments of skin, carried thither probably for the purpose of feeding their young; though I believe that most vultures, like pigeons, feed their progeny direct from the stomach.

There are several varieties of eagles in all parts of the Amazonian valley, mostly of the crested kinds, or harpy-eagles. These may at once be distinguished from the vultures by their appearing singly, or in pairs, which the last-named birds never do. Otherwise there is not so mighty a difference between the two classes as the book-men try to make out. The common crested eagle, *Thrysaëtus harpyia;* and the Guianan variety, *Morphuus guianensis*, for instance, might both be taken for vultures if seen sitting on a tree at thirty yards distance; and they are both dear lovers of a bit of putrid flesh, though they do not go to work systematically on carrion, like their near relatives the condors and vultures. How closely they resemble these is proved by the circumstance that the older naturalists, before the advent of Messrs. Huxley and Darwin, and their host of second-fiddlers, always described the condor as an eagle. But I am no slave of old school or new; and I quite admit they made a mistake on this point. The condor is a vulture with some strong resemblances to the eagles. It, however, goes in flocks, which no true eagle, or falcon, ever does.

Next to the condor, the crested eagle is the largest bird of prey in America, slightly exceeding in size the golden eagle of the north. I have shot them of about forty inches in length, with stronger-looking, bulkier bodies than other birds of the genus; but I cannot tell of which sex they were. In most eagles there is a considerable difference between the males and the females, the last being the larger.

In spite of their size, these birds do not prey on animals so large as those generally attributed to fall victims to their rapacity. They may occasionally pounce on the straggling young of deer, monkeys and peccaries; they dare not meddle with these when their mothers are at hand to defend them: for they have neither the strength nor the courage of the golden eagles. They may have been seen feasting on the carcasses of these animals slain by other creatures, or by accident—the terrible hail-storms of this country being responsible for the deaths of many large animals every year; and of men, too, who fail to find shelter in time. Horses and oxen, to say nothing of lesser cattle, are often killed by hail-stones. The yarns about harpy-eagles killing animals two or three times their own weight—are yarns: and that is all that need be said about it. As to the Primitive Peruvians of philosophic fame calling it "the bird of the wolf"; pray, where did the wolves come from? One may travel from Paramaribo to Tierra del Fuego, and remain innocent of such an animal.

I must hasten to mention one or two more birds that I think deserve a word of notice; though even to give a bare list of those that characterize the Amazonian region would take up half the pages of a volume.

Often at night-time I should be startled by the sound of a burst of insane laughter, followed by a mournful wail. Knowing what strange noises are emitted by the goat-suckers, or night-jars, of this region, the "willy-come-goes," *Chordeiles virginianus*; and "whip-poor-wills," *Antrostomus vociferus*, and a small host of others which I could not identify, I took but little notice, at first, of this unpleasant laughter, attributing it to one of these night-jarring gentry. One early morning, however, I was awoke by the horrible "Ah! ah! ah! Oh! oh! oh! Eh! eh! eh!" close over my head. I was very tired, and very cross at being disturbed; and I reached for my gun, exclaiming, "I'll give you something to laugh over, my little friend." Looking up, I perceived, by the moonlight, that "my little friend" was a great hulking owl, as big as a buzzard, perched not twelve feet above me. As I moved, it flew off into the shadows of night, but did not travel far: for presently I was saluted with a renewed outburst of maniacal merriment. I heard this bird often afterwards, and saw it once or twice, always in the middle of the night, or very early morning; and once I tried to shoot it, but missed in the uncertain light. So far as I can tell, it was a species of eagle-owl. These birds haunt the banks of the Amazon; and I have seen one or two fine specimens which were killed by other persons.

The common "horned owl," of precisely the same species as those found in England, was shot by me on the lower Amazon: and I have found this bird in widely separated districts in both great divisions of the American continent; having frequently seen it in Canada, several of the eastern, western, and southern States; and in Brazil and Bolivia. A third species, the common screech-owl of the northern States, completes the list of owls I have found in the Amazonian valley; but this genus of birds is not numerously represented in this region. The screech-owl cannot be mistaken. Those who have been used to its atrocious noises in the woods of the north will bless it wherever heard.

I attempt no description of the towns on the Amazon. Towns and cities are not in my line: besides, there is (or was at the time I visited them) nothing particular to describe concerning them. Some few were showing signs of eventually becoming places of importance, under the influence of Yankee and Teutonic push and energy—the Briton, I am sorry to record, was not conspicuous in any of these places.

Those who have seen a Spanish town may picture the urban collections of houses along the banks of the Amazon—they are all faithful reproductions of the old-world towns and cities—the houses and walls generally white-washed, or yellow-washed, but occasionally coloured with fancy tints. All buildings are flat-roofed; and as serious seismic disturbances are unknown along the course of the river, they are often built higher, and more substantially, than houses situated along the line of the Andes. Barra de Rio Negro, commonly called Manaos, the capital of the great province of the Amazonas, is situated a short distance up the Rio Negro; and with Obydos and Para, were the only places of real importance, and trade on a large scale, in 1884.

We sailed for days between forest-covered shores without seeing a town, house, clearing, or break of any kind; and unless we chanced to meet a ship or steamer, were to all intents and purposes in as isolated and wild a position as Orellana, when he dropped down this magnificent river 800 years ago. Some of the towns, also, are invisible from the centre of the stream, or nearly so, being situated a little way inland to avoid the swamps and seasonal inundation. What towns there are on the upper and central portions of the Amazon are frequently placed in groups, and very close together. This is the case with Santiago and San Borgia; San Ignacio and Barranon; Nauta and Omaguas; Yquitos and Puca-Allpa; Loreto, Tabatinga, and Marco; Cassara, Magueira, and Ega.

Ega, sometimes called Teffe, because it is situated on the river Teffe, a few miles from the south bank of the Amazon, is the place which the naturalist Bates made his head-quarters. I went up there especially to make enquiries about him; and to my surprise could find nobody who remembered him. There were no Indians living near the town, though a few were roving about the streets. I applied for information to some of the older men: no; they had never heard of Bates, or any other Englishman; nor could any of the head inhabitants, or priests, remember having seen him. Strange, and sad, that a worker in the paths of peace and knowledge should be so soon forgotten in the very place that he made the centre of his enquiries: and not very encouraging to those who follow in his footsteps. But, alas! I know something about this!

CHAPTER XXII

THE LOWER REACHES OF THE RIVER AMAZON

WE are drawing near the end of our journey, and a few general observations may be permitted. Throughout the whole course of the Amazon below Nauta there is not a single hill, or rise of the ground, on either bank, of sufficient importance to deserve particular notice. I cannot give the geological formations, that being a branch of knowledge in which I am, unfortunately, very deficient; but on the rivers Madeira and Tapajos; and at a few isolated spots that I have visited, a kind of granitic formation crops up in the form of isolated hills of no great elevation: and there are some heights, approximating mountains in extent, in the province of Para, which, it may be claimed, are within the Amazonian radius.

Of course, I am writing now of the main stream only, and excluding those mountain systems already described as the Cordillera Grande, and the plateaus of the Araguay and the Upper Tapajos. A few specimens which I collected within twenty miles of the banks of the Amazon proved to be of no particular interest or value. They were mostly crystals of aqueous origin, some of them brightly coloured. A green feldspar and a green madrepore were obtained on the upper reaches of the Purus, and on the tablelands just mentioned;

and on some other streams I obtained a few rubies of small value. So far as I could perceive there are no precious metals or stones in any of the waters of the great plain of Matto Grosso. What there may be in the upper waters of the Madeira, and the Araguay, and some of the smaller tributaries, I cannot tell; but I suspect a good deal.

There is certainly gold in the Cordillera Grande; but I could not find a rich vein. Probably it runs six to eight ounces to the ton of quartz: a company with capital would, therefore, do well, provided that John Portuguese granted a reasonable concession.

There are several spots in these highlands where there are diamonds; and I should be surprised if other precious stones were not found—perhaps of more value than diamonds: for I am not sure that these last are of good quality, though I think they may be of large size. I saw a good deal during the time I spent in Central Brazil; and I am not sure that some persons are not quietly making a little market for themselves. These people are of my opinion, that if the Government and the priests (who rule everything in Brazil, though they have not so much open authority as in Ecuador) learn of the knowledge that is in private possession at present, it will mean the effectual repression of individual enterprise. I have been watching for years for developments; but have heard nothing yet. This is surprising; and means that good prospects have suddenly failed, or a secret has been marvellously well kept.

To come back to mid-stream on the Amazon. I have read that after the rainy season the current on this great river runs four miles an hour. I have already said that there is no real rainy season in the Amazon valley. After storms and prolonged heavy rains there is certainly a great increase in the strength and rapidity of the current; but I do not think it is ever so much as four miles per hour, except, perhaps, after the waters of the Tapajos have joined it. All the great tributaries cause a very perceptible increase in the strength of the flow; but this gradually subsides as it runs downwards towards the sea. However, the great depth throughout the course of the Amazon, and its remarkable width, give an enormous body of water, the force of which is scarcely graspable by the human mind. At its mouth it has the tremendous power to push the sea back and aside; and I have myself drunk water drawn up over the side of a ship sixty miles from land, which was as clear and pure as spring water, and had not the slightest brackish flavour. At the meeting of the fresh water with the ocean, the roar and turmoil are equal to those which occur when a hurricane rages. The Amazonian current has not entirely lost its force 200 miles, in a straight line, out to sea.

In certain states of the weather a bore is apt to rush up the river. I saw one which was six feet high, and did terrible damage to small craft, swamping many boats, though as these were nearly all manned by Indians, half-breeds and negroes, who swim as if born to the water, the loss of life was not very great. This bore was felt as high up the Amazon as Serpa, which is only thirty miles below the mouth of the Madeira. High tides are felt as high up as this place; and ordinary tides to above Villa Nova, which is more than 400 miles from the mouth of the great river.

The favourite, and acknowledged, chief entrance to the Amazon is by the southern branch, very improperly called the Para river. The upper, or northern, fork is the true mouth; but it is blocked by a great number of large and small islands. The two branches embrace the large island of Marajo, or Joannes, which has a greater surface area than Wales. Actually the mouth of the river forms two great gulfs; and many miles before the sea is reached, and while the water is still perfectly fresh, a person on board a vessel in mid-stream cannot see either bank. These are low, it is true; but there are trees on them which are at least 150 feet high. I have several times had to use the expression "largest in the world," in describing objects and attributes in connection with the Amazon; and I must once more resort to a superlative. From Para downwards to the sea-coast, a distance of about eighty miles, it is not possible to see the opposite bank of the river, the stream varying in width from twenty to forty miles. On the other side of Marajo island, the true mouth of the Amazon, it is more than 120 miles. These then (the mouths of the Amazon and Para) are, beyond comparison, the two widest, and strongest, fresh-water currents in the world. At some distance off the coast the rush of fresh water is met by several cross-currents of the sea. The turmoil occasioned by these has just been described.

All the islands at the mouth of the Amazon were originally covered with dense forest; but their proximity to the sea made the timber valuable, as it was easily accessible; and much of it has been felled. All the larger islands are well watered. On Marajo there is a river exceeding 100 miles in length, besides nearly a dozen streams of twenty miles and upwards.

So vast a body of water as that contained in the Amazon and its tributaries would naturally be the home of many strange creatures. Amongst other animals worthy of notice this great fluvial system is the home of a species of dolphin, which is peculiar to it. Unfortunately, I did not see a great deal of this animal; but I think I may safely say that it was always confined to the lower reaches of the Amazon and some of its great tributaries. Most of my information about it was gathered from the Indians, and the people of the land. This I checked, as far as possible; but I do not like relying on the assertions of ignorant people, especially of those of uninformed coloured men—they are so very apt to say what they think you will be pleased to hear—true, or untrue.

However, this much is certain about the Amazonian dolphin—that it is so much like the common porpoise in appearance and habits and size, "breaching," or partially leaping from the water, like that animal, that I lost several good opportunities of studying its habits, I not knowing, at the time, that the river was the home of a special species of dolphin.

There seem to be several varieties of this animal; and it is asserted locally that none of them ever frequent the tidal portions of the Amazon. They ascend the Madeira as high as the first falls; but there are none above this point. As there are some in the Tapajos these must be a distinct variety, or it cannot be correct that it does not enter the tideway. I did not see any in the Purus; but a strange creature momentarily seen here, and which my man insisted was a mermaid, was probably a siren, or manati. Dolphins are found in the Rio Negro and Orinoco, and in the Amazon as high up as fifty or sixty miles above Nauta. None were seen in the upper reaches of the river, nor in the head-waters of any of the great tributaries. They swim together in herds of ten to forty, and are not numerous in any part of the river, as the Portuguese fishermen persecute them very much, as there is a market for their flesh and oil; and also because they devour large numbers of fish.

In length these dolphins do not much exceed six feet; but they are bulky animals, and are said to often weigh more than 300 pounds English. I was surprised to find that the Indians neglected so valuable an animal; and concluded that they disliked dolphin meat, or had a prejudice against it. Since leaving the country I have heard that this is the case.

Concerning the manati, or siren; this is a rare animal in the Amazon. I believe it was seen in the Purus, and it certainly was in the Javari; and in the tidal stream of the Amazon as low as the mouth of the Tapajos. It is a very different creature from the dolphin, though it is about the same size and length as that animal. If I were an evolutionist I should describe it as "a specialized seal"; but I know nothing about its cranial bumps, or dentition; and cannot say if it be mono-cusped, or bi-cusped, or tri-cusped, or not cusped at all; but I can tell that the fishermen of this region consider it a prize, and never lose an opportunity of capturing it, with the inevitable result that it is well on the way to extinction. While the dolphin certainly does destroy great quantities of fish, the siren is a most harmless animal, and strictly herbivorous. It has a very thick hide of a dark grey colour, which is wrinkled something like that of one of the great pachyderms, and sparsely sprinkled with very fine bristles, which stand upright. The common assertion that dolphins and sirens abound in the Amazonian region, and especially in the upper reaches, is incorrect, or was so in the years 1884–5.

Tons of fish captured in the Amazon, chiefly near its mouth, are annually exported to the United States, as well as to many other places in South America, Mexico, and the West India Islands. Some of it is previously cured; but great quantities are sent away alive in boats provided with wells for the purpose. Thousands of United Staters visit the towns on the lower reaches to enjoy the splendid fishing the river affords: for the vast quantities captured have not, as yet, produced a perceptible diminution of numbers.

But this trait of Uncle Sam of going abroad to catch fishes in other men's ditches was fated, many years afterwards, to tie me in a bit of a knot, as Pat would say. It happened thus: there are two very large fish in the Amazon, the tarpon and the arapaima. Now, Sam calls the tarpon the "king-herring." This must not be confounded with "the king-of-the-herrings," a fish which "belongs to quite another genus," and has no resemblance whatever to the tarpon; being, in fact, Mr. Banks's riband fish *Regalecus banksi;* while the tarpon is *Megalops atlanticus.* But all this I did not know in 1884, any more than I knew there were "authorities on fishes"; so when I was invited to join a party of affable southern gentlemen in a fishing excursion, and we caught an arapaima, *Arapaima gigas*, weighing nearly 500 pounds, and several tarpons of 89, 182, 168, and 222 pounds respectively, I was naturally much interested and surprised, never having seen or heard of these fish before. But these gentlemen, like myself, were not authorities and scientists; and when one of them remarked, "We call these fish king-herrings in Louisiana," and I could find no other names, native or otherwise, for them but "tarpon" and "arapaima," I naturally described them under these appellations: I did even worse. Having no fear of Cæsar before mine eyes, I *classed them together!* and sent an account of the fishing for them to the leading sporting paper! There, fortunately, my misdoing received a check. The gentleman who presides over the fishes at the British Museum saw my article, and sent a correction to the paper; and I now know more about *gigas* and *megalops* than I ever knew before. I am greatly indebted to the gentleman who so kindly corrected my error.

But among the things I learned was that the tarpon "is now becoming well known." Is it? Twenty years ago, and much more recently, I could not find anybody who had heard of the fish; and I do not believe that there was a museum in Europe that possessed a specimen of it; or a "natural history book" which contained the name! [I should like to know who "megalopsed" it.]

If the fish is becoming "well known" it is surprising that errors about it are spreading so rapidly. Among the things concerning the tarpon which require correcting are the assertions that it affords "excellent sport," leaping six feet out of the water when hooked. It does nothing of the kind. It is one of the tamest fish that swim. In America ladies habitually kill it: a child might do so. It usually sinks to the bottom when hooked: if it runs, it does so in a confused and uncertain way, turning frequently at right angles, and is soon exhausted. It may struggle a little when lifted into the boat; but often it does not even do this. I have seen many caught; have caught many myself: and not infrequently a forced run of half an hour will kill your fish without any further trouble.

The tarpon, like every other fish, varies in weight according to size, and other circumstances; but a full-grown fish in good condition is never under 200 pounds. The arapaima averages 400 to 500 pounds; but I assisted to kill one on the Rio Negro which scaled, even after it was cut in pieces, 628 pounds. I thought I had finished with the Amazonian superlatives; but I must endorse what a well-known naturalist has written, "the arapaima holds the proud position of being the largest fresh-water fish in the world." Both tarpon and arapaima are excellent fish for food. Many of the scales of the arapaima are five inches in diameter; and I have seen them an inch more. Those of the tarpon are half this size. Schomburgk describes the Indians as shooting the arapaima with arrows. I have only seen them captured with hook and line.

As the arapaima is a much larger, stronger, and pluckier fish than the tarpon, a big hook, and a substantial line, must be used; and the fisherman must be prepared for a considerable exertion of muscular power. The gape of the fish is very wide; it can, therefore, take a large bait, though I believe its usual food is very small, consisting of the fry of fishes, and particularly the young of crabs and lobsters. If I could find these, or a crab which had just changed its shell, and was in a soft condition, I always found it a very killing bait for tarpon: and arapaima, also, would readily take it. Failing these, I have used clams and large oysters, removed from the shells, of course.

The hook I used was four of the largest I could get, or make, tied together so that the barbs projected on every side—a sort of shark hook, in fact; with the bait securely tied on; and the line at least 200 yards long, and strong enough to bear the strain of a 600-pound fish. It is very desirable to have a quadruple hook, as the strain put on it is often tremendous: and it is a good plan to have a stout wooden bollard fixed in the boat, round which the rope can be passed two or three turns, to ease the pressure. The fish, when hooked, is almost sure to dash away at a great rate; but it does not leap from the water. It is game, and will show a lot of fight; and, if the boat can be got near enough, it is as well to kill it with a harpoon, or lance.

The tarpon is described as a sea fish, and the arapaima as strictly a fresh-water species. The tarpon is really an estuarine fish, often ascending large rivers far above the tide-limit; but never going far out to sea; although I have seen both these and arapaima far from the mouth of a river; but as they were always in an injured or dying condition it is probable they had been swept out to sea as a result of their helplessness. Arapaimas, however, come down into estuaries, and can exist in water that is brackish, if not absolutely salt; and I strongly suspect tarpons of taking journeys which partake of the character of migrations. There are several varieties of them; but I have only seen one arapaima, that which I have attempted to describe here, and which is certainly confined to the larger and deeper waters of the combined Amazon-Orinoco systems. I have never met with the least evidence that it enters the smaller and shallower streams; and I do not believe that it does do so. To read some accounts of it one would think he had but to look across the waters to see shoals of these fish and the Amazonian dolphins disporting themselves in every direction. He may look for weeks, and see nothing but the rippling waves and the dancing sunbeams: even the gigantic forest trees of the opposite shore are scarcely visible across the broad expanse of this vast river, and appear dimly, as a low, dark-coloured hedge.

Of the lesser fish it is hardly worth while to say anything, it is so exceedingly difficult to see what is taking place beneath the waters. There is no class of animals that more require a specialist to study them than fishes. A man must devote weeks and months to watching before he can learn a single habit of these creatures: and I had so much to see, and note, above water that I had no time to dive into its depths after knowledge.

All the fish, except three or four of the commonest kinds, of the Amazon are known by local and popular names which could convey no information to the students of system; but a few that I can mention may have a general interest, especially to lovers of the hook and line, who may contemplate a visit to this region.

A hundred pounds is not an uncommon weight for conger-eels in the lower reaches below Obydos, and especially in the Para river: and higher up, fresh-water eels are very numerous, attaining a length of six feet;

Photo Underwood & Underwood

A MAIL BOAT LEAVING THE AMAZON RIVER PORT OF SERPA

and are fierce enough to give a disciple of Old Izaak a lively time, if taken into the boat before they are disabled: and I have experienced some curious little adventures when fishing for congers in the lower reaches. I had one of these creatures make an attack on me, like a snake, and it very nearly succeeded in throwing me into the water. On another occasion one of monstrous size nearly upset the boat. He resisted so vigorously that we could not drag him inboard; and he finally got away with a large hook in his maw.

There is a huge "angel-fish" in the tidal waters, and a kind of cat-fish with a head as big as that of an ox. Higher up the stream there is a great variety of fishes, some kinds weighing as much as forty pounds per fish: others of twenty pounds are quite common. Some are of good flavour and are excellent food; others have such peculiar and unpleasant tastes and odours that we threw them overboard as soon as they had been examined. One of carp-like appearance, and twelve pounds weight, was a favourite with us; and was always dressed for the table when we could catch it. It is called a "berry-fish," on account of the large size of the grains of its roe. It does not appear in the lower reaches of the river.

The shoals of fish attract the gulls right up the Amazon, and I have seen large flocks of them hovering over the water far above Nauta, which is 2000 miles from the mouth: but we cannot return up-stream to watch these.

Those who wish to visit the Amazon on sport and pleasure bent, have no need to go farther than the towns near its mouth: for even a few miles from such places as Obydos, Santarem, Manaos, and Para there are miles of virgin forest which have never been penetrated by any feet but those of the prowling Indian and the sportsman. Here those who care for such expeditions may hire a boat, and, in the course of a day or two, find secluded nooks where they have no more fear of being interrupted, or disturbed, than Adam had in Eden. The explorer may bury himself in swamps where the Spanish moss hangs, not in festoons only, but in thick and wide sheets and masses from trees that are 200 feet high and more—specimens of arboreal growth of a tallness and spread of branches of which a European can have no conception; and the description of which, to him, must read like exaggeration. Here he will find creatures so unlike those to which he is accustomed, that he may easily dream he is in a fairy land.

If he be a true sportsman, and wants a spice of danger to actuate his pleasures, he can find it here; and this in a new guise. There are no mighty elephants, lions, and tigers to dance before his bullets; no huge bears to give him a crushing hug; but there is the cunning jaguar to drop on him unawares, the terrible cayman to upset his canoe, and gobble him up, after it has kept him hid in some mud-hole until he has, like a well-hung hare, acquired the proper flavour. There are huge boas, and anacondas, at least twenty feet long and, perchance, double that length, which will eye him with wonder, and very likely sample him. There are snakes hardly less in size than these, so deadly poisonous that the people of the land shudder at the mere mention of them. These are some of the things which will test his courage, and his nerve, if he goes into the wilderness in search of adventures.

But there are other things more beautiful, more wonderful, and not dangerous, to attract the attention of the lover of nature. There are the marvellous humming-birds, " living gems," as they have justly been called—the breathing jewels of the earth; moving masses of scarlet macaws, the most gorgeous of all flying creatures: clouds of mazarine-blue butterflies, rivalling the humming-birds in their amazing beauty: flowers, that for size, and variety of shape, and hue, throw those of all other parts of the earth into the shade; trees that are a forest in themselves, often growing, as parasites, one above another in three, and even four, layers: interminable forests of unrivalled works of the great Creator, incomparable in other quarters of the globe, and surpassed nowhere—on earth, at any rate. Skies of topaz—like heaven itself for magnificent clearness and purity: and through all, and around all, a New Rio La Plata—a winding, gleaming river of liquid silver tens of miles broad and thousands of miles in length—The Mightiest Stream on Earth.

THE END

INDEX

Lightning Source UK Ltd.
Milton Keynes UK
28 February 2011

168354UK00007B/20/A

9 780559 447341